Global Issues in Copyright Law

By

Mary LaFrance
William S. Boyd Professor of Law
William S. Boyd School of Law
University of Nevada, Las Vegas

AMERICAN CASEBOOK SERIES®

WEST®

A Thomson Reuters business

Mat #40748996

© 2009 Thomson Reuters

    610 Opperman Drive
    St. Paul, MN 55123
    1–800–313–9378

Printed in the United States of America

ISBN: 978–0–314–19447–3

To My Mother

*

Preface

International agreements such as the Berne Convention, the TRIPS Agreement, the WIPO Copyright Treaty and the WIPO Performances and Phonograms Treaty have led to significant harmonization of the domestic copyright laws of nations around the world. Nonetheless, important differences remain. In addition, copyright laws are dynamic rather than static. Developments in the copyright laws of one nation often influence the direction of copyright policy in other nations. Thus, copyright reforms tend to have a ripple effect throughout the world.

The materials presented in this text have been selected primarily to highlight differences between United States copyright law and the laws of other nations, and to stimulate discussion of the policy choices underlying these differences as well as the practical consequences that flow from them. In addition, some of the materials illustrate how the legal principles developed in one jurisdiction can influence the development of related doctrine in another jurisdiction.

This text is not a comprehensive overview of international copyright law. Rather, its purpose is to lend perspective to a study of United States copyright law by offering a glimpse of the alternative approaches which different nations have adopted when each is confronted with similar problems that call into question the proper scope and purpose of copyright.

*

Acknowledgments

The author gratefully acknowledges the assistance of Law Library Director Jeanne Price and reference librarians Jennifer Gross and Matthew Wright at the William S. Boyd School of Law. Additional assistance in manuscript preparation was provided by research librarian Gail Cline. Valuable consultation on matters of Japanese law was provided by Professor Toshiko Takenaka of the University of Washington School of Law and Waseda University, Tokyo.

*

Global Issues Series

Series Editor, Franklin A. Gevurtz

Titles Available Now

Global Issues in Civil Procedure by Thomas Main, University of the Pacific, McGeorge School of Law
ISBN 978–0–314–15978–6

Global Issues in Constitutional Law by Brian K. Landsberg, University of the Pacific, McGeorge School of Law and Leslie Gielow Jacobs, University of the Pacific, McGeorge School of Law
ISBN 978–0–314–17608–0

Global Issues in Contract Law by John A. Spanogle, Jr., George Washington University, Michael P. Malloy, University of the Pacific, McGeorge School of Law, Louis F. Del Duca, Pennsylvania State University, Keith A. Rowley, University of Nevada, Las Vegas, and Andrea K. Bjorklund, University of California, Davis
ISBN 978–0–314–16755–2

Global Issues in Copyright Law by Mary LaFrance, University of Nevada
ISBN 978–0–314–19447–3

Global Issues in Corporate Law by Franklin A. Gevurtz, University of the Pacific, McGeorge School of Law
ISBN 978–0–314–15977–9

Global Issues in Criminal Law by Linda Carter, University of the Pacific, McGeorge School of Law, Christopher L. Blakesley, University of Nevada, Las Vegas and Peter Henning, Wayne State University
ISBN 978–0–314–15997–7

Global Issues in Employee Benefits Law by Paul M. Secunda, Marquette University Law School, Samuel Estreicher, New York University School of Law, Rosalind J. Connor, Jones Day, London
ISBN 978–0–314–19409–1

Global Issues in Employment Discrimination Law by Samuel Estreicher, New York University School of Law and Brian K. Landsberg, University of the Pacific, McGeorge School of Law
ISBN 978–0–314–17607–3

ix

Global Issues in Employment Law by Samuel Estreicher, New York University School of Law and Miriam A. Cherry, University of the Pacific, McGeorge School of Law
ISBN 978–0–314–17952–4

Global Issues in Environmental Law by Stephen McCaffrey, University of the Pacific, McGeorge School of Law and Rachael Salcido, University of the Pacific, McGeorge School of Law
ISBN 978–0–314–18479–5

Global Issues in Family Law by Ann Laquer Estin, University of Iowa and Barbara Stark, Hofstra University
ISBN 978–0–314–17954–8

Global Issues in Freedom of Speech and Religion by Alan Brownstein, University of California, Davis, School of Law and Leslie Gielow Jacobs, University of the Pacific, McGeorge School of Law
ISBN 978–0–314–18454–2

Global Issues in Income Taxation by Daniel Lathrope, University of San Francisco School of Law
ISBN 978–0–314–18806–9

Global Issues in Labor Law by Samuel Estreicher, New York University School of Law
ISBN 978–0–314–17163–4

Global Issues in Legal Ethics by James E. Moliterno, College of William & Mary, Marshall–Wythe School of Law and George Harris, University of the Pacific, McGeorge School of Law
ISBN 978–0–314–16935–8

Global Issues in Property Law by John G. Sprankling, University of the Pacific, McGeorge School of Law, Raymond R. Coletta, University of the Pacific, McGeorge School of Law, and M.C. Mirow, Florida International University College of Law
ISBN 978–0–314–16729–3

Global Issues in Tort Law by Julie A. Davies, University of the Pacific, McGeorge School of Law and Paul T. Hayden, Loyola Law School, Los Angeles
ISBN 978–0–314–16759–0

Summary of Contents

        Page

PREFACE v
ACKNOWLEDGMENTS vii
TABLE OF CASES xvii

Chapter 1. Introduction 1

Chapter 2. Subject Matter 5
A. Copyright in Perfumes 6
B. Fashion Designs 18
C. Data Compilations 24
D. Copyright and Unfair Competition 62

Chapter 3. Authorship and Ownership 67
A. Introduction 67
B. Works Made for Hire 67
C. Joint Works 82
D. Cinematographic Works 88
E. Government Copyright 92
F. Term of Protection 95
G. Assignments 96

Chapter 4. Exclusive Rights 98
A. Introduction 98
B. Moral Rights 98
C. Rental and Lending Rights 122
D. Exhaustion of Rights 146
E. Resale Rights 167
F. Public Performance Rights 172
G. Cross–Border Infringement 188

Chapter 5. Fair Use 197
A. Treaty Provisions 197
B. European Union Directive 199
C. Statutes and Case Law 201

Chapter 6. Secondary Liability 229
A. Liability for "Authorizing" 229

Page

B. ISP Liability --- 234
C. Liability of Venues and Suppliers -------------------------------- 257

INDEX --- 267

Table of Contents

	Page
PREFACE	v
ACKNOWLEDGMENTS	vii
TABLE OF CASES	xvii

Chapter 1. Introduction — 1

Chapter 2. Subject Matter — 5

A. Copyright in Perfumes — 6
  - *Lancome Parfums et Beaute et Cie S.N.C. v. Kecofa B.V.* — 7
  - *Kecofa B.V. v. Lancome Parfums et Beaute et Cie S.N.C.* — 11
  - *Nejila X. contre Societe Haarmann & Reimer* — 14
  - *Beaute Prestige Int'l contre Societe Senteur Mazal* — 15
  - *Notes* — 16

B. Fashion Designs — 18
  - *Re Marcio X..., Roberts Y... A... and Olivier Z... Re Infringement of Copyright in Fashion Designs* — 18
  - *Notes* — 24

C. Data Compilations — 24
  - 1. The Decline of "Sweat of the Brow" — 24
    - *Notes* — 37
  - 2. The European Union Database Directive — 38
    - *Directive 96/9/EC of the European Parliament and of the Council of 11 March 1996 on the Legal Protection of Databases* — 38
    - *First Evaluation of Directive 96/9/EC on the Legal Protection of Databases* — 43
    - *Notes* — 61

D. Copyright and Unfair Competition — 62
  - *Judgment of Intellectual Property High Court* — 62
  - *Note* — 66

Chapter 3. Authorship and Ownership — 67

A. Introduction — 67

B. Works Made for Hire — 67
  - *Itar–Tass Russian News Agency v. Russian Kurier, Inc.* — 67
  - *Notes* — 80

C. Joint Works — 82
  - *Beckingham v. Hodgens* — 82
  - *Notes* — 87

D. Cinematographic Works — 88
  - *Maker of a Documentary Film* — 90
  - *Notes* — 92

Page

E. Government Copyright 92
F. Term of Protection 95
G. Assignments 96
   1. Economic Rights 96
   2. Moral Rights 97

Chapter 4. Exclusive Rights **98**
A. Introduction 98
B. Moral Rights 98
   1. Motion Picture Colorization 99
     Turner Entertainment Co. v. Huston 99
     Notes 107
   2. Editing for Commercials 108
     Claes Eriksson et al. v. TV 4 108
     Notes 113
   3. Moral Rights and Cultural Heritage 113
     Sehgal v. Union of India 113
     Notes 122
C. Rental and Lending Rights 122
   Metronome Musik GmbH v. Music Point Hokamp GmbH 124
   Directive 2006/115/EC of the European Parliament and of the Council of 12 December 2006 on rental right and lending right and on certain rights related to copyright in the field of intellectual property 130
   Commission of the European Communities v. Portuguese Republic 132
   Commission of the European Communities v. Portuguese Republic 138
   Notes 143
D. Exhaustion of Rights 146
   1. National Exhaustion 146
     Polo/Lauren Company LP v. Ziliani Holdings Pty Ltd 146
   2. Exhaustion in the European Union 153
     Laserdisken ApS v. Kulturministeriet 153
     Notes 162
   3. International Exhaustion 162
E. Resale Rights 167
   Directive 2001/84/EC of the European Parliament and of the Council of 27 September 2001 on the Resale Right for the Benefit of the Author of an Original Work of Art 167
   Notes 172
F. Public Performance Rights 172
   United States—Section 110(5) of the US Copyright Act 172
   Notes 186
G. Cross–Border Infringement 188
   Society of Composers, Authors & Music Publishers of Canada v. Canadian Assn. of Internet Providers 188
   Notes 195

Chapter 5. Fair Use **197**
A. Treaty Provisions 197
B. European Union Directive 199

Page

C. Statutes and Case Law ----- 201
  CCH Canadian Ltd. v. Law Society of Upper Canada ----- 201
  Notes ----- 210
  Fraser–Woodward Ltd v. British Broadcasting Corporation ----- 211
  Notes ----- 226

Chapter 6. Secondary Liability ----- **229**
A. Liability for "Authorizing" ----- 229
  CCH Canadian Ltd. v. Law Society of Upper Canada ----- 229
  Notes ----- 233
B. ISP Liability ----- 234
  Society of Composers, Authors & Music Publishers of Canada v. Canadian Assn. of Internet Providers ----- 234
  Notes ----- 249
  Directive 2000/31/EC of the European Parliament and of the Council of 8 June 2000 on Certain Legal Aspects of Information Society Services, in Particular Electronic Commerce, in the Internal Market ----- 249
  Note ----- 251
C. Liability of Venues and Suppliers ----- 257
  Infringement of Copyright by Singing at a Karaoke Outlet ----- 257
  Duty of Care of the Lessor of Karaoke Equipment for Business Use ----- 261
  Notes ----- 265

INDEX ----- 267

*

Table of Cases

The principal cases are in bold type. Cases cited or discussed in the text are in roman type. References are to pages. Cases cited in principal cases and within other quoted materials are not included.

Beaute Prestige Int'l contre Societe Senteur Mazal, Arret du 14 Fevrier 2007 (2007), **15**

Beckingham v. Hodgens, [2003] EWCA Civ 143, 2003 WL 270805 (CA Civ. Div. 2003), **82**

CCH Canadian Ltd. v. Law Society of Upper Canada, [2004] 1 S.C.R. 339, 2004 SCC 13 (S.C.C.2004), 25, 27, **201, 229**

Claes Eriksson et al. v. TV 4, Case No. T2117–06 (March 18, 2008), **108**

Commission of the European Communities v. Portuguese Republic, European Court of Justice (2006), **132, 138**

Dastar Corp. v. Twentieth Century Fox Film Corp., 539 U.S. 23, 123 S.Ct. 2041, 156 L.Ed.2d 18 (2003), 62

Desktop Marketing Systems Pty. Ltd. v. Telstra Corporation Ltd., [2002] FCAFC 112, 2002 WL 1005203 (FCA 2002), 29

Eastern Book Co. v. D.B. Modak, Appeal (Civil) 6472 of 2004 (Dec. 12, 2007), 28

Feist Publications, Inc. v. Rural Telephone Service Co., Inc., 499 U.S. 340, 111 S.Ct. 1282, 113 L.Ed.2d 358 (1991), 2, 25

Films by Jove, Inc. v. Berov, 341 F.Supp.2d 199 (E.D.N.Y.2004), 80

Fisher v. Brooker, [2007] F.S.R. 12, 2006 WL 3835218 (Ch. D. 2006), 87

Football League Ltd. v. Littlewoods Pools Ltd., [1959] Ch. 637, 1959 WL 19493 (Ch. D. 1959), 26

Fraser–Woodward Ltd. v. British Broadcasting Corporation, [2005] EWHC 472, 2005 WL 756056 (Ch. D. 2005), **211**

H. Blacklock & Co. Ltd. v. C. Arthur Pearson Ltd., [1915] 2 Ch. 376, 1915 WL 18767 (Ch. D. 1915), 26

IceTV Pty. Ltd. v. Nine Network Australia Pty. Ltd., [2009] HCA 14, 2009 WL 1059528 (HCA 2009), 29

Independent Television Publications Ltd. v. Time Out Ltd. and Elliott, [1984] F.S.R. 64, 1983 WL 216318 (Ch. D. 1983), 26

Itar–Tass Russian News Agency v. Russian Kurier, Inc., 153 F.3d 82 (2nd Cir.1998), **67**

Kecofa B.V. v. Lancome Parfums et Beaute et Cie S.N.C., First Chamber, No. C04327HR (2006), **11**

Ladbroke (Football) Ltd. v. William Hill (Football) Ltd., [1964] 1 All E.R. 465, [1964] 1 W.L.R. 273, 1964 WL 19516 (HL 1963), 26

Lancome Parfums et Beaute et Cie S.N.C. v. Kecofa B.V., Case No. C0200726/MA (2004), **7**

Laserdisken ApS v. Kulturministeriet, 2006 WL 2593844 (ECJ 2006), **153**

Marcio X..., Roberts Y... A... and Olivier Z... Infringement of Copyright in Fashion Designs, In re, [2008] E.C.C. 19, [2009] E.C.D.R. 1, 2008 WL 2976666 (Cass. 2008), **18**

Metronome Musik GmbH v. Music Point Hokamp GmbH (C200/96), Case–200/96, 1998 WL 1042900 (ECJ 1998), **124**

Nejila X. contre Societe Haarmann & Reimer, Arret No. 1006 du 13 Juin 2006 (Cass. 2006), **14**

Neudorf v. Nettwerk Productions Ltd., 71 B.C.L.R. (3d) 290, 1999 Carswell BC 2774, 1999 WL 33198299 (B.C. S.C.1999), 87

Peer International Corp. v. Termidor Music Publishers Ltd., 2003 E.M.L.R. 34, 2003 WL 21554794 (CA Civ. Div. 2003), 80

Polo/Lauren Company LP v. Ziliani Holdings Pty. Ltd., 2008 WL 5268577 (FCA 2008), **146**

Sarl Louis Feraud Intern. v. Viewfinder Inc., 2008 WL 5272770 (S.D.N.Y. 2008), 24

Sarl Louis Feraud Intern. v. Viewfinder Inc., 489 F.3d 474 (2nd Cir.2007), 228

Sarl Louis Feraud Intern. v. Viewfinder Inc., 406 F.Supp.2d 274 (S.D.N.Y. 2005), 24

Sehgal v. Union of India, [2005] F.S.R. 39, 2005 WL 2205308 (HC (Ind.) 2005), **113**

Society of Composers, Authors & Music Publishers of Canada v. Canadian Assn. of Internet Providers, 2004 SCC 45, [2004] S.C.R. 427 (S.C.C.2004), **188, 234**

Spraymiser Ltd. v. Wrightway Marketing Ltd., [2000] E.C.D.R. 349, 1999 WL 1489561 (Ch. D. 1999), 37

Tele–Direct (Publications) Inc. v. American Business Information Inc., 154 D.L.R. (4th) 328, 1997 WL 1926277 (Fed. C.A.1997), 38

Turner Entertainment Co. v. Huston, Chambre Civile (1994), **99**

Universal Music Australia Pty. Ltd. v. Australian Competition and Consumer Commission, [2003] FCAFC 193, 2003 WL 21996479 (FCA 2003), 165, 166

Video Ezy Int'l (NZ) Ltd v. Roadshow Ent. (NZ) Ltd., [2002] 1 N.Z.L.R. 855 (2002), 166

Weatherby & Sons v. International Horse Agency and Exchange Ltd., [1910] 2 Ch. 297, 1910 WL 15719 (Ch. D. 1910), 26

Global Issues in Copyright Law

*

Chapter 1

INTRODUCTION

Diversity of Copyright Regimes

In the United States, copyright law is designed primarily to protect economic rights—called "patrimonial rights" in many countries. For that reason, most of federal copyright law protects the rights of copyright *owners*—whether they are owners by virtue of authorship or by virtue of assignment. Authors, in contrast, have only a few inalienable rights—the termination right and, in the case of works of visual art, the moral rights of attribution and integrity. Under the work-made-for-hire rules, even the status of author may be "bargained for" in certain circumstances. This emphasis on the economic aspects of copyright law is also characteristic of other common law countries such as the United Kingdom and Australia.

In contrast, most civil law regimes (including those of continental Europe) protect works of creative expression under an "author's rights" ("droit d'auteur") regime. Under this approach, an author's inalienable moral rights (including at least the rights of attribution and integrity) are at least as important as the economic rights of the copyright owner, if not more so. Authorship cannot be bargained for; even where the law provides that the economic rights in a work vest initially in an employer or commissioning party (as is often the case with motion pictures, even in an author's rights regime), the individual creator of the work retains authorship status and the attendant moral rights. The modest degree of moral rights protection available in the United States bears little resemblance to moral rights protection overseas.

Several other types of protection play a more significant role in the copyright systems of other countries than in the United States. One—the public lending right—does not exist at all in the United States. Another—the resale right—exists only in California, and

1

arguably conflicts with federal copyright law. A third—rental rights—plays only a modest role in the United States, but is a significant revenue source for rightholders in other countries.

Outside the United States, the concept of "neighboring rights" applies to the rights of record producers, performers, and broadcasters. Although in the United States several of these rights are encompassed by the broad umbrella of copyright law, some of them are conspicuously excluded from federal copyright protection—notably, the general public performance right in sound recordings.

Throughout the European Union, and in several other countries as well, new legislative schemes have been enacted to protect factual compilations without regard to the originality of their selection or arrangement, in stark contrast to the position adopted by the United States Supreme Court in Feist Publications, Inc. v. Rural Telephone Serv. Co., 499 U.S. 340 (1991).

Today, cross-border transactions and digital communications ensure that copyrighted works will travel widely beyond the countries in which they originate. International differences in copyright regimes inevitably mean that some of these transnational activities will present copyright problems. For example, a work that is in the public domain in one country may still be copyrighted in another country. Different rules governing "fair use" may mean that an activity that is non-infringing in one country may be infringing in another. Restrictions on parallel imports may mean that a copy of a work that was lawfully made in one country cannot be transported to certain other countries. Differences in licensing rules or territorial copyright ownership could mean that a separate set of clearances is needed to exploit a given work in each of several countries. Awareness of these and other potential copyright issues is essential to modern copyright practice.

International Harmonization

The diversity of international approaches to copyright and authors' rights has been narrowed in recent decades as a result of a drive toward harmonization. A number of international agreements play a role in achieving this result. When a country that is a signatory to one of these agreements becomes the subject of a complaint that it has not fully implemented the mandatory provisions of the agreement in its domestic laws, some, but not all, of these agreements provide mechanisms for resolving these disputes. Some of the major agreements affecting copyright and neighboring rights are described below.

A key provision in each of these agreements is the nondiscrimination rule; with respect to the subject matter of the specific treaty, and subject to some significant exceptions, each signatory country is required to give the nationals of other signatory countries the benefit of the same rights that it extends to its own nationals. Thus, for the most part, a United States author will have the same copyright protection in France as a French author. Note, however, that this does *not* mean that the French copyright laws will be the same as the United States laws with which that author is probably more familiar.

The United States is a signatory to each of the following agreements except for the Maastricht Treaty and the Rome Convention.

1. *Berne Convention for the Protection of Literary and Artistic Works (1886; revised 1971)*

The Berne Convention establishes certain minimum standards for copyright protection. It has no enforcement mechanisms, but to the extent that its provisions are incorporated in TRIPS (see below), the enforcement mechanisms of the WTO Agreement apply. Berne is the leading treaty pertaining to copyright laws, with 164 countries as signatories.

2. *TRIPS Agreement (1994)*

The TRIPS (Agreement on Trade Related Aspects of Intellectual Property Rights) provisions of the WTO Agreement incorporate, *inter alia*, almost all of the Berne Convention. The only Berne provision not incorporated in TRIPS is Article 6bis, the moral rights provision. This was omitted from TRIPS at the insistence of the United States. WTO signatories can file complaints with the WTO if they believe that another signatory has failed to implement the TRIPS requirements in its domestic legislation, and violations can lead to trade sanctions.

3. *Rome Convention (1961)*

The International Convention for the Protection of Performers, Producers of Phonograms and Broadcasting Organizations ("Rome Convention," for short) is a neighboring rights treaty. It establishes minimum standards for protecting the rights of phonogram producers (with respect to reproduction, broadcasting, and public performance of their phonograms, *i.e.*, sound recordings), broadcasters with respect to their broadcasts, and performers with respect to their performances. The United States has not joined the Rome Convention because of the requirement for protecting public performance rights in sound recordings.

4. *Geneva Phonograms Convention (1971)*

The Convention for the Protection of Producers of Phonograms Against Unauthorized Duplication of Their Phonograms ("Geneva Convention," for short) focuses on record "piracy." It establishes minimum standards for protecting phonogram producers against the unauthorized reproduction of their sound recordings, and against importation and public distribution of unauthorized reproductions. It does not address public performance rights.

5. *WIPO Copyright Treaty (WCT) (1996)*

The WIPO Copyright Treaty incorporates and updates the Berne Convention. It sets minimum standards for, *inter alia*, rental rights, digital rights management (DRM) information, anticircumvention laws, databases, and the "making available" of works through individually accessible means such as the Internet.

6. *WIPO Performances and Phonograms Treaty (WPPT) (1996)*

The Performances and Phonograms Treaty sets minimum standards for protecting phonogram performers' moral and economic rights with respect to their performances, and for protecting phonogram producers' rights of reproduction and distribution. It also sets minimum standards for the rental rights and public performance rights of phonogram performers and producers, for their right of "making available" their works through individually accessible means such as the Internet, and for anticircumvention laws and DRM protection.

7. *Universal Copyright Convention (UCC) (1952; revised 1971)*

This early copyright convention is of little importance today, since it is largely superseded by the Berne Convention. Most UCC signatories are also signatories to Berne and/or the TRIPS Agreement.

8. *Maastricht (EU) Treaty (1992)*

The Maastricht Treaty (replacing the 1957 Treaty of Rome) binds the nations of the European Union (formerly the European Economic Community) into a federation in which trade barriers have been largely eliminated and, accordingly, many (but certainly not all) differences in copyright laws have been erased. The EU periodically issues legislation in the form of directives which establish legal rules to which all nations belonging to the European Community (EC) must conform, by amending their domestic laws if necessary. Several of these directives pertain to copyright and neighboring rights. Questions of compliance with the Maastricht Treaty and EU directives are addressed by the European Court of Justice (ECJ).

Chapter 2

SUBJECT MATTER

To some degree, international agreements have harmonized the scope of copyrightable subject matter. Article 2 of the Berne Convention mandates protection for the following categories of works:

> every production in the literary, scientific and artistic domain, whatever may be the mode or form of its expression, such as books, pamphlets and other writings; lectures, addresses, sermons and other works of the same nature; dramatic or dramatico-musical works; choreographic works and entertainments in dumb show; musical compositions with or without words; cinematographic works to which are assimilated works expressed by a process analogous to cinematography; works of drawing, painting, architecture, sculpture, engraving and lithography; photographic works to which are assimilated works expressed by a process analogous to photography; works of applied art; illustrations, maps, plans, sketches and three-dimensional works relative to geography, topography, architecture or science.

It also requires protection for "translations, adaptations, arrangements of music and other alterations of a literary or artistic work."

Among the categories not explicitly listed here are sound recordings ("phonograms," in European parlance), data compilations, and computer software (although the software's visual or audiovisual display will typically fall into one or more of the listed categories). Note, however, that the Berne Convention sets forth only a minimum standard for copyrightable subject matter. Signatories are free to extend copyright protection (or legal protection other than copyright) to other categories of works.

Under Article 4 of the WIPO Copyright Treaty, computer programs are "protected as literary works within the meaning of

Article 2 of the Berne Convention." Article 5 of the WIPO Treaty specifies that "compilations of data or other material, in any form, which by reason of the selection or arrangement of their contents constitute intellectual creations, are protected as such." Thus, WIPO signatories must extend copyright protection to software, but need only extend *some form* of intellectual property protection to the selection and arrangement of data compilations. Article 5 also makes clear that the protection it mandates does not extend to the data or other underlying material comprising the compilation. Similar provisions on software and data compilations are included in Article 10 of the TRIPS provisions of the WTO Agreement.

In many countries, including those of the European Union, sound recordings as well as broadcasts are protected under a regime of "neighboring rights." Although this protection is analogous to copyright, the specific terms of protection may differ. For example, a phonogram producer's right to prevent unauthorized reproduction, distribution, and public performance of a sound recording is protected for only 50 years in the European Union (although newly proposed legislation would extend this to 70 years), while the copyright in the underlying musical composition lasts for the life of the author plus 70 years.

The WIPO Performances and Phonograms Treaty addresses neighboring rights. It gives phonogram producers certain exclusive rights (reproduction, public distribution, rental, public performance and transmission) in their sound recordings, and gives phonogram performers (*i.e.,* musicians) certain economic and moral rights in their recorded performances, for a period of 50 years.

Neighboring rights are also included in Article 14 of TRIPS, which gives phonogram producers reproduction and rental rights, and gives phonogram performers the same economic rights as under the WIPO agreement, for a 50–year term. Article 14(3) extends certain economic rights to broadcasters, although only for 20 years, and with a proviso that signatories can choose to extend these rights only to the owners of the copyrighted content of the broadcast rather than to the broadcasters themselves.

Even with the degree of harmonization imposed by these agreements, there remain intriguing differences in the scope of copyrightable subject matter around the world. This chapter highlights several interesting examples—copyright in perfumes, fashion designs, and data compilations.

A. COPYRIGHT IN PERFUMES

Several European courts have considered the question whether copyright extends to fragrances. Each of the decisions excerpted below, issued by courts in the Netherlands and France, bases its resolution of this question on the language of the relevant copyright statutes. The first opinion is from a Dutch appellate court, and the second opinion is the decision of the Dutch Supreme Court in the appeal of that case. The third opinion is from the highest court in France, and the fourth is from a French appellate court, one year later, in a separate case presenting the same general question but in a very different context. How does the analysis differ in each of these cases? How would this issue be analyzed under U.S. law?

LANCOME PARFUMS ET BEAUTE ET CIE S.N.C. v. KECOFA B.V.

Court of Appeal in 's Hertogenbosch, 2004
Case No. C0200726/MA

* * *

In its judgment of April 18, 2002, the district court ordered Lancome to establish that:

> (1) The scent combination which it offers under the Tresor mark satisfies the criteria for copyright protection, in particular the requirement that it possess an original character and that it carry the stamp of its creator;

> (2) Lancome should be considered the creator of this scent combination;

> (3) The scent combination sold under the Female Treasure mark should be considered a copy or imitation that infringes the copyright in the combination sold under the Tresor mark.

* * *

In ground II of its cross-appeal, Kecofa challenges the district court's conclusion that the 1912 Copyright Act does not foreclose copyright protection for a scent combination if the requirements for copyright protection are otherwise satisfied.

* * *

Copyright Law Protection

This litigation centers on the question whether Lancome's Tresor qualifies for copyright protection. In this regard it must be determined whether (a) a work of this nature is eligible for copyright protection, and (b) whether the work in question has a sufficiently original character and carries the stamp of its creator.

(a) Nature of the work

In the appellate court's opinion, Kecofa is correct in asserting that one must distinguish between the perfume (a substance whose composition gives off a scent and which is manufactured and used for that purpose) and the scent (that which humans can perceive through their senses). The court of appeal interprets Lancome's arguments referencing "its Tresor perfume" as indicating that the protection sought was for the perfume—that is, the substance contained in the bottles sold under the Tresor mark.

It is unnecessary to consider Kecofa's argument that a scent as such is by its nature too volatile, too variable, and too dependent on environmental factors to constitute a work in the sense of copyright law, because Lancome invokes this protection not for the mere scent of its product but for the perfume—the substance, which Lancome indicates means its composition (a substance which the court will hereinafter call "Tresor perfume").

Thus, that for which Lancome invokes copyright protection is not only perceptible by the senses, as required, but also, in the view of this court, sufficiently concrete and stable to be considered as a work within the meaning of copyright law.

Kecofa's argument that a scent is subjective does not alter this conclusion, because human perception always involves a degree of subjectivity, and because the work in question is not the scent itself but the specific composition which can be objectively determined.

(b) Original Character

In support of its argument that Tresor perfume has its own original character and carries the stamp of its creator, Lancome asserts, inter alia, that Tresor perfume:

-results from a highly creative development process: from hundreds of possible scents the creator selected, as the court understands it, about 25 scents, resulting in a unique combination;

-combines, among others, a fresh floral aroma of white roses and lilies-of-the-valley, the powdery aroma of iris, apricot flower, and heliotrope, against a background of amber [Ed. note: a commonly used fragrance combination derived from storax], sandalwood, and musk;

-results from Lancome's deliberate effort to make it a remarkable and unique perfume;

-enjoyed immediate success due to its fragrance.

These facts, which are largely uncontested by Kecofa, support the conclusion that Tresor perfume possesses the requisite degree of originality and individual creative stamp.

Kecofa has argued that, at the time of its creation, Tresor perfume (i) conformed to a long tradition of feminine, fruity, and floral fragrances, (ii) was comparable to Calvin Klein's existing "Eternity" fragrance, and (iii) was itself based on the "Exclamation" fragrance previously created by the perfume maker Grosjman.

To be eligible for copyright, a work need not be objectively novel, but need only be original in a subjective sense (that is, from the point of view of its creator). The fact that a similar work already existed is relevant to originality only if the creator of the later work copied from the earlier work, an argument which must be argued and proved by the defendant.

The fact that a perfume conforms to a particular style or tradition because of several of its general characteristics does not, by itself, establish that the composition of the perfume is not original. For the same reason, the argument that Tresor perfume is comparable to an earlier perfume is unavailing. Kecofa's argument that Tresor perfume was derived from "Exclamation" perfume implies that Tresor was copied from that perfume, but Kecofa has provided insufficient support for this allegation. Based on the specific and unrefuted assertions in which Lancome has described the creative process and the original character of Tresor perfume, the court of appeals finds that Kecofa needed to make a stronger showing to support the alleged derivation which Lancome denies, and Kecofa has failed to do so.

Accordingly, the court concludes that Tresor perfume is original and carries the stamp of its creator. Tresor perfume is therefore eligible for copyright protection.

* * *

Infringement

The next issue is whether Kecofa's Female Treasure fragrance infringes the copyright in Tresor perfume.

In this context it must be determined whether Female Treasure possesses enough of the copyrightable aspects of Tresor that the overall impressions of the two works are insufficiently different to support the conclusion that Female Treasure was created independently.

To support its allegation that Female Treasure is an imitation of Tresor, Lancome has submitted, *inter alia,* a technical report dated December 17, 2003, prepared by the French firm of Breese & Majerowicz (B & M), with a Dutch translation on which the court of appeal relies.

* * *

The report contained a chemical analysis of the two perfumes. It states, *inter alia,* that:

> The two perfumes have 24 olfactory elements in common. Tresor contains two elements not present in Female Treasure, while Female Treasure contains one element not present in Tresor. However, the latter is a low-cost substitute for the corresponding element in Tresor (Musk Ketone).
>
> Two perfumes sharing a large number of olfactory elements convey the same aromatic impression, and this is not a coincidence. In other words, the fact that they share a considerable number of olfactory elements raises a strong inference that one is copied from the other, or at least is an effort to imitate the other.
>
> Certain elements are found in only one of these perfumes. However, if the different element found in the second perfume has the same characteristics as the elements used in the first perfume, then this substitution has no impact on the impression which the fragrance makes on the consumer. Such is the case with the musk element provided by "Musk Ketone" in Tresor and by Gamma Dodelacton in Female Treasure.
>
> [Based on the number of olfactory elements available to perfume creators, the report calculated that the statistical probability of two independently created perfumes differing by only two olfactory elements was 1 in 10 to the 23rd power.]
>
> In conclusion, almost all of the raw materials contained in Tresor are present in Female Treasure, either identically or in the form of a substitute. The similarities in the raw materials are confirmed by the similarities in sensory effect.
>
> [Survey results indicated that, in a random sample, ¾ of the participants were unable to distinguish between the two perfumes.]

* * *

Accordingly, the court of appeal concludes that Female Treasure may be considered an unlawful reproduction of the copyrighted Tresor perfume, and that Kecofa, the seller of Female Treasure, has infringed Lancome's copyright. * * *

KECOFA B.V. v. LANCOME PARFUMS ET BEAUTE ET CIE S.N.C.

Supreme Court of the Netherlands, 2006
First Chamber, No. C04327HR

[In this appeal from the decision reproduced above, the Supreme Court reviewed the analysis of the Court of Appeals as well as Kecofa's assertions of error, then held as follows:]

Count 1 challenges jur.gr. 4.11. The complaints as to law and reasoning in a. and b. imply that while ignoring the limits of the litigation and/or by reason of an incomprehensible interpretation of the allegations of Lancôme the Appeal Court found that in this dispute Lancôme invokes the protection under copyright law not for the scent of the perfume Trésor (which can be perceived by humans with their olfactory sense), but for the (composition of) the olfactory substance (the olfactory source), as it is found in the bottles marketed under the trademark Trésor, and the Appeal Court thus gave a surprise decision, since Lancôme did not raise the issue of the similar components in the respective perfume liquids until oral arguments on appeal and Kecofa did not accept the litigation on this point. In c. and d., the count develops this with complaints about incorrectness and/or incomprehensibility of the opinion of the Appeal Court, because the composition of the olfactory substance as such is in principle not open to protection as "work" in the sense of the Auteurswet, and the same or almost identical scent (message) can be produced by olfactory substances of a very different nature or composition and, conversely, a rather small difference in the concentration or proportions of the same type of components may result in a significantly and even essentially different scent. * * *

Upon examining this count it is a priori that it does not contest that a scent—including a scent combination—may qualify for protection under copyright law. This starting-point is correct. The description laid down in Art. 10 Auteurswet, next to the non-exhaustive listing of types of works, of what must be understood to be a "work" in the sense of this Act, is put in general wording and does not preclude protection for a scent. This implies that as to the question of whether or not a scent qualifies for protection under copyright law, the determinative questions are whether the product is open to human perception and whether it has an original character of its own and bears the personal stamp of the maker. The notion of "work" in the Auteurswet does find its limits where the original character is no more than what is required to achieve a technical effect, but seeing that in case of a perfume there is no purely technical effect, this last condition does not prevent the award of protection under copyright law to the scent of a perfume.

The circumstances that the properties of the human olfactory sense put limits to the ability to distinguish scents and that the level to which one can distinguish different scents differs from one person to another, does not alter the above, nor does the circumstance that due to the specific nature of scents not all provisions and restrictions in the Auteurswet can directly apply—for example, because the use of perfume by the ordinary user by its nature necessarily implies dissemination of the scent.

For copyright law to apply, a scent cannot be limited to the substance or substances which make the scent. The substance or substances operate as an—not necessarily exclusive—incorporation of the work which is the scent, and they also ensure that the scent should not be excluded from protection under copyright law for being too volatile or unstable. In a perfume the scent therefore has to be distinguished from the mixture of substances which the perfume is composed of, and which the gaseous olfactory substances which can be perceived with the olfactory organ are released from when exposed to the open air.

To the extent that the complaints of count 1 are founded on the opinion that the Appeal Court interpreted the Lancôme's position as invoking protection under copyright law only for the composition of the olfactory substance of its perfume Trésor, they lack basis in fact. To the extent that count 1.a. complains that the Appeal Court gave an incomprehensible interpretation of the ground of the claim of Lancôme and its allegations, it is founded, seeing that these allegations do not allow any interpretation other than that Lancôme looks for protection for the scent of the perfume Trésor (the position endorsed above). Nevertheless this error is too insignificant to warrant reversal. As appears from jur.gr. 4.11.2–4.11.4 the Appeal Court expressed, although in less fortunate wordings, that the scent is entitled to copyright protection, as incorporated in the olfactory substance contained in the perfume bottles. Upon examining the infringement question the Appeal Court next rightly examined whether the scent Female Treasure should be considered to be a reproduction of the work Trésor (jur.gr. 4.16–4.16.1 and 4.16.6). * * *

* * *

Count 2.b furthermore challenges with independent complaints the opinion laid down in jur.gr. 4.12–4.13 concerning the original nature of the perfume Trésor. The Appeal Court discussed in jur.gr. 4.12.3–4.12.5 the allegations by which Kecofa countered the allegations of Lancôme in this respect—said argumentation boiling down to the argument that the perfume Trésor fits within a long existing tradition of perfumes having a specific scent character, that it is comparable with the perfume already previously existing "Eternity" and is an adaptation of the perfume "Exclamation"—and dismissed these allegations in a manner which does not demonstrate an incorrect conception of the law, nor is incomprehensible. That such parenthood with an existing scent tradition does exist in the perfume Trésor, even if this allegation was sufficiently substantiated with the "scent atlas" submitted by Kecofa, does not alter this. The mere circumstance that a creation fits within an existing tradition of similar works does not hinder the possibility of protection under copyright law thereof. That is why the Appeal Court could reject the offer of Kecofa to furnish proof.

The complaint in (iii) also fails, since in the light of that considered in respect of complaint (ii) it is not relevant that, as the complaint implies, the allegations of Lancôme leave room for the possibility that the scent of Trésor has too few features relevant to copyright law to distinguish it as a work in the sense of the Auteurswet from the scents of similar perfumes within the tradition referred to by Kecofa. The complaint in (iv) argues that the Appeal Court omitted to verify "empirically" whether the scent Trésor has an original character of its own and bears the personal stamp of the maker. This argument is answered by that considered by the Appeal Court in jur.gr. 4.124–4.12.5—not contested in cassation—*i.e.*, that protection under copyright law does not require that the work is new in an objective sense, but that it suffices that it is original in a subjective sense, *i.e.*, seen from the perspective of the maker, that it is up to the one who contests such originality to allege and to prove that the maker derived his work from an earlier work, and that in this respect Kecofa alleged too little, or did not sufficiently substantiate its allegations respectively.

Count 2.c argues that the opinion of the Appeal Court on the question whether the scent of Female Treasure infringes the copyright vested in Lancôme relating to the scent of the perfume Trésor is incorrect, or else incomprehensible for several reasons. The complaint reads (i) that without any verification of its own, at least not without any further reasoning than invoking the report [of Lancome's expert B & M], the Appeal Court could not reach the opinion that, to put it briefly, Female Treasure infringes Trésor * * *.

* * *

Faced with the question of whether Female Treasure constitutes a reproduction or adaptation of the work Trésor, the Appeal Court held on the basis of the criterion stated in jur.gr. 4.16.1—and (rightly) not contested in cassation—that a court could conclude from the B & M report that this was the case. Contrary to what the count contends, the judges did not have to make their own observations as well. Without any further allegation of defect, it cannot be understood why this report, which is founded both on a physical chemical analysis and on a sense survey methodologically founded among 66 test persons, be less reliable than the personal observation by judges of scents of only both perfumes in question next to each other, even apart from the fact that as appears from the advertising claims cited by Lancôme and not contested by Kecofa, that the latter aims at denying all differences between its perfumes and the perfumes it competes with, like Trésor, save where it concerns its price. The complaint of the count fails by reason of the above.

* * *

NEJILA X. CONTRE SOCIETE HAARMANN & REIMER

Cour de Cassation, Premiere Chambre Civile

Arret No. 1006 du 13 Juin 2006

Mme. X. appeals from the decision below (Versailles, March 5, 2002), which dismissed her request for compensation from Haarmann & Reimer for the perfumes that she created for them, holding that such creations do not qualify for copyright protection. She argues that the provisions of the Intellectual Property Code of France protect the rights of authors of every kind of work of the mind, regardless of genre, form of expression, merit, or purpose; that the Code provides a non-exhaustive list of things that qualify as works of the mind; that the fragrance of a perfume, as an intellectual creation, can therefore, provided that it is original, qualify as a work of the mind protected by copyright; that accordingly, Mme. X. requested compensation for the perfumes which she created, as she is entitled to under the Code; and that, in deciding that the creation of perfumes was not encompassed by copyright, the court of appeal violated Articles L.112–1 and L.112–2 of the Intellectual Property Code.

However, the fragrance of a perfume, which results from the mere implementation of know-how, does not, within the meaning of these Code provisions, constitute a form of expression that is entitled to copyright protection; from which it follows that the appeal has no foundation.

For these reasons: The appeal is rejected.

BEAUTE PRESTIGE INT'L CONTRE
SOCIETE SENTEUR MAZAL

Cour d'Appel de Paris
4eme Chambre—Section A
Arret du 14 Fevrier 2007

[Beaute Prestige International petitions the court of appeal to confirm the holding of a lower court that the products "J.P. L'Homme" and "Inmate for Men" sold by Societe Senteur Mazal infringe the copyright of Beaute Prestige International in its fragrance "Le Male." Societe Senteur Mazal argues that the fragrance of a perfume, which results from the mere application of know-how, is not copyrightable expression.]

* * *

Article L.112–2 of the Intellectual Property Code does not provide an exhaustive list of works eligible for copyright protection and does not exclude things perceivable by smell; furthermore, under the terms of Article L.112–1 of the Code, copyright extends to all works of the mind, regardless of genre, form of expression, merit, or purpose.

Fixation of a work is not a prerequisite to copyright protection as long as the form is perceivable; a fragrance, the olfactory composition of which is determinable, meets this requirement even though it is perceived in a different way, just like literary, pictorial, or musical works which, likewise, require a certain know-how.

The existence of perfume "families" does not preclude copyright protection for a fragrance that shares dominant components with those families, provided that it is the product of a deliberate combination of ingredients in such proportions that the resulting aroma reflects the creative input of the author, which is the case here.

A perfume may therefore qualify as a work of the mind protectable under the Intellectual Property Code, provided that, by reflecting the personal stamp of its author, it is original.

[Because Beaute Prestige International submitted an analysis of Le Male identifying specific components of the fragrance, and the defendant submitted no evidence indicating that Le Male was unoriginal, the court held that Le Male was protected by copyright. An expert's gas chromatographic analysis of Le Male and Inmate for Men indicated that 80% of the components are the same. The expert testified that this analysis showed numerous and important similarities between the products, and concluded that there was a significant risk of consumer confusion between the two fragrances.

Likewise, chromatographic analysis of J.P. L'Homme revealed that 66% of the components are the same, leading the expert to conclude that J.P. L'Homme is similar in the top notes and the background, so that there is a significant risk of consumer confusion.]

Considering that the selection of these common components cannot be coincidental;

Considering, by way of consequence, that by importing and commercializing the two perfumes on the French market, Senteur Mazal infringed the copyright of Beaute Prestige International in its fragrance;

The decision below is confirmed.

* * *

Notes

1. *Perfume Copyrights in the Netherlands:* Under Dutch law, does copyright subsist in the aroma of the perfume, the composition of the liquid that produces the aroma, or both? Does one approach make more sense than the other in terms of copyright policy? Could infringement liability arise from reproducing the same aroma by using a different formula?

2. *Perfume Copyrights in France:* Prior to 2006, at least two appellate courts in France had held that perfumes were eligible for copyright protection. In 2006, France's highest court, the Cour de Cassation, reached the opposite conclusion in *Nejila X.*, a typically brief decision. However, decisions of the Cour de Cassation have no precedential effect, and in 2007 two more appellate courts in France held that perfumes are copyrightable, as illustrated by the *Beaute Prestige* decision. Due to these conflicting opinions, the copyrightability of perfumes under French law remains unsettled. Compare *Nejila X.* and *Beaute Prestige* with the analyses of the Dutch courts, and with the most likely analysis under U.S. law.

3. Article L.112–1 of the French Intellectual Property Code states:

> The provisions of this Code protect the rights of authors of all types of works of the mind, regardless of genre, form of expression, merit, or purpose.

Article L.112–2 provides:

> For purposes of this Code, works of the mind include:
>
> 1. Books, pamphlets, and other literary, artistic, and scientific writings;
>
> 2. Lectures, speeches, sermons, arguments, and similar works;
>
> 3. Dramatic or dramatico-musical works;

4.   Choreographic works, circus acts and feats, pantomimes, the execution of which is fixed in writing or otherwise;

5.   Musical compositions with or without words;

6.   Cinematographic works and other works consisting of sequences of moving images, with or without sound, referred to collectively as "audiovisual works";

7.   Drawings, paintings, architectural works, sculptures, engravings, lithographs;

8.   Graphical and typographical works;

9.   Photographic works and works produced by analogous techniques;

10.   Works of applied art;

11.   Illustrations, geographical maps;

12.   Plans, sketches and three-dimensional works relating to geography, topography, architecture, and science;

13.   Software, including the preparatory design material;

14.   Creations of the seasonal industries of clothing and other fashion articles. Industries included in this category are those which, because of the exigencies of style, frequently change the form of their products, particularly including the making of dresses, furs, lingerie, embroidery, fashion, shoes, gloves, leather goods, the manufacture of fabrics with high novelty or of special use in high fashion dressmaking, the products of makers of high fashion goods and of footwear and upholstery fabrics.

Leaving aside perfume, what types of works are copyrightable under French law but not under U.S. law?

4.   Article 2(2) of the Berne Convention provides:

(2) It shall * * * be a matter for legislation in the countries of the Union to prescribe that works in general or any specified categories of works shall not be protected unless they have been fixed in some material form.

Under Article L.112–2 of the French Intellectual Property Code, must a work be fixed in order to be protected by copyright?

5.   Nejila X. was invoking a right to compensation from her employer. Because France has no work-made-for-hire provisions, presumably an employee who creates a copyrightable fragrance is considered the author of that fragrance, and hence the owner of the economic and moral rights. It is possible that another French court might disagree with the decision in *Nejila X.*, and recognize an employee as the author of a fragrance (because the Cour de Cassation's decision has no precedential effect). Indeed, this outcome would be consistent with the perfume industry's argument that perfumes are copyrightable. In that event, how could the French perfume industry protect itself against

after-the-fact compensation claims such as the one advanced by Nejila X.?

6. If perfume is copyrightable, does the person wearing it commit infringement by disseminating the fragrance to the public? Does the interaction of the wearer's body chemistry with the raw fragrance create an infringing derivative work? Even if the perfume maker is unlikely to raise such a claim against its own customer, what if the wearer has purchased a knock-off perfume instead?

7. If fragrances are copyrightable, does this conclusion apply also to the aromas of food and wine?

B. FASHION DESIGNS

RE MARCIO X. . ., ROBERTS Y. . . A. . . AND OLIVIER Z. . . RE INFRINGEMENT OF COPYRIGHT IN FASHION DESIGNS

Cour de Cassation (France)
Criminal Chamber, 2008

[2008] E.C.C. 19, [2009] E.C.D.R. 1

The Cour de Cassation, Chambre Criminelle, delivered the following judgment in the appeals brought by Marcio X. . ., Roberts Y. . . A. . ., Olivier Z. . . from the judgment of the Paris Court of Appeal, 13th Chamber, dated January 17, 2007, which imposed a fine of €8,000.00 on the first two, [and] a fine of €3,000.00 on the third one, for infringement of copyright through circulation of intellectual property, ordered the judgment to be published, and ruled on civil damages.

* * *

The reasons for the decision were that fashion creations and fashion shows are, under the terms of arts L.112–1[1] and 112–2[2] of the Intellectual Property Code, intellectual property that is

1. Art. L.112–1 provides:

   The provisions of this Code shall protect the rights of authors in all works of the mind, whatever their kind, form of expression, merit or purpose.

2. Art. L.112–2, para. 14, provides, in relevant part:

   The following, in particular, shall be considered works of the mind within the meaning of this Code:

   * * *

   14. creations of the seasonal industries of dress and articles of fashion.

Industries which, by reason of the demands of fashion, frequently renew the form of their products, particularly the making of dresses, furs, underwear, embroidery, fashion, shoes, gloves, leather goods, the manufacture of fabrics of striking novelty or of special use in high fashion dressmaking, the products of manufacturers of articles of fashion and of footwear and the manufacture of fabrics for upholstery shall be deemed to be seasonal industries.

protected under the provisions of Book I of the said Code, and that fashion houses have a copyright over those creations and shows insofar as they have an original character, which is not disputed in the present case as regards the fashion shows which took place in Paris from March 6 to 10, 2003. On that basis, they have the right to authorise or not the reproduction and circulation of these creations. In the present case, the complaint against the defendants is that they circulated, in the case of Marcio X. . . and Roberts Y. . ., or sold to be circulated, in the case of Olivier X. . ., on the internet site of the Viewfinder company, "firstview.com", photographs, reproductions of pictures or designs during the fashion shows without authorisation from the copyright holders.

On the material element of the offence, it is established that photographs taken during the relevant shows, especially by Marcio X. . ., manager of the Zeppelin company, but also by Roberts Y. . . and Olivier X. . ., were handed over to the Zeppelin company where they were transcribed onto CD ROM, then duplicated and directly transferred to the computer of the Viewfinder company, situated in New York, where they were made available to the public on the firstview.com internet site a few hours after the fashion show. The material element of circulation, established from the moment the photos were handed over to the Zeppelin company for the purpose of communicating them to the public, is therefore shown as against Marcio X. . ., who, as the manager of the company responsible for the communication of the photographs for the purpose of putting them online, was personally giving instructions to that effect, as against Roberts Y. . . who handed over his photos to the Zeppelin company with full knowledge of their destination, even if some of them could not be made immediately available online for technical reasons, and as against Olivier Z. . . who cannot pretend to have handed over his photos without considering that they could be circulated. This circulation took place without the authorisation of the holders of the relevant copyrights. Such authorisation could not be implied from the [press] accreditation enjoyed by the accused which allowed them to be present at the fashion shows and to take photographs, it being given only for the members of the media which had applied for it.

It is in vain that the accused claim not to be bound by the terms of the undertaking given by the press, of which they claim they never had any knowledge, and not to have signed the exclusive agreement as regards their photographs since they knew they were invited within the framework of a press accreditation. Marcio X. . . who had unsuccessfully applied for an accreditation for the Viewfinder company, is ill-founded to claim he did not know of the system put into place under the aegis of the Couture Federation. Even assuming they had been invited to the fashion shows in their personal capacity because of their notoriety, the submissions do not show that any one [of] them had received any kind of mandate from the fashion houses involved to make their creations available to the public. Marcio X... and Roberts Y..., directors of the Viewfinder company, knew [of] the decisions delivered in 2001 by the Tribunal de Grande Instance [Paris District Court] which had been personally served upon them, under the terms of which the circulation of photographs taken during other fashion shows was recognised as an infringement act. * * *

Finally, Marcio X..., Roberts Y... and Olivier Z..., being professional photographers of long standing, not unaware of the rules of fashion houses or of the rules applying to their own copyright, knew that they were neither entitled to use photographs of designs over which they had no rights nor to give them another destination than that authorised by their creators. It follows that the material element of the offence of infringement is proved against them. The moral element of the offence is established as against Marcio X..., Roberts Y... and Olivier Z..., who cannot rely on any authorisation to circulate and do not submit any evidence as to their good faith; on the contrary, the first two knew that they had not been granted the accreditation requested for Viewfinder, and Olivier Z..., although aware of the existence of firstview.com, took no steps to prevent the posting of his photos online. Good faith could not result from the American court decision which held that the acts complained of were not unlawful on the territory of the State of New York since the elements constituting the offence were committed on French soil; they knew that the acts were unlawful in France from the judgments referred to above and delivered in 2001.

[The Cour de Cassation summarized the photographers' arguments in the paragraphs numbered 1–5 below.]

1.   The offence of infringement of copyright requires a preliminary characterisation of a work as presenting an original character, without which there can be no copyright. Olivier Z..., Marcio X... and Roberts Y... were charged with infringement in respect of the shows of ready-to-wear fashion which took place between March 6 and 10, 2003, as well as of the ready-to-wear designs shown, through divulging photos reproducing them. In stating in a purely theoretical and general manner that fashion creations are works of intellectual property over which fashion houses have a copyright if they are original, and that this originality was not disputed in the present case, despite the accused disputing the material element of the offence, the Court of Appeal (which was obligated to make specific findings as to each element of the offense, the material one[s] in particular, in order to deliver a guilty verdict) failed to justify its decision in law.

2. According to the new art. L.122–5, 9°[³] of the Intellectual Property Code, resulting from art.1(1) of Act 2006–961 of 3 August 2006 (France), which is pertinent to the facts of the present case in that it sets up a new exception to copyright, the author cannot forbid the reproduction or representation, in full or in part, of a graphic, visual or architectural work of art, by way of written, audiovisual or online press, for the exclusive purpose of immediate information and in direct connection with the latter, subject to clearly indicating the name of the author. In not considering whether this provision, removing all copyright protection and therefore [negating] the criminal nature of the defendants' acts, was applicable to the circulation online, which took place immediately after their being taken, and at the time of the event, of the photographs of the fashion creations involved, on an online information site dedicated to fashion and haute couture, the Court of Appeal failed to justify its decision in law.

3. A circulation, limited in time and number, of reproductions made by a professional photographer of works presented at an event at which he has been invited by their creators, reproductions which the latter allow in order to have a media coverage of the event, does not require an authorisation. The decision below found that the photographs complained of were taken during fashion shows to which their authors, all well-known professional photographers, had been invited, together with other representatives from the press, that they were allowed to take photographs, and that they had not entered into any agreement under which they would refrain from publishing those photographs immediately after the events in order to ensure an attendance at those shows. The circulation of the reproductions complained of was limited to the posting online by the internet fashion magazine firstview.com for the purpose of covering this current event of the fashion world. In not considering whether it followed from those circumstances that the fashion houses which organised those shows had intended to permit the circulation of the photographs complained of in order to ensure a certain amount of publicity for their shows, their collections and their names, and whether therefore the online publication of the pictures was lawful even in the absence of an express authorisation, the Court of Appeal failed to justify its decision in law.

4. Inviting a professional photographer to an event in the course of which works are presented to the press, which he is

---

3. Art. L.122–5, para. 9, provides that the author cannot prevent the reproduction or communication to the public, in whole or in part, of a graphic, plastic or architectural artistic work, in the written, audiovisual or online press, for the exclusive purpose of immediately informing and in direct relation with this information, as long as the author's name is clearly indicated.

allowed to reproduce, amounts to an implicit authorisation to circulate the reproductions for the information of the public. The findings of the judgment show that the accused are professional photographers, that they had been invited by the fashion houses to attend the presentation to the press of their fashion shows and their collections, and that they were allowed to take photographs for the purpose of information, from which it follows that they had an implicit authorisation to circulate for information purposes the reproductions of the works thus presented. In requiring a specific publication authorisation to avoid liability for infringement of the rights of the fashion houses, when such an authorisation was already implied by the circumstances in which the accused had been invited to the fashion shows, the Court of Appeal failed to justify its decision in law.

5. Criminal infringement of copyright is an intentional offence requiring * * * the existence of a guilty intention, even if presumed. The judgment below states that Olivier Z..., who limited himself to selling his photographs to the Zeppelin company, which itself transferred them to the Viewfinder company, had not taken any steps to avoid the posting online of his photographs by the latter company of whose existence of he was aware. In thus reproaching Olivier Z... for committing an imprudence, to find him guilty of the offence of infringement of copyright, the Court of Appeal did not justify its decision in law.

[The Cour de Cassation then delivered its opinion:]

The decision below and the parties' filings indicate that, on March 11, 2003, the French Couture Federation and several companies involved in haute couture, ready-to-wear or fashion design, filed a formal complaint against an unnamed person, for infringement of copyright by publishing works of intellectual property in disregard of the rights of the authors, with the central squad for the prosecution of industrial and artistic infringements of copyright, producing two reports of March 7 and 10, 2003, from the Programmes Protection Agency, which showed that the American company Viewfinder Inc., set up between Marcio X... and Roberts Y... A..., circulated on the internet site "Firstview.com" the ready-to-wear fashion shows which had taken place in Paris from March 6 to 10, 2003. On March 11, 2003, police officers stopped Marcio X..., Roberts Y... A... and Olivier Z..., an independent photographer having, like they had, a press accreditation from the French Couture Federation, at the premises where a fashion show organised by the Chanel company was taking place. A search at the registered office of the Zeppelin company, of which Marcio X... is a manager and to which Olivier Z... sells his photos, then enabled them to seize CD–ROMs including the photographs taken between March 6 and 10, 2003, during the ready-to-wear fashion shows and to discover a transfer being carried out of the files of photographs of the fashion show of the Lanvin couture house to the Viewfinder company. At the end of the enquiry, Marcio X..., Roberts Y... A... and Olivier Z... were called by the prosecution service before the criminal court (*tribunal correctionnel*) charged with infringement of copyright through circulation of intellectual works disregarding the rights of the authors. The criminal court discharged them and dismissed the claims of the French Federation for couture, ready-to-wear, fashion houses and designers, and 12 fashion designer companies, appearing as civil parties. The prosecution and the civil parties appealed from these decisions.

In order to overturn the judgment, to declare the accused guilty of the offence they were charged with and to order them jointly to compensate 10 out of the 13 civil parties, the judgment, after having stated that fashion designs and shows are works of intellectual property in respect of which fashion houses have a copyright protected by the Intellectual Property Code, found, for reasons taken up in the ground of appeal, that in taking photographs of several fashion shows and in contributing from the French territory to the circulation online of the pictures thus obtained, without authorisation from the holders of copyright in the designs they reproduced, on a site to which the benefit of the press accreditations they had been granted had not been extended, that Olivier Z..., Marcio X... and Roberts Y... A... were guilty of the offence of infringement of copyright of intellectual works in breach of the authors' rights. The court added that Marcio X... who had unsuccessfully applied for an accreditation for the Viewfinder company, Roberts Y... A... who could not ignore that refusal to give an accreditation, and Olivier Z... who had taken no step to avoid the putting online of his photographs, did not show any evidence of their good faith.

Given these findings, resulting from its power of final appreciation of facts and circumstances of the case, as well as the submitted evidence which had been examined by both sides, the court of appeal justified its decision.

It follows that the ground of appeal, which fails in its claims that the defence provided by art. L.122–5, 9° of the Intellectual Property Code, is applicable to creations of the clothing and jewellery seasonal industries, protected by art. L.122–2 of the said Code, cannot succeed.

* * *

Notes

1. How does the French approach to copyright in fashion designs differ from that of the U.S.?

2. A number of countries now provide *sui generis* protection for fashion designs. Should the U.S. adopt such legislation? What type and degree of protection should such legislation provide?

3. The American decision referred to by the Cour de Cassation is Sarl Louis Feraud Int'l v. Viewfinder, Inc., 406 F.Supp.2d 274 (S.D.N.Y. 2005), *vacated*, 489 F.3d 474 (2d Cir. 2007). The district court in that case held that the French court's judgment against Viewfinder in this case (a default judgment, because Viewfinder failed to respond to the complaint) could not be enforced in the United States because doing so would violate the First Amendment. The Second Circuit vacated and remanded, with instructions to consider whether the publication of the photographs would qualify as fair use under section 107 and, if so, whether French copyright law provides protection comparable to fair use. On remand, the district court denied the plaintiff's motion for summary judgment, holding that a reasonable fact finder could conclude that the defendant was entitled to a fair use defense. Sarl Louis Feraud Int'l v. Viewfinder, Inc., 2008 WL 5272770 (S.D.N.Y. Dec. 19, 2008). This aspect of the case will be discussed in Chapter 5, Fair Use.

4. Does the *Marcio X.* case recognize copyright only in the fashion designs, or in the runway shows themselves? How would a claim of copyright in a runway show be addressed under U.S. law?

5. Consider the question of copyright in stage direction. In Sweden, Denmark, Norway, and Finland, it appears that copyright protects stage direction to the extent that a director adds "something new" to the dramatic work, in which case the stage direction is protected as an adaptation. *See* Anna Hammaren, *The Copyrightability of Stage Direction*, Scandinavian Studies in Law, Vol. 42—Intellectual Property (2002). In France, a 1971 case indicates that a director can be considered the "author" of his or her stage direction if there is sufficient originality, at least where the visual aspects of a performance are significant. *Id.* (citing the *Bataclan* case, RIDA 75 (1973), p.134 (Cour d'Appel de Paris, July 8, 1971)). How would this be addressed under U.S. law?

C. DATA COMPILATIONS

1. THE DECLINE OF "SWEAT OF THE BROW"

While the "authors' rights" jurisdictions of continental Europe have generally applied a relatively high standard of "originality" to all categories of copyrightable works, in the case of fact-based works countries with copyright traditions rooted in English law have tended to adhere to the "sweat of the brow" or "industrious collection" approach which the U.S. Supreme Court rejected in Feist Publications, Inc. v. Rural Telephone Service Co., 499 U.S. 340 (1991).

The Berne Convention does not directly address copyright in data compilations. Article 2(5) could be read as supporting a requirement for originality in selection and arrangement:

> (5) Collections of literary or artistic works such as encyclopaedias and anthologies which, by reason of the selection and arrangement of their contents, constitute intellectual creations shall be protected as such, without prejudice to the copyright in each of the works forming part of such collections.

However, Berne sets only a *minimum* standard for copyright protection. Thus, nothing in Berne prevents signatories from expanding the scope of copyrightable subject matter under their domestic laws to include, *inter alia*, unoriginal selections and arrangements of data.

The contrasting European approaches have been described as follows:

> The idea of "intellectual creation" was implicit in the notion of literary or artistic work under the Berne Convention for the Protection of Literary and Artistic Works (1886), to which Canada adhered in 1923, and which served as the precursor to Canada's first Copyright Act, adopted in 1924. Professor Ricketson has indicated that in adopting a sweat of the brow or industriousness approach to deciding what is original, common law countries such as England have "depart[ed] from the spirit, if not the letter, of the [Berne] Convention" since works that have taken time, labour or money to produce but are not truly artistic or literary intellectual creations are accorded copyright protection.

> In the international context, France and other continental civilian jurisdictions require more than mere industriousness to find that a work is original. "Under the French law, originality means both the intellectual contribution of the author and the novel nature of the work as compared with existing works". This understanding of originality is reinforced by the expression *"le droit d'auteur"*—literally the *"author's* right"*— the term used in the French title of the [Canadian] Copyright Act. The author must contribute something intellectual to the work, namely skill and judgment, if it is to be considered original.

CCH Canadian Ltd. v. Law Society of Upper Canada, (2004) SCC 13, paras. 19–20 (citations omitted).

However, as discussed in C.2. below, within the European Union the Database Directive has eliminated many of these differences, at least in the context of fact compilations. Outside the EU, the courts in nations that derive their copyright tradition from England—Canada, India, and Australia—have been retreating from the "sweat of the brow" approach in the aftermath of *Feist,* although they have stopped short of a wholehearted embrace of *Feist.*

Prior to the Database Directive, English courts adhered firmly to the "sweat of the brow" doctrine, and failed to distinguish between the labor invested in *creating* facts and the labor invested in *compiling* them. In 1910, the English courts upheld copyright in a comprehensive list of all thoroughbred brood mares at stud in England; the court reasoned that significant effort had gone into collecting this information. Weatherby & Sons v. International Horse Agency & Exchange Ltd, [1910] 2 Ch 297. Similarly, in H. Blacklock & Co. Ltd v. C. Arthur Pearson Ltd, [1915] 2 Ch 376, the court held that the copyright in a comprehensive railroad timetable (listing station names in alphabetical order) was infringed even though the defendant reproduced only the names of the stations. In Football League Ltd v. Littlewoods Pools Ltd, [1959] 1 Ch 637, a chronological list of football (*i.e.,* soccer) fixtures (*i.e.,* match-ups) was held to be copyrightable, because the effort that went into deciding the fixture schedule should not be distinguished from the effort that went into expressing them in the form of a list. In 1964, the House of Lords applied this same analysis to football betting coupons, finding them copyrightable even though far more effort went into developing the odds than into reproducing them on paper. Ladbroke (Football) Ltd. v. William Hill (Football) Ltd., [1964] 1 All E.R. 465 (HL), [1964] W.L.R. 273. In 1984, it was held that infringement occurred when a weekly magazine copied information from broadcasters' television listings; these listings were held to be copyrightable because of the skill and labor invested in creating the program schedules. Independent Television Publications Ltd v. Time Out Ltd, [1984] FSR 64. In 2000, a leading treatise summarized British law on compilation copyrights as follows:

> A compilation is a work consisting of a collection of materials, and its merit normally resides in the painstaking labour which has been expended in assembling the facts (as in the case of a directory); or in the skill, judgment and knowledge involved in selecting those things which are to be included (as in the case of an anthology); or both. Consequently the copyright in such a work may be infringed by appropriating an undue amount of the material, although the language employed be different or the order of the material be altered. Were the law otherwise

copyrights in compilations would be of little or no value. The point is succinctly stated in two dicta which have frequently been approved: "No man is entitled to avail himself of the previous labours of another for the purpose of conveying to the public the same information": and "The true principle in all these cases is that the defendant is not at liberty to use or avail himself of the labour which the plaintiff has been at for the purpose of producing his work; that is, in fact, merely to take away the result of another man's labour or, in other words, his property."

* * *

In *Football League Ltd v. Littlewoods Pools Ltd* it was left as an open question whether a copyist might legitimately take the contents of a compilation by rearranging the order of the words. It is submitted that the result of the authorities ... is that he may not do so if he is still appropriating for himself a substantial amount of the pains, skill, judgment, knowledge and so on of the original author. Where, however, the originality resides in the order of the material, and the effect of the rearrangement is to destroy this, so that he is no longer appropriating a substantial part of the author's work, the process is legitimate.

H. Laddie, P. Prescott, M. Vitoria, A. Speck and L. Lane, The Modern Law of Copyright and Designs (3rd ed., 2000), paras. 3.88 and 3.90.

In Canada, the Supreme Court in CCH Canadian Ltd. v. Law Society of Upper Canada, (2004) SCC 13, announced that, while it would not adopt the exact standard of *Feist,* it would no longer apply the traditional "sweat of the brow" standard derived from English law. Instead, the Court equated originality with the exercise of "skill and judgment":

For a work to be "original" within the meaning of the Copyright Act, it must be more than a mere copy of another work. At the same time, it need not be creative, in the sense of being novel or unique. What is required to attract copyright protection in the expression of an idea is an exercise of skill and judgment. By skill, I mean the use of one's knowledge, developed aptitude or practised ability in producing the work. By judgment, I mean the use of one's capacity for discernment or ability to form an opinion or evaluation by comparing different possible options in producing the work. This exercise of skill and judgment will necessarily involve intellectual effort. The exercise of skill and judgment required to produce the work must not be so trivial that it could be characterized as a purely mechanical exercise. For example, any skill and judgment that might be involved in simply changing the font of a work to produce "another" work would be too trivial to merit copyright protection as an "original" work.

CCH, para. 16. The Court viewed its new standard as falling somewhere between *Feist* and the "sweat of the brow" approach:

> The "sweat of the brow" approach to originality is too low a standard. It shifts the balance of copyright protection too far in favour of the owner's rights, and fails to allow copyright to protect the public's interest in maximizing the production and dissemination of intellectual works. On the other hand, the [*Feist*] creativity standard of originality is too high. A creativity standard implies that something must be novel or non-obvious—concepts more properly associated with patent law than copyright law. By way of contrast, a standard requiring the exercise of skill and judgment in the production of a work avoids these difficulties and provides a workable and appropriate standard for copyright protection that is consistent with the policy objectives of the Copyright Act.

Id., para. 24. Is this a fair characterization of *Feist*'s creativity standard?

A 2007 decision from the Supreme Court of India also rejects the "sweat of the brow" approach. In Eastern Book Co. v. D.B. Modak, Appeal (Civil) 6472 of 2004 (Dec. 12, 2007), the Court compared the English "sweat of the brow" precedents with both *Feist* and *CCH Canadian*, and opted for an approach similar to Canada's. Where the work in question consisted of published law reports, the court concluded that some, but not all, of the annotations added by the publisher to the public domain opinions issued by the Indian courts involved "skill and judgment" as well as a "minimum amount of creativity," *id.*, para. 41, thus giving rise to a copyrightable derivative work:

> Although for establishing a copyright, the creativity standard applied is not that something must be novel or non-obvious, but some amount of creativity in the work to claim a copyright is required. It does require a minimal degree of creativity. Arrangement of the facts or data or the case law is already included in the judgment of the court. * * * To support copyright, there must be some substantive variation and not merely a trivial variation, not the variation of the type where limited ways/unique of expression available and an author selects one of them which can be said to be a garden variety. Novelty or invention or innovative idea is not the requirement for protection of copyright but it does require minimal degree of creativity.

Id., para. 40.

The standard of originality in Australia is currently in flux, but recent developments suggest that the "sweat of the brow" theory is in its final throes. Until 2009, the leading case was Desktop Marketing Systems Pty Ltd v. Telstra Corp. Ltd, [2002] FCAFC 112, in which the Federal Court of Australia (one step below the nation's highest court) expressly declined to adopt *Feist*, and reiterated its commitment to the "sweat of the brow" approach, holding that a telephone directory was "original" because the plaintiff undertook "substantial labour and expense" in "compiling and presenting the details of telephone subscribers," and that the defendant infringed when it appropriated the benefit of that labor and expense.

In April of 2009, however, Australia's High Court (the equivalent of the U.S. Supreme Court) issued its decision in IceTV Pty Ltd v. Nine Network Australia Pty Ltd, [2009] HCA 14. The High Court rejected a television network's claim that the defendant's digital television guide infringed the copyright in the network's program listings. However, the standard for subsistence of copyright was not squarely at issue, because the defendant conceded that the network's program listings were copyrightable. For that reason, the defendant did not copy directly from the network's listings, but employed a more circuitous route to predict the program schedule. The opinion explains:

> * * * Approximately two weeks prior to the commencement of each week of broadcasting, an employee of [plaintiff] Nine supplies certain third parties known as "Aggregators" with a schedule of programmes to be broadcast on Nine Network stations in that week (a "Weekly Schedule"). Each Weekly Schedule is produced from the Nine Database.
>
> Each Weekly Schedule contains various elements, including particulars of the time and title of programmes to be broadcast ("time and title information"). The Aggregators use the Weekly Schedule, together with comparable material provided by other Australian television broadcasters and independently obtained material, to produce "Aggregated Guides", which are schedules of programmes to be broadcast on various television stations, for publication in various media.
>
> * * *
>
> The primary business of [defendant] IceTV is the provision, via the Internet, of a subscription-based electronic programme guide for television known as the "IceGuide". When downloaded onto certain devices, which are available for purchase by consumers in Australia, the IceGuide displays details of programmes scheduled to be broadcast by free-to-air televi-

sion stations for the coming six to eight days, including stations in the Nine Network.

Over the period relevant to this appeal, when preparing the information to be included in the IceGuide for a given day, employees of IceTV used information included in the IceGuide for a previous day and then compared this with published Aggregated Guides. Where there was a discrepancy as to the time and title information, the IceGuide was amended to reflect the Aggregated Guides in almost all cases. It is this use of the Aggregated Guides that is in issue in this appeal.

IceTV, paras. 1–5.

On advice of counsel, who no doubt relied on *Desktop*'s reaffirmation of the "sweat of the brow" theory of copyright, the defendant went to great lengths to avoid copying directly from the network's published guides. This included a great deal of time watching television:

> * * * The objective of IceTV had been to start with "a clean sheet of paper" and develop an EPG [Electronic Program Guide] without infringing third party intellectual property rights. IceTV obtained legal advice as to how this might be done and began by creating templates of the daily programming of the Sydney channels Nine, Ten and Seven ("the Sydney templates"). The author of the Sydney templates was IceTV's Content Manager, Mr. Mitchell Rilett.
>
> The Sydney templates included seven spreadsheets populated with time and title information and additional programme information for programmes broadcast by TCN–9 on each day of the broadcast week. Nine alleged at trial that this information had been copied from the publicly available guides. However, Bennett J. found that Mr. Rilett created the Sydney templates by watching television over a period of three weeks in August 2004 and recording the time and title of the programmes then broadcast; his evidence of that experience and description of it as "torture" were found by her Honour to be compelling. The primary judge went on to find that Mr. Rilett compared his templates with the publicly available guides in September 2004, noted a "slight variation" in the time and title information, and amended the Sydney templates accordingly.
>
> In this Court, the alleged copying of time and title information was identified not in the creation or amendment of the Sydney templates, but in the making and updating of successive IceGuides built upon those templates. This commenced in October 2004, when Mr. Rilett transposed the information in the Sydney templates into a computer database maintained by

IceTV ("the Ice Database") and began using IceTV's software to compile 24–hour guides for the commercial networks for each day of the calendar week, six days ahead of when the programmes were scheduled for broadcast.

The findings of the primary judge and the evidence supported the identification of three tasks required to populate the IceGuide schedules with time and title information for the Sydney station, TCN–9.

Task one was to cause IceTV's software to create a "starting template" populated with time and title information copied from a past IceGuide schedule for TCN–9 Sydney for the same day of a previous week. This was done by Mr. Rilett or one of two other IceTV staff, Ms. Suzanne Langford or Ms. Samantha Tai. By way of example, the primary judge explained:

"Mr. Rilett used the IceGuide for TCN–9 Sydney for Saturday, 16 September 2006 as the source schedule to create an IceGuide for TCN–9 Sydney for Saturday, 23 September 2006. 'Predicting over' the source schedule using Ice[TV]'s software caused the starting template for 23 September 2006 to contain the same program listings information as the source schedule, save for date and episode information."

This process was referred to within IceTV as "predicting it over" and relied on the assumption, noted earlier in these reasons, that the TCN–9 programming for any given day was likely to be substantially the same as it was on the same day of the previous week. While that assumption was made good for "strip programs" broadcast by TCN–9 in the same timeslots, 6:00 am to 7:00 pm, Mondays to Fridays, "predicting it over" could not accommodate movies, one-off programmes or other changes in programming from week to week.

For that reason, task two was necessary. This was to check the time and title information in the starting template with at least three online published guides. In the event of the published guides indicating a variation in programming from the previous week, Mr. Rilett, Ms. Tai or Ms. Langford typically amended the starting template to reflect the time and title information in the published guides.

To illustrate the extent of amendments made, Bennett J. found that it was necessary for Mr. Rilett to amend the time and title information for 17 out of 31 timeslots in the starting template for TCN–9 for Saturday, 23 September 2006. However, the primary judge also found that fewer amendments were necessary for weekdays because of strip and series programmes. Thus, her Honour's reasons recorded the making of changes to programme title, time or episode for 13 out of 29 timeslots when creating an IceGuide schedule for TCN–9 for Monday, 2 October 2006.

The nature of amendments made to the starting template was further illustrated by the setting out by the primary judge of each change made by Mr. Rilett in creating the IceGuide schedule for TCN–9 for 23 September 2006. By way of example of five such changes, Mr. Rilett:

"• changed the start time for *Nightline* from 12:25 am to 12:15 am to reflect the information in published guides;

• deleted the movie *Lansky*, which was scheduled to appear at 12:55 am in the IceGuide but was not in the published guides;

• added the movie *The Inspectors* at 12:45 am to the IceGuide, based on the information in the published guides;

• changed the start time in the IceGuide for the *Late Show with David Letterman* from 3:05 am to 2:35 am, based on the information in the published guides;

• added the program *Entertainment Tonight* to the IceGuide at 3:30 am, based on the information in the published guides".

However, the evidence also showed that the time and title information was not universally amended to reflect the published guides. For example, in the course of making the amendments just described, Bennett J. explained that Mr. Rilett:

"ignored the published guides' indication that *The Batman* would be broadcast at 8:05 am, 8:40 am and 9:20 am and instead left the IceGuide starting template's indication that *Classic Looney Tunes* would be broadcast at these times. Mr. Rilett disregarded the published guides as he determined that TCN–9 Sydney may not broadcast *The Batman* at that time by reason of the program not being suitably rated for viewing during children's hours".

To amend the time and title information in the starting template, Bennett J. found that IceTV staff searched the Ice Database for programmes or episode titles previously included in that database. This was done by causing IceTV's software to generate an on-screen list of available programme titles. Start times could be selected or amended using on-screen "drop-down boxes", while mouse-clicking buttons marked "Revise" or "Update Show" caused the software to insert new starting times or programme titles into the IceGuide schedule. Episode titles were similarly presented by IceTV's software in a list available to the operator and available for selection for inclusion in the IceGuide schedule. If, at the time of amendment of the starting template, the programme or episode had not been previously added to the Ice Database, it could be added using IceTV's software.

The third and final task was to capture late changes to Nine's programming. The primary judge found that this was done by Ms. Langford, who undertook a daily comparison of the time and title information in the IceGuide schedule with the listings in the YourTV Guide for the up-coming 60–hour period. Late changes were also inserted by Mr. Rilett in response to information obtained from his review of a website styled *Television Programming News* and from messages posted by subscribers on an online forum maintained on IceTV's website.

The evidence showed the same three tasks were performed to create IceGuide schedules for other stations in the Nine Network, subject to one variation in task one. This comprised the use of a different channel within the Nine Network as the source schedule. Thus, IceGuide schedules for GTV–9 in Melbourne were made by "predicting over" time and title information derived from the IceGuide schedule for TCN–9 for the same day. In the expectation that the same episodes would be shown by the various stations in the Nine Network, episode titles were retained by IceTV's software where the source schedule channel was different from the destination channel. The evidence included a chart prepared by Mr. Rilett documenting the relevant "source schedule" for the various stations within the Nine Network. However, for each new schedule, it remained necessary to repeat task two and cross-check the time and title information with online, publicly available guides.

One further point concerning the making and updating of the IceGuide should be noted. This concerns the source of the IceGuide synopses. Bennett J. found that the synopses appearing in the IceGuide for the Nine Network were drafted by two IceTV staff, Ms. Madeleine Doyle and Ms. Kiriaki Orfanos. Reference books such as *Halliwell's Film & Video Guide 2002* and websites were consulted for this purpose, but Ms. Doyle and Ms. Orfanos were not permitted to have regard to the published guides. * * * "

IceTV, paras. 173–184.

Even these extraordinary efforts did not immunize IceTV from the wrath of the Nine Network, which forced IceTV into a protracted battle all the way up to Australia's highest court. Although

IceTV prevailed in the trial court, the Federal Court of Appeal reversed, applying the "sweat of the brow" standard it had recently reaffirmed in *Desktop Marketing*. The High Court later summed up the philosophical difference between the trial judge and the court of appeal as follows:

> Both the primary judge and the Full Court essentially approached the question of whether IceTV had reproduced a substantial part of any Weekly Schedule by identifying the "skill and labour" which was expended on creating the Weekly Schedules, then asking whether IceTV had "appropriated" Nine's skill and labour. The primary judge and the Full Court reached opposite conclusions on the point essentially because of different approaches to identifying the relevant skill and labour in question: the primary judge considered that skill and labour in making programming decisions was not relevant and that there was not a reproduction of a substantial part; the Full Court considered that this skill and labour was relevant and that there was a reproduction of a substantial part.

Id., para. 8.

On appeal to the High Court, IceTV conceded that Nine Networks' program listings were copyrightable. Therefore, the High Court focused its analysis on whether, despite the defendant's effort to recreate the program listings (program title, episode title, date, and time of broadcast) through its elaborate process of independent observation and predictive methods, the defendant's activity amounted to copying a "substantial part" of the copyrighted compilation. Although the six Justices ruled unanimously that the defendant did not infringe, there was no majority rationale. Instead, the Justices split 3–3 between two opinions.

Three of the Justices held that, while the defendant appropriated the plaintiff's "skill and labor," that skill and labor was not directed to the *form* of the plaintiff's expression, but to creating its informational content. In other words, the plaintiff had invested skill and labor in making its programming decisions, and it was this skill and labor that the defendant appropriated, rather than skill and labor invested in expressing those programming decisions. Thus, these Justices distinguished the effort which Nine Network invested in *deciding* the schedule from the effort that it invested in *expressing* the schedule:

> In the context of infringement, in particular the determination of whether a part reproduced is a "substantial part", a matter often referred to is whether there has been an "appropriation" of the author's skill and labour. As already noted, both the primary judge and the Full Court adopted that approach in this case. However, it is always necessary to focus on

the nature of the skill and labour, and in particular to ask whether it is directed to the originality of the particular form of expression.

* * *

Rewarding skill and labour in respect of compilations without any real consideration of the productive effort directed to coming up with a particular form of expression of information can lead to error. The error is of a kind which might enable copyright law to be employed to achieve anti-competitive behaviour of a sort not contemplated by the balance struck in the Act between the rights of authors and the entitlements of the reading public. The Act mandates an inquiry into the substantiality of the part of the work which is reproduced. A critical question is the degree of originality of the particular form of expression of the part. Consideration of the skill and labour expended by the author of a work may assist in addressing that question: that the creation of a work required skill and labour may indicate that the particular form of expression adopted was highly original. However, focussing on the "appropriation" of the author's skill and labour must not be allowed to distract from the inquiry mandated by the Act. To put aside the particular form of expression can cause difficulties, as evidenced by *Desktop Marketing Systems Pty Ltd v. Telstra Corporation Ltd*.

It is not seriously in dispute that skill and labour was expended on producing the Weekly Schedules (and the Nine Database). The evidence disclosed considerable skill and labour involved in programming decisions. There was a contest about whether it mattered if some of the skill and labour expended was directed to business considerations. Plainly, the skill and labour was highly relevant to matters such as advertising revenue. It is not difficult to understand that questions of the timing of particular broadcasts are crucial for advertising revenues. The fact that business considerations inform the decision to adopt a particular form of expression will not necessarily detract from the originality of that form of expression.

However, the critical question is whether skill and labour was directed to the particular form of expression of the time and title information, including its chronological arrangement. The skill and labour devoted by Nine's employees to programming decisions was not directed to the originality of the particular form of expression of the time and title information. The level of skill and labour required to express the time and title information was minimal. That is not surprising, given that, as explained above, the particular form of expression of the time and title information is essentially dictated by the nature of that information.

Id., paras. 49–54.

In their separate opinion, the three remaining Justices noted that, in the absence of database legislation comparable to the EU Database Directive, the question of copyright in a factual compilation "cannot be resolved by concluding, as did the Full Court [of Appeals], that Ice appropriated 'the fruits of Nine's skill and labour.'" *IceTV*, para. 139. They agreed with the defendant that:

> [T]he originality of the compilation being the [plaintiff's] Weekly Schedule lay not in the provision of time and title information, but in the selection and presentation of that information together with additional programme information and synopses, to produce a composite whole.

Id., para. 152. Rejecting the analysis of the appellate court, they agreed instead with the trial judge:

> The primary judge approached the issue of substantiality correctly when she stressed that the detailed and lengthy preparatory work involved * * * was directed to the conduct of the business of the Nine Network in broadcasting programmes which would attract viewers. Likewise the making of late programme changes, as Mr. Healy explained.
>
> There remained what the Full Court accepted was "the extremely modest skill and labour" in setting down the programmes already selected * * *.
>
> If the Weekly Schedule be seen in that light, several propositions advanced by Ice should be accepted. First, it ought, in a case such as the present, * * * to be clearly established by Nine that, looking at the Weekly Schedule as a whole, there has been a substantial reproduction in the particular use by IceTV of the Aggregated Guides to access the time and title information.
>
> Secondly, in assessing the quality of the time and title information, as components of the Weekly Schedule, baldly stated matters of fact or intention are inseparable from and co-extensive with their expression. It is difficult to discern the expression of thought in statements of which programmes will be broadcast and when this will occur. If the facts be divorced from the other elements constituting the compilation in suit, as is the case with the use by IceTV of the time and title information, then it is difficult to treat the IceGuide as the reproduction of a substantial part of the Weekly Schedule in the qualitative sense required by the case law.

Thirdly, it is important also to ask whether IceTV acted as it did in preparing the IceGuide with *animus furandi*, to take from the Aggregated Guides the time and title information to save itself from effort on its part. This invites further attention to the business plan and methods adopted by Ice and to the matter of "predictions".

Id., paras. 167–71. Finally, at the urging of an amicus, these three justices addressed the possibility that their analysis constituted a rejection of *Desktop Marketing* and an endorsement of *Feist*. Their response was oblique:

One final point should be made. This concerns the submission by the Digital Alliance that this Court consider the Full Court's decision in *Desktop Marketing* and, to the contrary of *Desktop Marketing*, affirm that there must be "creative spark" or exercise of "skill and judgment" before a work is sufficiently "original" for the subsistence of copyright.

It is by no means apparent that the law even before the 1911 [English Copyright] Act was to any different effect to that for which the Digital Alliance contends. It may be that the reasoning in *Desktop Marketing* with respect to compilations is out of line with the understanding of copyright law over many years. These reasons explain the need to treat with some caution the emphasis in *Desktop Marketing* upon "labour and expense" per se and upon misappropriation. However, in the light of the admission of Ice that the Weekly Schedule was an original literary work, this is not an appropriate occasion to take any further the subject of originality in copyright works.

IceTV, paras. 187–188.

Notes

1. Is there anything left of the "sweat of the brow" standard in Australia? Will businesses like IceTV continue having to use circuitous methods to re-create a network's program listings, or will they be able to simply copy time and title information from the network's guides? Will a "white pages" telephone directory have any copyright protection in Australia?

2. Would the principle that copyright arises from skill and industry permit a copyist, or a maker of a scale model, to assert copyright based on the skill and effort expended in making a precise replica? According to Spraymiser Ltd. v. Wrightway Mktg. Ltd., [2000] ECDR 349 (High Court, Chancery Division, 1999), the answer under English law is no. Why?

3. Canada's copyright law, as amended in 1993 to conform with Article 1705 of the North American Free Trade Agreement, defines a

"compilation" as "a work resulting from the selection or arrangement of data." Sec. 2, Copyright Act 1985 (as amended in 1993). In Tele–Direct Pubs., Inc. v. American Business Information, Inc., 154 DLR(4th) 328 (1997), which foreshadowed *CCH Canadian*, the Canadian Federal Court of Appeal held that a Yellow Pages directory was entitled to copyright as a compilation only to the extent that it manifested originality in the selection and arrangement of information. Judge Decary's opinion noted:

> [T]he addition of the definition of "compilation" in so far as it relates to "a work resulting from the selection or arrangement of data" appears to me to have decided the battle which was shaping up in Canada between partisans of the "creativity" doctrine— according to which compilations must possess at least some minimal degree of creativity—and the partisans of the "industrious collection" or "sweat of the brow" doctrine—wherein copyright is a reward for the hard work that goes into compiling facts.

4.   The WIPO Copyright Treaty (Art. 5) requires signatories to protect data compilations to the extent that they "constitute intellectual creations" by virtue of "the selection or arrangement of their contents." Protection does not extend to the data itself.

2.   THE EUROPEAN UNION DATABASE DIRECTIVE

Prior to 1996, the nations belonging to the European Union had adopted varying approaches to copyright in data compilations. Several employed an originality test similar to that of *Feist*. The United Kingdom, in contrast, adhered to its traditional "sweat of the brow" or "industrious collection" approach. Other approaches fell somewhere between these perspectives. In 1996, in an effort to harmonize these approaches, the European Council and the European Parliament adopted Directive 96/9/EC, and required member states to adopt implementing legislation by 1998. In 2005, the European Commission issued a report evaluating the impact of the Directive on the production of databases in Europe. Excerpts from the Directive and the 2005 report are reproduced below.

DIRECTIVE 96/9/EC OF THE EUROPEAN PARLIAMENT AND OF THE COUNCIL OF 11 MARCH 1996 ON THE LEGAL PROTECTION OF DATABASES

CHAPTER I: SCOPE

Article 1: Scope

1.   This Directive concerns the legal protection of databases in any form.

2.   For the purposes of this Directive, "database" shall mean a collection of independent works, data or other materials arranged

in a systematic or methodical way and individually accessible by electronic or other means.

3.   Protection under this Directive shall not apply to computer programs used in the making or operation of databases accessible by electronic means.

Article 2: Limitations on the scope

This Directive shall apply without prejudice to Community provisions relating to:

(a) the legal protection of computer programs;

(b) rental right, lending right and certain rights related to copyright in the field of intellectual property;

(c) the term of protection of copyright and certain related rights.

CHAPTER II: COPYRIGHT

Article 3: Object of protection

1.   In accordance with this Directive, databases which, by reason of the selection or arrangement of their contents, constitute the author's own intellectual creation shall be protected as such by copyright. No other criteria shall be applied to determine their eligibility for that protection.

2.   The copyright protection of databases provided for by this Directive shall not extend to their contents and shall be without prejudice to any rights subsisting in those contents themselves.

Article 4: Database authorship

1.   The author of a database shall be the natural person or group of natural persons who created the base or, where the legislation of the Member States so permits, the legal person designated as the rightholder by that legislation.

2.   Where collective works are recognized by the legislation of a Member State, the economic rights shall be owned by the person holding the copyright.

3.   In respect of a database created by a group of natural persons jointly, the exclusive rights shall be owned jointly.

Article 5: Restricted acts

In respect of the expression of the database which is protectable by copyright, the author of a database shall have the exclusive right to carry out or to authorize:

(a) temporary or permanent reproduction by any means and in any form, in whole or in part;

(b) translation, adaptation, arrangement and any other alteration;

(c) any form of distribution to the public of the database or of copies thereof. The first sale in the Community of a copy of the database by the rightholder or with his consent shall exhaust the right to control resale of that copy within the Community;

(d) any communication, display or performance to the public;

(e) any reproduction, distribution, communication, display or performance to the public of the results of the acts referred to in (b).

Article 6: Exceptions to restricted acts

1. The performance by the lawful user of a database or of a copy thereof of any of the acts listed in Article 5 which is necessary for the purposes of access to the contents of the databases and normal use of the contents by the lawful user shall not require the authorization of the author of the database. Where the lawful user is authorized to use only part of the database, this provision shall apply only to that part.

2. Member States shall have the option of providing for limitations on the rights set out in Article 5 in the following cases:

(a) in the case of reproduction for private purposes of a non-electronic database;

(b) where there is use for the sole purpose of illustration for teaching or scientific research, as long as the source is indicated and to the extent justified by the non-commercial purpose to be achieved;

(c) where there is use for the purposes of public security or for the purposes of an administrative or judicial procedure;

(d) where other exceptions to copyright which are traditionally authorized under national law are involved, without prejudice to points (a), (b) and (c).

3. In accordance with the Berne Convention for the protection of Literary and Artistic Works, this Article may not be interpreted in such a way as to allow its application to be used in a manner which unreasonably prejudices the rightholder's legitimate interests or conflicts with normal exploitation of the database.

CHAPTER III: SUI GENERIS RIGHT

Article 7: Object of protection

1. Member States shall provide for a right for the maker of a database which shows that there has been qualitatively and/or quantitatively a substantial investment in either the obtaining, verification or presentation of the contents to prevent extraction and/or re-utilization of the whole or of a substantial part, evaluated qualitatively and/or quantitatively, of the contents of that database.

2.   For the purposes of this Chapter:

(a) "extraction" shall mean the permanent or temporary transfer of all or a substantial part of the contents of a database to another medium by any means or in any form;

(b) "re-utilization" shall mean any form of making available to the public all or a substantial part of the contents of a database by the distribution of copies, by renting, by on-line or other forms of transmission. The first sale of a copy of a database within the Community by the rightholder or with his consent shall exhaust the right to control resale of that copy within the Community;

Public lending is not an act of extraction or re-utilization.

3.   The right referred to in paragraph 1 may be transferred, assigned or granted under contractual licence.

4.   The right provided for in paragraph 1 shall apply irrespective of the eligibility of that database for protection by copyright or by other rights. Moreover, it shall apply irrespective of eligibility of the contents of that database for protection by copyright or by other rights. Protection of databases under the right provided for in paragraph 1 shall be without prejudice to rights existing in respect of their contents.

5.   The repeated and systematic extraction and/or re-utilization of insubstantial parts of the contents of the database implying acts which conflict with a normal exploitation of that database or which unreasonably prejudice the legitimate interests of the maker of the database shall not be permitted.

Article 8: Rights and obligations of lawful users

1.   The maker of a database which is made available to the public in whatever manner may not prevent a lawful user of the database from extracting and/or re-utilizing insubstantial parts of its contents, evaluated qualitatively and/or quantitatively, for any purposes whatsoever. Where the lawful user is authorized to extract and/or re-utilize only part of the database, this paragraph shall apply only to that part.

2.   A lawful user of a database which is made available to the public in whatever manner may not perform acts which conflict with normal exploitation of the database or unreasonably prejudice the legitimate interests of the maker of the database.

3.   A lawful user of a database which is made available to the public in any manner may not cause prejudice to the holder of a copyright or related right in respect of the works or subject matter contained in the database.

Article 9: Exceptions to the sui generis right

Member States may stipulate that lawful users of a database which is made available to the public in whatever manner may, without the authorization of its maker, extract or re-utilize a substantial part of its contents:

(a) in the case of extraction for private purposes of the contents of a non-electronic database;

(b) in the case of extraction for the purposes of illustration for teaching or scientific research, as long as the source is indicated and to the extent justified by the non-commercial purpose to be achieved;

(c) in the case of extraction and/or re-utilization for the purposes of public security or an administrative or judicial procedure.

Article 10: Term of protection

1.   The right provided for in Article 7 shall run from the date of completion of the making of the database. It shall expire fifteen years from the first of January of the year following the date of completion.

2.   In the case of a database which is made available to the public in whatever manner before expiry of the period provided for in paragraph 1, the term of protection by that right shall expire fifteen years from the first of January of the year following the date when the database was first made available to the public.

3.   Any substantial change, evaluated qualitatively or quantitatively, to the contents of a database, including any substantial change resulting from the accumulation of successive additions, deletions or alterations, which would result in the database being considered to be a substantial new investment, evaluated qualitatively or quantitatively, shall qualify the database resulting from that investment for its own term of protection.

Article 11: Beneficiaries of protection under the sui generis right

1.   The right provided for in Article 7 shall apply to database[s] whose makers or rightholders are nationals of a Member State or who have their habitual residence in the territory of the Community.

2.   Paragraph 1 shall also apply to companies and firms formed in accordance with the law of a Member State and having their registered office, central administration or principal place of business within the Community; however, where such a company or firm has only its registered office in the territory of the Communi-

ty, its operations must be genuinely linked on an ongoing basis with the economy of a Member State.

* * *

FIRST EVALUATION OF DIRECTIVE 96/9/EC ON THE LEGAL PROTECTION OF DATABASES

Commission of the European Communities
Brussels, 12 December 2005

1. INTRODUCTION

1.1. The scope and purpose of this evaluation

The purpose of this evaluation is to assess whether the policy goals of Directive 96/9/EC on the legal protection of databases (the "Directive") have been achieved and, in particular, whether the creation of a special "sui generis" right has had adverse effects on competition. This is the first time that the Directive is subject to an evaluation.

The aim of the Directive was to remove existing differences in the legal protection of databases by harmonising the rules that applied to copyright protection, safeguard the investment of database makers and ensure that the legitimate interests of users to access information compiled in databases were secured.

At the time of its adoption, the Commission reasoned that differences in the standard of "originality" required for a database to enjoy copyright protection impeded the free movement of "database products" across the Community. In particular, the Commission argued that the difference between the lower "sweat of the brow" copyright standard (*i.e.* involving considerable skill, labour or judgment in gathering together and/or checking a compilation) that applied in common law Member States and the higher "intellectual creation" standard that applied in *droit d'auteur* Member States created distortion of trade in "database products".

In essence, the Directive sought to create a legal framework that would establish the ground rules for the protection of a wide variety of databases in the information age. It did so by giving a high level of copyright protection to certain databases ("original" databases) and a new form of "sui generis" protection to those databases which were not "original" in the sense of the author's own intellectual creation ("non-original" databases).

The approach chosen in the Directive was to harmonise the threshold of "originality". Those "non-original" databases that did not meet the threshold would be protected by a newly created right.

– In a first step, this was done by adopting the higher standard that applied in *droit d'auteur* countries, which had the effect of

protecting fewer databases by copyright (which was now limited to so-called "original" databases);

– In a second step, for those databases that would previously
have enjoyed protection under the "sweat of the brow" copyright, but no longer according to the harmonised "originality"
standard, a new right was created—the "sui generis" right to
prevent extraction and reutilisation of the whole or a substantial part of the contents of a database in which there has been
substantial investment ("non-original" databases).

While "original" databases require an element of "intellectual
creation", "non-original" databases are protected as long as there
has been "qualitatively or quantitatively a substantial investment
in either the obtaining, verification or presentation of the contents"
of a database. The "sui generis" right is a Community creation
with no precedent in any international convention. No other jurisdiction makes a distinction between "original" and "non-original"
databases.

1.2. What was evaluated?

The evaluation focused on the issue of whether the Directive
has created a legal framework that would establish the ground
rules for the protection of a wide variety of databases in the
information age. In particular, the evaluation focused on whether
the European database industry's rate of growth increased after the
introduction of the new right; whether the beneficiaries of the new
right produced more databases than they would have produced in
the absence of this right; and whether the scope of the right was
drafted in a way that targets those areas where Europe needs to
encourage innovation.

Its detractors have criticised the "sui generis" right for the
following reasons:

(1) The new "sui generis" protection was unclear in scope and
ill-suited to target areas where innovation and growth should
have been stimulated;

(2) The new form of protection locks up data and information
to the detriment of the academic community or other industries that depend on the availability of data and information to
conduct their business or research;

(3) The new form of protection is too narrow in scope and thus
fails to adequately protect investors in database products.

This report evaluates these criticisms. In doing so, it analyses:

(1) The impact of the judgments delivered by the ECJ in

November 2004[3], the effect of which is to significantly curtail the scope of "sui generis" protection;

(2) Whether the objectives of the Directive have been achieved effectively and efficiently, that is, without triggering unnecessary costs for the academic community or industries that depend on the availability of data and information;

(3) The evolution of EU database production in order to determine whether this sector of the EU economy has grown subsequent to the adoption of the Directive.

* * *

1.4. What evidence was found?

The economic impact of the "sui generis" right on database production is unproven.

Introduced to stimulate the production of databases in Europe, the new instrument has had no proven impact on the production of databases. Data taken from the *GDD* show that the EU database production in 2004 has fallen back to pre-Directive levels: the number of EU-based database "entries" into the *GDD* was 3095 in 2004 as compared to 3092 in 1998. In 2001, there were 4085 EU-based "entries" while in 2004 there were only 3095.

Is "sui generis" protection therefore necessary for a thriving database industry? The empirical evidence, at this stage, casts doubts on this necessity. The European publishing industry, which was consulted in a restricted online survey, however, produced strong submissions arguing that "sui generis" protection was crucial to the continued success of their activities.

In addition, most respondents to the on-line survey believe that the "sui generis" right has brought about legal certainty, reduced the costs associated with the protection of databases, created more business opportunities and facilitated the marketing of databases.

1.5. What conclusions were drawn?

At this stage, the evaluation concludes that repealing the Directive altogether or repealing the "sui generis" right in isolation would probably lead to considerable resistance by the EU database industry which wishes to retain "sui generis" protection for factual compilations. While this resistance is not entirely based on empirical data (many factual compilations would, most likely, remain protected under the high standard of "originality" introduced by

---

3. Cases C–46/02 (*Fixtures Marketing Ltd v. Oy Veikkaus Ab*); C–203/02 (*The British Horseracing Board Ltd and Others v. William Hill Organisation Ltd*); C–338/02 (*Fixtures Marketing Limited v. AB Svenska Spel*) and C–444/02 (*Fixtures Marketing Ltd v. Organismos prognostikon agonon podosfairou AE— "OPAP"*).

the Directive), this evaluation takes note of the fact that European publishers and database producers would prefer to retain the "sui generis" protection in addition to and, in some instances, in parallel with copyright protection.

With regard to Member States, those that would be most affected by a repeal of the sui generis right would be the common law jurisdictions.

On the one hand, a repeal of the "sui generis" right would enable these jurisdictions to reintroduce "sweat of the brow" copyright; but on the other, these jurisdictions could also decide to maintain the higher level of protection, thereby limiting protection to "original" databases.

But repealing the "sui generis" right has its obvious drawbacks. It would require withdrawing, or "reverse", legislation and that might reopen the original debate on the appropriate standard of "originality".

Equally, any attempt to reformulate the scope of the "sui generis" right will require the Community legislator to revisit the compromise underlying the two-tier protection introduced by the Directive where a distinction is made between "original" databases that have to comply with a high standard of "originality" and "non-original" databases that enjoy a form of "sui generis" protection.

The paper therefore concludes that leaving the Directive unchanged is an additional policy option for the Commission. The argument could be made that, despite its limited effectiveness in creating growth in the production of European databases, the Directive does not impose significant administrative or other regulatory burdens on the database industry or any other industries that depend on having access to data and information.

In addition, the ECJ in November 2004 significantly curtailed the scope of "sui generis" protection, thereby pre-empting concerns that the right negatively affects competition.

2. OBJECTIVES OF THE DIRECTIVE

The Commission adopted a proposal for a Council Directive on the legal protection of databases on 13 May 1992.

The aim of the proposal was to remove existing differences in the legal protection of databases by harmonising the rules that applied to copyright protection. The aim was also to safeguard the investment of database makers and ensure that the legitimate interests of users of information contained in databases were secured.

* * *

2.1. Eliminate the differences in the legal protection of authors of databases

Prior to the adoption of the Directive, national laws in different Member States differed with respect to the level of "originality" which was used to determine whether a database was protectable or not under copyright law. In particular, the threshold of "originality" for the copyright protection of compilations in common law jurisdictions was lower than the threshold of "originality" that prevailed elsewhere in the Community and in particular in the *droit d'auteur* Member States:

– While *droit d'auteur* Member States protected only "original" databases that required an element of "intellectual creation", the common law Member States also protected "non-original" databases involving considerable skill, labour or judgment in gathering together and/or checking a compilation ("sweat of the brow" copyright).

– In practice, the higher standard of "originality" that applied in *droit d'auteur* countries had the effect of protecting fewer databases by copyright (protection was limited to so called "original" databases). The best known examples of compilations of data or information which were granted copyright protection under the "sweat of the brow" criterion as they did not display any "originality" are the television programme listings which were the subject of the action in the case of *Magill*[8].

– In certain Member States' legislation there were other unique forms of protection[9].

---

8. Judgment of 6 April 1995, *Radio Telefis Eireann (RTE) and Independent Television Publications Ltd (ITP) v. Commission of the European Communities*, (Joined cases C–241/91 P and C–242/91 P). In the *Magill* case the European Commission found that three public television broadcasters whose images were broadcast in Ireland had abused their dominant position on the Irish broadcasting market in refusing to licence Magill to publish in its magazine a comprehensive weekly television guide, given that information about TV programme timings was indispensable to allow a firm to compete in the market for TV listings magazines. See also two earlier judgments, *Van Dale Lexicografie BV v. Rudolf Jan Romme and Feist Publications Inc. v. Rural Telephone Service Co. Inc.* where, respectively, the Dutch Hooge Raad and the U.S. Supreme Court did not apply the "sweat of the brow" criteria to a dictionary and a telephone directory, but clearly required "originality" in the copyright sense as a condition for protection.

9. Denmark, Finland and Sweden protected "a catalogue, a table or another similar production in which a large number of information items have been compiled" under the so-called "catalogue rule". At the time of the adoption of the proposal in 1992, Finland and Sweden had not yet acceded to the Community but did so in 1995. Norway and Iceland (EFTA States) also have sui generis regimes. The Netherlands protected under copyright certain "non-original writings" ("*Onpersoonlijke geschriftenbescherming*").

In 1992, the Commission argued that such differences in legal protection between common law and *droit d'auteur* Member States had negative effects on the free movement of "database products", the provision of information services and the freedom of establishment within the Community. The Commission observed that undertakings producing databases in countries with clear and established protection for databases seemed to be in a more favourable position than those in countries in which protection was uncertain. Figures showed that the UK alone produced 50% of European on-line database services.

The Directive attempts to establish a uniform threshold of "originality" for "original" databases. This level of protection has the effect that the United Kingdom and Ireland, which applied a lower threshold of "originality", were required to "lift the bar" and accord copyright protection to only those databases which were "original" in the sense of the author's own intellectual creation. As a result, databases which qualified for copyright protection under the "sweat of the brow" regime would no longer be protected. In exchange, and in order to compensate for the loss of the "sweat of the brow" protection, the "sui generis" form of protection for "non-original" databases was introduced as an entirely novel form of intellectual property.

2.2. Stimulate database creation by means of a "sui generis" right

In 1992, the Commission reasoned that the growth in the market for data required considerable investment (both human and financial) in producing and marketing of databases and that, consequently, the maker of such database product needed protection at [the] European level.

The Commission recognised that copyright protection based on the standard of "originality" alone might not be an adequate tool to protect these often considerable investments. Therefore, in order to protect the selection or arrangement of the contents of a database which did not meet the standard of being "original", the Commission considered it appropriate to provide a form of "sui generis" protection for the investment involved in the making of a database.

The Commission believed that there was a need to protect investment in the creation of databases against parasitic behaviour by those who seek to misappropriate the results of the financial and professional investment made in obtaining and collection of data and information. While "original" databases require an element of "intellectual creation", "nonoriginal" databases are protected as long as there has been "qualitatively or quantitatively a substantial investment in either the obtaining, verification of presentation of the contents" of a database (Article 7.1).

The Commission argued that the introduction of a stable and uniform legal regime for the protection of database makers would increase the level of investments in information storage and processing systems. The scope of "sui generis" protection was intended to ensure protection of any investment in "obtaining, verifying or presenting the contents of a database" for the 15 year duration of the right, without giving rise to the creation of a new right in the works, data or material themselves.

2.3. Safeguard the legitimate interests of lawful users

The Community legislator also felt the need to find an appropriate balance between the legitimate interests of database authors/makers and users[11]. Notwithstanding the exclusive rights of authors and database makers, the Community legislator felt the need to allow lawful users[12] to continue to perform certain acts necessary to access the contents of databases and facilitate the dissemination of information.

The issue of access to "information" is of concern to various categories of users as it may involve information in the public domain (*e.g.* an electoral register); information where the database constitutes the only available source of that information (*e.g.* a telephone directory); information pertaining to academic and scientific research and [to] other public interest users such as consumers, the disabled, libraries; information which is "created" independently of any other activities where the primary purpose or principal activity is the creation of a database whether using [one's] own data or data acquired from another source (*e.g.* an encyclopaedia); information which is generated from "spin-off" databases[13] (*e.g.* football fixtures lists). [Ed. note: "Fixtures lists" are lists of scheduled matches.]

11. Under the original proposal, a licence had to be granted on fair and non-discriminatory terms when the works or materials contained in a database could not be independently created, collected or obtained from any other source—that is, when the database is the only source of a work of material and when the database maker is a statutory public body; the database had to be made publicly available and Member States had to provide for arbitration with respect to the conditions for granting licences. However, the provisions on non-voluntary licensing were deleted as a result of a compromise reached in the Council.

12. The Directive does not provide a definition of "lawful user". Recital 34 refers to a user authorised by agreement with the rightholder to access and use the database. The original proposal for the Directive referred to a "person having acquired a right to use the database".

13. That is, databases which are by-products of a main or principal activity. The "spin-off" theory has been developed by the doctrine and case law of certain Member States; under such theory, "spin-off" databases do not enjoy "sui generis" protection.

With a view to safeguarding the legitimate interests of lawful users, an exhaustive list of optional exceptions to both copyright (Article 6) and the "sui generis" right (Article 9) was introduced and mandatory provisions in favour of lawful users were provided (Articles 6.1, 8 and 15).

2.4. Increase the EU database production as compared to the US

Finally, the Community argued that investments in the production of databases could not achieve adequate returns unless databases manufactured in the EU were awarded protection on a par with the protection awarded by its major trading partners.

An imbalance in the level of investment between the Community and the world's largest database-producing third countries was observed. This conclusion was drawn in spite of the fact that the U.S. did not protect "non-original" compilations, a stance confirmed by the Supreme Court's ruling in *Feist Publications v. Rural Telephone Service Company*.

The creation of the "sui generis" right thus also aimed at enhancing global competitiveness of the European database industry in particular by filling in the gap between the EU and the U.S.

3. MEASURES

* * *

The Directive provides a two-tier protection: a harmonised level of protection of "original" databases under copyright (Articles 3–5) and the introduction of a new "sui generis" right to protect investments in databases (Articles 7, 10 and 11). Both rights differ in terms of criteria for protection, duration, acts prohibited, the exceptions or limitations that apply and the person or persons (both natural and legal) in whom each right vests (Articles 6, 8, 9 and 15). Article 1 defines a "database" for the purposes of the Directive and applies to both copyright and "sui generis" protection. The proposal for the Directive was originally limited to electronic databases but now includes analogue, including hard copy or traditional print media, and electronic forms, including digital or online.

4. IMPACT

The data reported here were collected from a restricted on-line survey addressed to the European database industry and from the *GDD*; the Internal Market and Services Directorate General has drawn its conclusions from the views expressed by stakeholders, interested parties, Member States and its own views and analysis.

4.1. Has the Directive eliminated the differences that existed between Member States in the legal protection of databases?

4.1.1. Transposition into national laws

All 25 Member States have transposed the Directive into national law. * * *

4.1.2. Application of the Directive by national courts and authorities

National case-law shows that the notion of "database" has been interpreted widely so as to include listings of telephone subscribers; compilations of case-law and legislation; websites containing lists of classified advertisements; catalogues of various information; lists of headings of newspaper articles. The ECJ has stressed the broad definition of "database" in the Directive.

But national case law has also highlighted the textual ambiguities of the "sui generis" right. Battles have erupted over the precise meaning of "substantial investment" as contained in Article 7 of the Directive.

While the District Court of The Hague held that the cost of collecting and maintaining up-to-date information concerning several thousands of real estate properties amounted to a "substantial investment," the President of the District Court of Rotterdam held that newspaper headlines were a mere "spinoff" of newspaper publishing and therefore did not reflect a "substantial investment."

Where the Court of Appeal of Düsseldorf held that there has been no proven "substantial investment" in a website containing information on building construction, the German Supreme Court found recently that collecting and verifying data for the weekly German "Top 10" hit chart of music titles requires "substantial investment" and that a "substantial part" of the contents of the plaintiff's database had been "extracted" by the defendant who published his own compilation in printed form and on CD–Rom.

Other divergent judgements concern "spin-off" databases—that is, databases which are byproducts of a main or principal activity—especially where the database is a single source database[18].

Another area of divergent case-law concerns the exploitation of on-line databases and Internet-related activities such as "hyper linking" or "deep-linking" using search engines[19] (there have been no references to the ECJ on this issue).

---

18. The "spin-off" theory has been developed by the doctrine and case law of certain Member States (in particular, the Netherlands); under such theory, "spin-off" databases do not enjoy "sui generis" protection.

19. Linking occurs when a connection is made between pages within a

In some cases, the heading, the Internet address (URL) and a brief summary of a press article have been held not to constitute a substantial part of a database and the hyper linking of headings of press articles has been held not to infringe the owner's "sui generis" right. However, in most cases the systematic bypassing of the homepage of the database maker (including banner advertisements) was found to be an infringement of the database maker's "sui generis" right.

* * *

4.1.4.   Has the ECJ's interpretation of the scope of the "sui generis" right devalued the uniform levels of protection achieved for "non-original" databases?

Four cases concerning single-source databases of sports information in the areas of football and horseracing have been referred to the ECJ. The references came from national courts in Greece, Finland, Sweden and the United Kingdom. The ECJ gave its judgments in these cases on 9 November 2004.[24]

With respect to the extensive lists of runners and riders drawn up by the British Horseracing Board (the "BHB") in its function as the governing body for the British horseracing industry, the ECJ simply stated that:

> "The resources used to draw up a list of horses in a race and to carry out checks in that connection do *not* constitute investment in the *obtaining* and *verification* of the contents of the database in which that list appears[.]" (emphasis added)

The ECJ thus distinguishes between the resources used in the "creation" of materials that make up the contents of a database and the *obtaining* of such data in order to assemble the contents of a database. Only the latter activity is protected under the "sui generis" right. This leaves no protection for bodies like the BHB which "create" the data that makes up the contents of their database. Arguably, other industries like the publishers of directories, listings or maps, remain protected as long as they do not "create" their own data but *obtain* these data from others.

The ECJ distinction between "creation" and *obtaining* of data means that sports bodies such as the BHB cannot claim that they *obtained* the data within the meaning of the Directive. Therefore, such bodies cannot license their own data to third parties.

single web site or another website by the use of hypertext mark up language, *i.e.*, highlighted to identify the link. Clicking on a link transfers the user from the website to that of the linked page and the Uniform Resource Locator (URL). A

"deeplink" bypasses the homepage of the URL to link directly with embedded web site pages.

24.   See footnote 3.

While going against the Commission's original intention of protecting "non-original" databases in a wide sense, the judgements have the merit of pointing to the serious difficulties raised by attempting to harmonise national laws by recourse to untested and ambiguous legal concepts ("qualitatively or quantitatively substantial investments in either the obtaining, verification or presentation of contents").

The ECJ's judgment would probably apply to the databases created by broadcasting organisations for the purposes of scheduling programmes: they would not be able to assert a "sui generis" right in the contents of such databases.

In addition, the European Court ruled that on-line betting activities on football matches and horse races carried out by betting companies such as Svenska Spel or William Hill, did not affect the whole or a substantial part of the contents of the plaintiffs' databases as they did not prejudice the substantial investment of the latter in the creation of their databases.

On 13 July 2005, the British Court of Appeal applied the above interpretation, albeit on a slightly different basis, in its judgment in the *British Horse Racing Board v. William Hill*. The British Court dismissed the BHB's arguments aimed at showing that its database was protectable by the "sui generis" right under Article 7(1) of the Directive.

These rulings imply that sports bodies like the BHB can only claim protection under the "sui generis" right where they have made a "substantial investment" in seeking existing material and collecting, verifying and presenting it in their databases. As the scope of the "sui generis" protection does not include, in the view of the Court, the "creation" of the underlying data[26], a soccer fixture list would usually not be protected under the "sui generis" right.

Commentators perceive the Court's judgments as a major blow to funding plans envisaged by sports bodies. BHB was hoping to generate more than £100 million (around 142m euros) a year in revenue by selling data on the runners and riders (so-called "data-licensing"). Football's governing bodies will very likely lose substantial revenue by not being able to charge for information contained in football fixtures lists.

---

26. For example, the national football bodies establish the annual "football calendar" by pairing the teams, setting up home and away matches. This activity which comprises the basic activity of organising soccer tournaments involves the "creation" of data. The collection and verification of the data in order to set up the fixture list is only a by-product of this basic activity, but the by-product requires relatively little investment.

Nevertheless, the Commission Services' online survey reveals that 43% of the respondents believe that the legal protection of their databases will be the same as before the ECJ rulings (or even reinforced); only 36% believe that the scope of protection will be either weakened or removed.

On the other hand, 54% believe that fewer databases will be protected by the "sui generis" right. This view is expressed not only by the companies which have been primarily affected by the Court's rulings, but also by other companies, such as database publishers and information suppliers, from both the *droit d'auteur* and common law Member States.

Other industries where data is "created" and concurrently stored and processed in a database, such as real estate or employment agencies, could be affected by the Court's rulings. There is a risk that national courts applying the European Court's case-law will conclude that relatively little of the investment in establishing a database appears to have been in collecting and verifying the information displayed on a website containing data on, *e.g.*, real estate or job advertisements.

On the other hand, the ECJ's narrow interpretation of the "sui generis" protection for "nonoriginal" databases where the data were "created" by the same entity as the entity that establishes the database would put to rest any fear of abuse of a dominant position that this entity would have on data and information it "created" itself (so-called "single-source" databases).

At national level, only few cases have been reported where owners of the "sui generis" right in a dominant position have been required to license their databases under certain conditions[28].

* * *

4.2. Has the provision of uniform protection in all Member States stimulated investments into the creation of databases?

[Although the Directive's sui generis protection was intended to stimulate the production of databases in Europe, it has had no proven impact. Empirical research indicates that the number of databases generated in the EU has not increased since Directive

---

28. See, for instance, Supreme Court of Austria, 9 April 2002, *Republic of Austria v. Compass Publishing Company*, where the Austrian public authority, holder of the sui generis right upon the official company register, was required to license its database under certain conditions to a competitor; Nederlandse mededingingsautoriteit, NMa, 10 September 1998, *De Telegraaf v. NOS and HMG*, where the Dutch competition authority ruled that, by refusing to license its own radio and TV programme listings, the Dutch broadcasting company had abused its dominant position. In both decisions, the national courts and authorities have made reference to the *Magill* case.

was implemented by the Member States. Nevertheless, the European publishing and database industries continue to claim that "sui generis" protection is crucial to the continued success of their activities.

The UK remains the Member State with the highest relative database production. Reasons for this success may be the relative maturity of the UK database industry and the success of databases that are produced in English.]

* * *

4.3. Has the balance between the legitimate interests of manufacturers and lawful users of databases been safeguarded?

Certain rightholders (publishers, public rightholders, private users of databases) interviewed in the context of an independent study finalised in 2002 were of the opinion that the Directive—with certain exceptions—achieves a satisfactory balance between the legitimate interests of rightholders and users and expressed the view that the Directive should remain unchanged since it has proved to be an incentive for the further development of an Internal Market in databases. Publishers claim that the "sui generis" right provides an incentive for wide dissemination of information and encourages specialisation and differentiation on the market. At the same time, certain users (libraries, academic organisations, lotteries, public users of databases) have expressed concern as to whether the scope of the "sui generis" right has led to an over-broad protection. Fewer concerns have been expressed in relation to databases protected by copyright. Certain users have pleaded for an extension in the scope of the exception for private purposes to digital databases, but rightholders (in particular, publishers) fear that such a move would lead to abuse and would increase the risks of theft and piracy.

Certain members of the academic and scientific community were concerned that the exceptions to the "sui generis" right were too restrictive with regard to the access to and use of data and information for scientific and educational purposes.

Claims were also made for the enlargement of the scope of certain exceptions (*e.g.*, in support of the private use of digital databases), for the application of traditional exceptions also to the "sui generis" right (*i.e.*, exception for fair dealing reporting of current events, in particular in the field of sports data) and for the introduction of new exceptions (*i.e.*, for the benefit of the physically disabled). Certain libraries claim that the "sui generis" right has resulted in a concentration of leading database producers, for example electronic journals, monopolizing information.

Furthermore, there is an increasing demand for consumer access to information contained in databases owned by public bodies, such as weather data, maps and statutory registers[40]. It has been observed that the complexity of the "sui generis" regime due to the two tier approach of the Directive has caused confusion among users as the same database can be protected by both copyright and [the] "sui generis" right. In particular, the association of European academies represented by ALLEA ("All European Academies") revealed serious concerns about the effect of the Directive upon scientific research. The main concern is that the Directive limits access and the use of data and information for scientific and educational purposes. This is held to impede research and reduce the public benefit which might otherwise be derived from research. In the view of ALLEA, the Directive is designed for the commercial sector whilst scientific data and the way in which scientists have traditionally used it is different in many ways.

Furthermore, the reports of two workshops organised by the Commission's Research Directorate General revealed that in both the U.S. and in Europe there is reluctance to use the "sui generis" right due to its complexity and its limitations.

It is noteworthy that the ECJ and some national judges appear to fear that the balance between users and rightholders is inappropriate. Indeed, the interpretation adopted by the European Court may have been influenced by the concern that the "sui generis" right might otherwise significantly restrict access to information. Thus, for instance, the ECJ has ruled that the mere act of consultation of a database is not covered by the database maker's exclusive rights[43].

* * *

40. The re-use of public sector information is now the subject of Directive 2003/98/EC. Under such Directive, Member States are required to ensure that the documents held by public sector bodies shall be re-usable for commercial or non-commercial purposes. The Directive is without prejudice to Directive 96/9 and does not apply to documents for which third parties hold intellectual property rights and the obligations imposed must be compatible with the Berne Convention and the TRIPS Agreement.

43. "However, it must be stressed that the protection of the *sui generis* right concerns only acts of extraction and re-utilisation as defined in Article 7(2) of the directive. That protection does not, on the other hand, cover consultation of a database. Of course, the maker of a database can reserve exclusive access to his database to himself or reserve access to specific people. However, if he himself makes the contents of his database or a part of it accessible to the public, his *sui generis* right does not allow him to prevent third parties from consulting that base", case C–203/02, n. 54, 55.

4.4. Has the EU database production increased as compared to the U.S.?

[Since the implementation of the Directive, the EU's share of global database production has not substantially increased. In fact, the ratio of European to U.S. database production has *decreased*.]

* * *

5. ANALYSIS

From the outset, there have been problems associated with the "sui generis" right: the scope of the right is unclear; granting protection to "non-original" databases is perceived as locking up information, especially data and information that are in the public domain; and its failure to produce any measurable impact on European database production.

5.1. The "sui generis" right is difficult to understand

First and foremost is the lack of clarity in the text of the relevant provisions of the Directive. The "sui generis" right is formulated as follows in Article 7 of the Directive:

> Member States shall provide for a right for the maker of a database which shows that there has been qualitatively and/or quantitatively a substantial investment in either the obtaining, verification or presentation of the contents to prevent extraction and/or reutilisation of the whole or a substantial part, evaluated qualitatively and/or quantitatively, of the contents of that database.

None of these terms has a precise legal meaning and none of them has an established tradition in copyright law. Sections 4.1.2. and 4.1.4. demonstrate how national courts and the ECJ have struggled over the precise meaning of the "sui generis" protection.

But the November 2004 decisions of the ECJ restrict the scope of protection for "nonoriginal" databases by introducing a distinction between "creation" of data and *obtaining* it.

The Court thereby refuses to count any investment before or at the time of "creating" data as constituting a substantial investment in the database itself. It can be expected that database makers will devise legal strategies to get around the distinction drawn in the ECJ judgments and that this might result in online databases increasingly being secured by systems of access control.

5.2. "Sui generis" protection comes close to protecting data as property

There is a long-standing principle that copyright should not be extended to cover basic information or "raw" data. However, as evidenced by the ECJ's differentiation between the "creation" of data and its *obtaining* demonstrate, the "sui generis" right comes precariously close to protecting basic information.

The United States has rejected a similar course. In *Feist Publications v. Rural Telephone Service Company*, the Supreme Court found that the "bits of information" contained in a telephone directory are not protected under copyright laws. Moreover, the Court held that the arrangement of the data in a telephone book was dictated by the identities of its subscribers and the need for alphabetization, making it "devoid of even the slightest trace of creativity." In conclusion, third parties were free to copy or make other use of this information as they wished. The *Feist* case is often interpreted as the culmination of a gradual trend in copyright law. In recent years, fewer and fewer courts have been willing to protect compilations solely under the "sweat of the brow" doctrine.

Nevertheless, as the figures discussed below demonstrate, there has been a considerable growth in database production in the U.S., whereas, in the EU, the introduction of "sui generis" protection appears to have had the opposite effect. With respect to "non-original" databases, the assumption that more and more layers of IP protection means more innovation and growth appears not to hold up.

5.3. The economic impact of the "sui generis" right is unproven

The second problem with the "sui generis" right is that its economic impact on database production is unproven. Introduced to stimulate the growth of databases in Europe, the new instrument has had no proven impact on the production of databases. According to the *Gale Directory of Databases*, the number of EU-based database "entries" was 3095 in 2004 as compared to 3092 in 1998 when the first Member States had implemented the "sui generis" protection into national laws. More significantly, the number of database "entries" dropped just as most of the EU–15 Member States had implemented the Directive into national laws in 2001. In 2001, there were 4085 EU-based "entries" while in 2004 there were only 3095.

Nevertheless, the Internal Market and Services Directorate General has received strong representations from the European publishing industry that "sui generis" protection is crucial to the continued success of their activities. In addition, 75% of respondents to the on-line survey are aware of the existence of the "sui generis" right; among these, 80% feel "protected" or "well protected" by such right. 90% believe that database protection at EU level, as opposed to national level, is important and 65% believe that today the legal protection of databases is higher than before harmonisation. In the opinion of respondents, the "sui generis" right has brought about legal certainty, reduced the costs associated with the protection of databases, created more business opportunities and facilitated the marketing of databases.

While this endorsement of the "sui generis" right is somewhat at odds with the continued success of U.S. publishing and database production that thrives without "sui generis" type protection, the attachment to the new right is a political reality that seems very true for Europe.

6. POLICY OPTIONS

6.1. Option 1: Repeal the whole Directive

Withdrawing the Directive in its entirety would allow Member States to revert to the situation that applied in national law prior to the adoption of the Directive. This would allow *droit d'auteur* Member States to keep their threshold of "originality", to protect "original" databases under copyright law and to choose other means, *e.g.*, unfair competition or the law of misappropriation, to protect "non-original" compilations. Common law Member States, for their part, would be allowed to revert to the "sweat of the brow" standard as a relevant copyright test.

But withdrawing the Directive in its entirety would give rise to a pre-directive scenario where Member States could protect "original" databases under diverging levels of "originality". In particular, the UK and Ireland would be allowed to revert to the "sweat of the brow" copyright test and Sweden, Denmark and Finland (and Norway and Iceland) would be allowed to revert to their "catalogue rule".

In this scenario, one could expect that the terms of use for collections of data or compilations would be dealt with only by contract law and right-holders would increasingly protect their databases (especially online databases) by means of access control systems. However, this option would have the disadvantage of doing away with the harmonised level of copyright protection for "original" databases which has not caused major problems so far.

6.2. Option 2: Withdraw the "sui generis" right

Another possibility would therefore be to withdraw the "sui generis" right in isolation and thus maintain the harmonised level of copyright protection for "original" databases.

Arguably, this partial withdrawal would still allow *droit d'auteur* Member States to keep their threshold of "originality", to protect "original" databases under copyright law and to choose other means, *e.g.*, unfair competition or the law of misappropriation to protect "non-original" compilations. It would also allow common law Member States to revert to the "sweat of the brow" standard as a relevant test to protect "non-original" compilations.

The arguments for partial withdrawal would largely be based on a strict application of the "better regulation" principles. These principles would probably suggest that the "sui generis" right be withdrawn as it has revealed itself to be an instrument that is ineffective at encouraging growth in the European database industry and, due to its largely untested legal concepts, given rise to significant litigation in national and European courts. Empirical data underlying this evaluation show that its economic impact is unproven. In addition, no empirical data that proves that its introduction has stimulated significant growth in the production of EU databases could be submitted so far.

Furthermore, withdrawal of the "sui generis" right appears to be in line with an emerging trend in common law jurisdictions as the high standard of "originality" introduced by the Directive would put them on a par with the U.S., thereby protecting fewer rather than more Databases[45]. It may thus well be that even the common law jurisdictions within the Community (UK and Ireland) would maintain the higher threshold for protection, thereby only protecting "original" databases. The ruling in the *Feist* case and the economic evidence that points at the U.S. as being a leader in database production could lead to significant reluctance in reintroducing "sweat of the brow".

Finally, withdrawing the "sui generis" right would still leave companies with factual compilations that may not be fully protected under the standard of "originality" as prescribed in copyright law, free to protect their works by other means such as contract law or use of technological protection measures or other forms of access control when the work is delivered on-line. It would also [allow] producers of compilations to claim protection by stating that their arrangements met the threshold of "originality". However, this paper acknowledges that European publishers and database producers would clearly prefer to retain the "sui generis" protection.

6.3.   Option 3: Amend the "sui generis" provisions

Another option would be to amend and clarify the scope of protection awarded under the "sui generis" provisions. Attempts could be made to reformulate the scope of the "sui generis" right in order to also cover instances where the "creation" of data takes place concurrently with the collection and screening of it. Amend-

---

45. Canada, as the other common law jurisdiction affected, has also now adopted the high level of "originality" in its case law.

ments could also clarify the issue of what forms of "official" and thereby single source lists would be protected under the "sui generis" provisions.

Amendments could also be proposed to clarify the scope of protection and clarify whether the scope would only cover "primary" producers of databases (*i.e.*, those producers whose main business is to collect and assemble information they do not "create" themselves) or would also include producers for whom production of a databases is a "secondary" activity (in other words, a spin-off from their main activity). Amendments could, in addition, clarify the issue of what actually constitutes a substantial investment in either the obtaining, verification or presentation of the contents of a database. On the other hand, reformulating the scope of the "sui generis" right entails a serious risk that yet another layer of untested legal notions would be introduced that will not withstand scrutiny before the ECJ.

6.4. Option 4: Maintaining the status quo

On the other hand, even if a piece of legislation has no proven positive effects on the growth of a particular industry, withdrawal is not always the best option. Removing the "sui generis" right and thereby allowing Member States to revert to prior forms of legal protection for all forms of "non-original" databases that do not meet the threshold of "originality", might be more costly than keeping it in place. Arguably, the limitations imposed by the judgments of the ECJ mean that the right is now only available to "primary" producers of databases and not those who for whom databases are a "secondary" activity.

* * *

Notes

1. Why would the European database industry favor retention of the *sui generis* right if it has not enhanced their productivity? Does this suggest something about the limitations of incentive-based intellectual property regimes?

2. In recent years Congress has considered several proposals for *sui generis* protection for databases. How might the European experience influence future consideration of such proposals?

3. Does Article 10(3) of the Database Directive raise the spectre of perpetual protection for certain databases?

D.   COPYRIGHT AND UNFAIR COMPETITION

In light of the Supreme Court's decision in Dastar Corp. v. Twentieth Century Fox Film Corp., 539 U.S. 23 (2003), together with federal preemption doctrine, it is increasingly difficult to utilize federal or state unfair competition laws to protect material that Congress has deliberately excluded from the protection of United States copyright laws. As illustrated by the following case from Japan, copyright laws in other countries may not have the same preemptive effect.

JUDGMENT OF INTELLECTUAL PROPERTY HIGH COURT*

Fourth Division
Case No. 2005(Ne) No.10095 (March 15, 2006)

Summary of the Judgment:

This is a case where the plaintiff, an attorney belonging to the Daiichi Tokyo Bar Association, who had written books (the Plaintiff's Books) designed to explain legal issues to layman readers, asserted that the defendant corporation's act of publishing similar books (the Defendant's Books) constituted an infringement of the plaintiff's copyright (rights of reproduction and adaptation) and moral rights (rights to determine the indication of the author's name and to maintain integrity). The plaintiff demanded (1) an injunction against the publication, sale, and distribution, etc., of the Defendants' Books under Article 112, para.1 of the Copyright Act, (2) damages under Article 709 of the Civil Code, and (3) an apology advertisement under Article 115 of the Copyright Act, and further claimed the remedies mentioned in the above (1) through (3) also with regard to Defendant X and Defendant Y, who, the plaintiff asserted, were the authors of the Defendants' Books.

In response, the defendants argued that the publication of the Defendants' Books did not infringe the copyright and moral rights of the plaintiff * * *.

The plaintiff filed this lawsuit on June 4, 2003. On May 17, 2005, the court of the first instance handed down a judgment that partially accepted the plaintiff's claim (The court ordered an injunction against the publication and distribution of some of the Defendants' Books and payment of 269,881 yen as well as delayed damages). The plaintiff appealed on May 30, 2005, while the defendants filed an incidental appeal on September 2 in the same year.

* Translation provided courtesy of the   Institute of Intellectual Property, Tokyo.

This court judged as follows:

[1] Dependency

A close comparison between the Plaintiff's Books and the Defendants' Books revealed that the two groups of books were extremely similar in terms of the structure and sentences, etc., to such a degree that it could not be explained only by the fact that they had the same target readers and the same purpose and nature. These books were the same even in parts that could not be the same if written by different authors. It was therefore reasonable to assume that the Defendants' Books were based entirely on the Plaintiff's Books, as found by the first instance.

[2] Copyright infringement

This court upheld the judgment of the court of the first instance concerning copyright infringement that the expressions in the Defendants' Books (Defendants' Expressions) did not infringe the reproduction right and adaptation right of the plaintiff, except for three passages included in the Defendants' Expressions.

Although the court of the first instance judged that the three passages included in the Defendants' Expressions constituted an infringement of the reproduction right of the plaintiff, this court found that those three passages, as well as the other expressions included in the Defendant's Expressions, did not infringe the plaintiff's reproduction right and adaptation right, on the ground that the three passages could not be considered as creative works because they were a type of expression describing with ordinary words the findings naturally derived from the interpretation of laws and regulations as well as of judicial precedents and academic theories and from their application to practices.

[3] General torts

(1) The plaintiff claimed damages for torts under Article 709 of the Civil Code, not only for the defendants' infringement of the plaintiff's copyright, but also for the defendants' acts of deliberately or negligently imitating the books written by the plaintiff with great efforts, and publishing and distributing the resulting books without the plaintiff's consent. As discussed below, the court examined whether the latter acts really constituted torts (hereinafter referred to as "General Tort Liability" in order to distinguish it from the tort liability claimed by the plaintiff based on the alleged copyright infringement).

(2) The author of a book which was designed to explain legal issues to layman readers, such as the Plaintiff's Books, needed to use various writing techniques to make his/her book readable to

those who had no background in legal study. It appears that, in the Plaintiff's Books, the plaintiff used such techniques. However, the plaintiff failed to use any technique that can be evaluated as something exceeding the ordinarily conceivable ones, and therefore failed to use any expression that can be regarded as something other than commonplace expression. For this reason, the defendants' acts cannot be regarded as infringing the Plaintiff's Books, as explained in section 2 above. In general, it is inevitable that a book designed to explain specific subjects to layman readers will sacrifice originality, which would be protected under the Copyright Act, in exchange for readability and simplicity. This is because the more the author of such book tries to increase its readability and simplicity, the more he/she tends to utilize commonplace expressions, unless he/she makes special efforts to use creative and ingenious expressions. The Plaintiff's Books were not an exception. [They] cannot be found to contain expressions that were particularly creative or ingenious.

However, the fact that the expressions included in the Plaintiff's Books were not protected under the Copyright Act did not necessarily mean that no act of tort was committed by the defendants who, deliberately or negligently, wrote and published books extremely similar to the Plaintiff's Books. Every author is entitled to the economic benefits from the publication and distribution of his own work, and such economic benefits deserve to be protected under the law. Therefore, the act of writing a book by depending entirely on another author's work, and then publishing it, cannot be qualified as a fair and socially acceptable act of competition, and should be regarded as constituting a tort, as long as such act is committed for the purpose of gaining profits, and may be regarded as making profits by unfairly taking advantage of another person's work in light of the similarity of descriptions and overall impression given by the structure and headings of the book.

(3) From the perspective described above, the court examined whether the defendants' acts really gave rise to General Tort Liability.

The defendant corporation was a juridical person engaging in the publication and sale of books and magazines, including a paperback book series entitled "Commuters' University Legal Study Course." The Defendants' Books were published as a part of the series. Like the Plaintiff's Books, the Commuters' University Legal Study Course consisted of books designed to explain legal issues to laypersons in a simple and easy-to-understand language with many figures and tables.

The Defendants' Books were derived entirely from the Plaintiff's Books, as found in section 1 above. They were extremely similar not only in the basic structure and the order of chapters but also in the headings and the order of descriptions. In addition, most of the expressions as well as the figures and tables contained in the Defendants' Books and the Plaintiff's Books were similar to each other. In some parts of the Defendants' Books, passages similar to, or even the same as, those in the Plaintiff's Books took up an entire page or two. In consideration of these facts, it would be reasonable to conclude that the Defendants Books used the parts of the Plaintiff's Books where the plaintiff tried to increase the readability for lay readers by choosing plain expressions or simplifying expressions, carefully choosing the order of descriptions and the method of classification, and using many figures and tables. The defendant made almost no changes to those parts except for some alterations in the order or wording of expressions. Thus, the Defendants' Books were found to contain many writing techniques used by the plaintiff in writing the Plaintiff's Books.

Without depending entirely on the Plaintiff's Books in the above-mentioned manner, the defendants would have been unable to write and publish the Defendants' Books within a short period of time after the publication of the Plaintiff's Books. In addition, such total dependence on the Plaintiff's Books enabled the defendants to write and publish the Defendants' Books without paying any compensation for an author.

Accordingly, it should be found that the defendants wrote and published the Defendants' Books, which were extremely similar to the Plaintiff's Books in terms of the expressions used therein and also the overall impression given by the structure and headings, for the same target readers as those of the Plaintiff's Books, within a very short period of time after the publication of the Plaintiff's Books, and it therefore should be concluded that the defendants gained profits by taking unfair advantage of the works of the plaintiff.

Since the defendants' act of writing and publishing the Defendants' Books by depending entirely on the Plaintiff's Books amounts to an act of gaining profits by taking unfair advantage of the plaintiff's works for the purpose of profit, it cannot be regarded as a fair and socially acceptable act of competition and should be regarded as constituting a tort (constructive joint and several liability for a joint tort under Article 719, para. 1 of the Civil Code).

[4] Damages

As it was extremely difficult to prove to what extent the publication of the Defendants' Books affected the sales of the Plaintiff's Books, the court calculated the reasonable amount of damages under Article 248 of the Code of Civil Procedure with regard to the part that could not be substantiated by specific evidence, and concluded that the reasonable amount of damages for property loss incurred by the plaintiff was 242,638 yen. Then, the court rejected the plaintiff's claim for non-pecuniary damage. The court calculated the reasonable amount for the attorney's fee as 20,000 yen in connection with the defendants' acts.

Note

How would a United States court analyze a tort or unfair competition claim based on copying (1) a plaintiff's writing style, or (2) a plaintiff's use of commonplace forms of expression or arrangement of material?

Chapter 3

AUTHORSHIP AND OWNERSHIP

A. INTRODUCTION

Questions of authorship and copyright ownership receive little attention in international copyright treaties. The Berne Convention does not define authorship. It addresses ownership only with respect to copyright in cinematographic works, but expressly notes that this is "a matter for legislation in the country where protection is claimed." Art. 14bis(2)(a). Neither the TRIPS provisions of the WTO Agreement nor the WIPO treaties constrain the freedom of signatories to establish their own rules for authorship and ownership of copyrighted works.

Some concepts with respect to which nations have established divergent rules include works made for hire, authorship and ownership of cinematographic works, and joint authorship. As the *Itar–Tass* case illustrates, in cross-border disputes choice-of-law questions must sometimes be addressed before substantive questions of authorship and copyright owner can be resolved. This is because copyright is a territorial concept; in other words, the owner of a copyright in one country may not be the owner of copyright in that same work in a different country.

B. WORKS MADE FOR HIRE

ITAR–TASS RUSSIAN NEWS AGENCY
v. RUSSIAN KURIER, INC.

United States Court of Appeals, Second Circuit, 1998
153 F.3d 82

NEWMAN, Circuit Judge:

This appeal primarily presents issues concerning the choice of law in international copyright cases and the substantive meaning of

Russian copyright law as to the respective rights of newspaper reporters and newspaper publishers. The conflicts issue is which country's law applies to issues of copyright ownership and to issues of infringement. The primary substantive issue under Russian copyright law is whether a newspaper publishing company has an interest sufficient to give it standing to sue for copying the text of individual articles appearing in its newspapers, or whether complaint about such copying may be made only by the reporters who authored the articles. Defendants-appellants Russian Kurier, Inc. ("Kurier") and Oleg Pogrebnoy (collectively "the Kurier defendants") appeal from the March 25, 1997, judgment of the District Court for the Southern District of New York (John G. Koeltl, Judge) enjoining them from copying articles that have appeared or will appear in publications of the plaintiffs-appellees, mainly Russian newspapers and a Russian news agency, and awarding the appellees substantial damages for copyright infringement.

On the conflicts issue, we conclude that, with respect to the Russian plaintiffs, Russian law determines the ownership and essential nature of the copyrights alleged to have been infringed and that United States law determines whether those copyrights have been infringed in the United States and, if so, what remedies are available. We also conclude that Russian law, which explicitly excludes newspapers from a work-for-hire doctrine, vests exclusive ownership interests in newspaper articles in the journalists who wrote the articles, not in the newspaper employers who compile their writings. We further conclude that to the extent that Russian law accords newspaper publishers an interest distinct from the copyright of the newspaper reporters, the publishers' interest, like the usual ownership interest in a compilation, extends to the publishers' original selection and arrangement of the articles, and does not entitle the publishers to damages for copying the texts of articles contained in a newspaper compilation. We therefore reverse the judgment to the extent that it granted the newspapers relief for copying the texts of the articles. However, because one non-newspaper plaintiff-appellee is entitled to some injunctive relief and damages and other plaintiffs-appellees may be entitled to some, perhaps considerable, relief, we also remand for further consideration of this lawsuit.

Background

The lawsuit concerns *Kurier,* a Russian language weekly newspaper with a circulation in the New York area of about 20,000. It is published in New York City by defendant Kurier. Defendant Pogrebnoy is president and sole shareholder of Kurier and editor-in-chief of *Kurier.* The plaintiffs include corporations that publish, daily or weekly, major Russian language newspapers in Russia and

Russian language magazines in Russia or Israel; Itar–Tass Russian News Agency ("Itar–Tass"), formerly known as the Telegraph Agency of the Soviet Union (TASS), a wire service and news gathering company centered in Moscow, functioning similarly to the Associated Press; and the Union of Journalists of Russia ("UJR"), the professional writers union of accredited print and broadcast journalists of the Russian Federation.

* * *

[It was undisputed that the Kurier defendants copied substantial amounts of copyrighted material from the plaintiffs' publications without the plaintiffs' consent. Pogreboy claimed that he received permission from the authors of several of the copied articles, but the District Court held, for reasons discussed below, that their consent was not pertinent.]

Preliminary injunction ruling. After a hearing in May 1995, the District Court issued a preliminary injunction, prohibiting the Kurier defendants from copying the "works" of four plaintiff news organizations. *See ITAR–TASS Russian News Agency v. Russian Kurier Inc.,* 886 F.Supp. 1120, 1131 (S.D.N.Y.1995) (*"Itar–Tass I"*). Since the Court's analysis framed the key issue that would be considered at trial and is raised on appeal, the Court's opinion and the Russian statutory provisions relied on need to be explained.

Preliminarily, the Court ruled that the request for a preliminary injunction concerned articles published after March 13, 1995, the date that Russia acceded to the Berne Convention. *See id.* at 1125. The Court then ruled that the copied works were "Berne Convention work[s]," 17 U.S.C. § 101, and that the plaintiffs' rights were to be determined according to Russian copyright law. *See Itar–Tass I,* 886 F.Supp. at 1125–26.

The Court noted that under Russian copyright law authors of newspaper articles retain the copyright in their articles unless there has been a contractual assignment to their employer or some specific provision of law provides that the author's rights vest in the employer. *See id.* at 1127. Since the defendants alleged no claim of a contractual assignment, the Court next considered the provision of the 1993 Russian Federation Law on Copyright and Neighboring Rights ("Russian Copyright Law") (World Intellectual Property Organization (WIPO) translation) concerning what the United States Copyrights Act calls "works made for hire," 17 U.S.C. § 201(b). *See* Russian Copyright Law, Art. 14(2). That provision gives employers the exclusive right to "exploit" the "service-related work" produced by employees in the scope of their employment, absent some contractual arrangement. However, the Court noted, Article 14(4) specifies that subsection 2 does not apply to various categories of works, including newspapers. *See Itar–Tass I,* 886

F.Supp. at 1127. Accepting the view of plaintiffs' expert, Professor Vratislav Pechota, Judge Koeltl therefore ruled that the Russian version of the work-for-hire doctrine in Article 14(2), though exempting newspapers, applies to press agencies, like Itar–Tass. *See id.*

Turning to the rights of the newspapers, Judge Koeltl relied on Article 11, captioned "Copyright of Compiler of Collections and Other Works." This Article contains two subsections. Article 11(1) specifies the rights of compilers generally:

> The author of a collection or any other composite work (compiler) shall enjoy copyright in the selection or arrangement of subject matter that he has made insofar as that selection or arrangement is the result of a creative effort of compilation.

> The compiler shall enjoy copyright subject to respect for the rights of the authors of each work included in the composite work.

> Each of the authors of the works included in the composite work shall have the right to exploit his own work independently of the composite work unless the author's contract provides otherwise.

* * *

Russian Copyright Law, Art. 11(1). Article 11(2), the interpretation of which is critical to this appeal, specifies the rights of compilers of those works that are excluded from the work-for-hire provision of Article 14(2):

> The exclusive right to exploit encyclopedias, encyclopedic dictionaries, collections of scientific works—published in either one or several installments—newspapers, reviews and other periodical publications shall belong to the editor[1] thereof. The editor shall have the right to mention his name or to demand such mention whenever the said publications are exploited.

> The authors of the works included in the said publications shall retain the exclusive rights to exploit their works independently of the publication of the whole work.

Id., Art. 11(2). In another translation of the Russian Copyright Law, which was in evidence at the trial, the last phrase of Article 11(2) was rendered "independently from the publication as a whole." Russian Copyright Law, Art. 11(2) (Newton Davis translation). Because the parties' experts focused on the phrase "as a whole" in the Davis translation of Article 11(2), we will rely on the

---

1. The Newton Davis translation, which was an exhibit at trial, renders   this word "publisher."

Davis translation for the rendering of this key phrase of Article 11(2), but all other references to the Russian Copyright Law will be to the WIPO translation.

The District Court acknowledged, as the plaintiffs' expert had stated, that considerable scholarly debate existed in Russia as to the nature of a publisher's right "in a work as a whole." *See Itar–Tass I*, 886 F.Supp. at 1128. Judge Koeltl accepted Professor Pechota's view that the newspaper could prevent infringing activity "sufficient to interfere with the publisher's interest in the integrity of the work." *Id*. Without endeavoring to determine what extent of copying would "interfere with" the "integrity of the work," Judge Koeltl concluded that a preliminary injunction was warranted because what *Kurier* had copied was "the creative effort of the newspapers in the compilation of articles including numerous articles for the same issues, together with headlines and photographs." *Id*. The Court's preliminary injunction opinion left it unclear whether at trial the plaintiffs could obtain damages only for copying the newspapers' creative efforts as a compiler, such as the selection and arrangement of articles, the creation of headlines, and the layout of text and graphics, or also for copying the text of individual articles.

Expert testimony at trial. At trial, this unresolved issue was the focus of conflicting expert testimony. The plaintiffs' expert witness at trial was Michael Newcity, coordinator for the Center for Slavic, Eurasian and East European Studies at Duke University and an adjunct member of the faculty at the Duke University Law School. He opined that Article 11(2) gave the newspapers rights to redress copying not only of the publication "as a whole," but also of individual articles. He acknowledged that the reporters retained copyrights in the articles that they authored, but stated that Article 11(2) created a regime of parallel exclusive rights in both the newspaper publisher and the reporter. He rejected the contention that exclusive rights could not exist in two parties, pointing out that co-authors share exclusive rights to their joint work.

Newcity offered two considerations in support of his position. First, he cited the predecessor of Article 11(2), Article 485 of the Russian Civil Code of 1964. That provision was similar to Article 11(2), with one change that became the subject of major disagreement among the expert witnesses. Article 485 had given compilers, including newspaper publishers, the right to exploit their works "as a whole." The 1993 revision deleted "as a whole" from the first paragraph of the predecessor of Article 11(2), where it had modified the scope of the compiler's right, and moved the phrase to the second paragraph of revised Article 11(2), where it modifies the reserved right of the authors of articles within a compilation to exploit their works "independently of the publication as a whole."

Though Newcity opined that even under Article 485, reprinting of "one or two or three, at most," articles from a newspaper would have constituted infringement of the copyright "as a whole," he rested his reading of Article 11(2) significantly on the fact that the 1993 revision dropped the phrase "as a whole" from the paragraph that specified the publisher's right. This deletion, he contended, eliminated whatever ambiguity might have existed in the first paragraph of Article 485.

* * *

Defendants' experts presented a very different view of the rights of newspapers. Professor Peter B. Maggs of the University of Illinois, Urbana–Champaign, College of Law, testifying by deposition, pointed out that Article 11(2) gives authors the exclusive rights to their articles and accords newspaper publishers only the "exclusive rights to the publication as a whole, because that's the only thing not reserved to the authors." He opined that a newspaper's right to use of the compiled work "as a whole" would be infringed by the copying of an entire issue of a newspaper and probably by copying a substantial part of one issue, but not by the copying of a few articles, since the copyright in the articles belongs to the reporters. He also disagreed with Newcity's contention that exclusive rights to individual articles belonged simultaneously to both the newspaper and the reporter. Exclusive rights, he maintained, cannot be held by two people, except in the case of co-authors, who have jointly held rights against the world.

The defendants' first expert witness at trial was Michael Solton, who has worked in Moscow and Washington as an associate of the Steptoe & Johnson law firm. Under Article 11, he testified, authors retain exclusive rights to their articles in compilations, the compiler acquires a copyright in the selection and creative arrangement of materials in the compilation, and a newspaper publisher typically acquires the limited rights of the compiler by assignment from the compiler. The publisher, he said, does not acquire any rights to the individual articles. Solton declined to attach any significance to the decision issued by the [Russian] Informational Disputes Chamber because, he explained, the bylaws of that body accord it authority only over limited matters concerning the mass media and explicitly preclude it from adjudicating matters that Russian law refers to courts of the Russian Federation, such as copyright law.

The defendants' second expert trial witness was Svetlana Rozina, a partner of the Lex International law firm, who has consulted for the Russian government. She wrote the first draft of what became the 1993 revision of the Russian Copyright Law. She also testified that authors of works in compilations retain the exclusive right to their works, and that publishers of compilations do not have any rights to individual articles. Turning to the change in the placement of the phrase "as a whole" from Article 11(1) to Article 11(2), she explained that no substantive change was intended; the shift was made "[f]or the purpose of Russian grammar." She also agreed with Solton that the Informational Disputes Chamber renders advice on matters concerning freedom of mass information and lacks the competence to adjudicate issues of copyright law.

Trial ruling. The District Court resolved the dispute among the experts by accepting Newcity's interpretation of Russian copyright law. As he had previously ruled in granting the preliminary injunction, Judge Koeltl recognized that newspapers acquire no rights to individual articles by virtue of Article 14 since the Russian version of the work-for-hire doctrine is inapplicable to newspapers. Nevertheless, Judge Koeltl accepted Newcity's view of Article 11, relying on both the movement of the phrase "as a whole" from the first paragraph of Article 11(2) to the second paragraph of Article 11(2), and the opinion of the Informational Disputes Chamber. He also reasoned that publishers have "the real economic incentive to prevent wholesale unauthorized copying," and that, in the absence of assignments of rights to individual articles, widespread copying would occur if publishers could not prevent *Kurier*'s infringements.

[The District Court held that Kurier had willfully infringed, and calculated an award of actual damages, as well as an award of statutory damages for the articles for which the plaintiffs had obtained U.S. copyright registrations; to avoid duplicative recovery, the court gave the plaintiffs a choice between these awards.]

* * *

Discussion

I.   Choice of Law

The threshold issue concerns the choice of law for resolution of this dispute. That issue was not initially considered by the parties, all of whom turned directly to Russian law for resolution of the case. Believing that the conflicts issue merited consideration, we requested supplemental briefs from the parties and appointed Professor William F. Patry as Amicus Curiae. Prof. Patry has submitted an extremely helpful brief on the choice of law issue.

Choice of law issues in international copyright cases have been largely ignored in the reported decisions and dealt with rather cursorily by most commentators. Examples pertinent to the pending appeal are those decisions involving a work created by the employee of a foreign corporation. Several courts have applied the United States work-for-hire doctrine, *see* 17 U.S.C. § 201(b), without explicit consideration of the conflicts issue. *See, e.g., Aldon Accessories Ltd. v. Spiegel, Inc.,* 738 F.2d 548, 551–53 (2d Cir.1984) (U.S. law applied to determine if statuettes crafted abroad were works for hire); *Dae Han Video Productions, Inc. v. Kuk Dong Oriental Food, Inc.,* 19 U.S.P.Q.2d 1294 (D.Md.1990) (U.S. law applied to determine if scripts written abroad were works for hire); *P & D International v. Halsey Publishing Co.,* 672 F.Supp. 1429, 1435–36 (S.D.Fla.1987) (U.S. work-for-hire law assumed to apply). Other courts have applied foreign law. *See Frink America, Inc. v. Champion Road Machinery Ltd.,* 961 F.Supp. 398 (N.D.N.Y.1997) (Canadian copyright law applied on issue of ownership); *Greenwich Film Productions v. DRG Records Inc.,* 1992 WL 279357 (S.D.N.Y. Sept. 25, 1992) (French law applied to determine ownership of right to musical work commissioned in France for French film); *Dae Han Video Production Inc. v. Dong San Chun,* 17 U.S.P.Q.2d 1306, 1310 n. 6, 1990 WL 265976 (E.D.Va. June 18, 1990) (foreign law relied on to determine that alleged licensor lacks rights); *see also Autoskill, Inc. v. National Educational Support Systems, Inc.,* 994 F.2d 1476, 1489 n. 16 (10th Cir.1993) (U.S. work-for-hire law applied where claim that contrary Canadian law should apply was belatedly raised and for that reason not considered); *Pepe (U.K.) Ltd. v. Grupo Pepe Ltda.,* 24 U.S.P.Q.2d 1354, 1356 (S.D.Fla.1992) (congruent foreign and U.S. law both applied). In none of these cases, however, was the issue of choice of law explicitly adjudicated. The conflicts issue was identified but ruled not necessary to be resolved in *Greenwich Film Productions S.A. v. D.R.G. Records, Inc.,* 25 U.S.P.Q.2d 1435, 1437–38 (S.D.N.Y.1992).

The Nimmer treatise briefly (and perhaps optimistically) suggests that conflicts issues "have rarely proved troublesome in the law of copyright." *Nimmer on Copyright* § 17.05 (1998) (*"Nimmer"*) (footnote omitted). Relying on the "national treatment" principle of the Berne Convention[6] and the Universal Copyright Convention[7] ("U.C.C."), *Nimmer* asserts, correctly in our view, that "an author who is a national of one of the member states of either Berne or the U.C.C., or one who first publishes his work in any such member state, is entitled to the same copyright protection in each other member state as such other state accords to its own nationals." *Id.* (footnotes omitted). *Nimmer* then somewhat overstates the national treatment principle: "The applicable law is the copyright law of the state in which the infringement occurred, not that of the state of which the author is a national, or in which the work is first published." *Id.* (footnote omitted). The difficulty with this broad statement is that it subsumes under the phrase "applicable law" the law concerning two distinct issues—ownership and

---

6. *See* Berne Convention Art. 5(1) (Paris text 1971).

7. *See* Universal Copyright Convention (Paris text 1971).

substantive rights, *i.e.,* scope of protection.[8] Another commentator has also broadly stated the principle of national treatment, but described its application in a way that does not necessarily cover issues of ownership. "The principle of national treatment also means that both the question of whether the right exists and the question of the scope of the right are to be answered in accordance with the law of the country where the protection is claimed." S.M. Stewart, *International Copyright and Neighboring Rights* § 3.17 (2d ed. 1989). We agree with the view of the Amicus that the Convention's principle of national treatment simply assures that if the law of the country of infringement applies to the scope of substantive copyright protection, that law will be applied uniformly to foreign and domestic authors. *See Murray v. British Broadcasting Corp.,* 906 F.Supp. 858 (S.D.N.Y.1995), *aff'd,* 81 F.3d 287 (1996).

Source of conflicts rules. Our analysis of the conflicts issue begins with consideration of the source of law for selecting a conflicts rule. Though *Nimmer* turns directly to the Berne Convention and the U.C.C., we think that step moves too quickly past the Berne Convention Implementation Act of 1988, Pub. L. 100–568, 102 Stat. 2853, 17 U.S.C. § 101 note. Section 4(a)(3) of the Act amends Title 17 to provide: "No right or interest in a work eligible for protection under this title may be claimed by virtue of ... the provisions of the Berne Convention.... Any rights in a work eligible for protection under this title that derive from this title ... shall not be expanded or reduced by virtue of ... the provisions of the Berne Convention."[9] 17 U.S.C. § 104(c).

We start our analysis with the Copyrights Act itself, which contains no provision relevant to the pending case concerning conflicts issues.[10] We therefore fill the interstices of the Act by developing federal common law on the conflicts issue. * * *

---

8. Prof. Patry's brief, as Amicus Curiae, helpfully points out that the principle of national treatment is really not a conflicts rule at all; it does not direct application of the law of any country. It simply requires that the country in which protection is claimed must treat foreign and domestic authors alike. Whether U.S. copyright law directs U.S. courts to look to foreign or domestic law as to certain issues is irrelevant to national treatment, so long as the scope of protection would be extended equally to foreign and domestic authors.

9. Other pertinent provisions are:

Section 2(2), which provides: "The obligations of the United States under the Berne Convention may be performed only pursuant to appropriate domestic law."

Section 3(a)(2), which provides: "The provisions of the Berne Convention ... shall not be enforceable in any action brought pursuant to the provisions of the Berne Convention itself."

Section 3(b)(1), which provides: "The provisions of the Berne Convention ... do not expand or reduce the right of any author of a work, whether claimed under Federal, State, or the common law ... to claim authorship of the work."

10. The recently added provision concerning copyright in "restored works," those that are in the public domain because of noncompliance with

* * *

The choice of law applicable to the pending case is not necessarily the same for all issues. *See* Restatement (Second) of Conflict of Laws § 222 ("The courts have long recognized that they are not bound to decide all issues under the local law of a single state."). We consider first the law applicable to the issue of copyright ownership.

Conflicts rule for issues of ownership. Copyright is a form of property, and the usual rule is that the interests of the parties in property are determined by the law of the state with "the most significant relationship" to the property and the parties. *See id.* The Restatement recognizes the applicability of this principle to intangibles such as "a literary idea." *Id.* Since the works at issue were created by Russian nationals and first published in Russia, Russian law is the appropriate source of law to determine issues of ownership of rights. That is the well-reasoned conclusion of the Amicus Curiae, Prof. Patry, and the parties in their supplemental briefs are in agreement on this point. In terms of the United States Copyrights Act and its reference to the Berne Convention, Russia is the "country of origin" of these works, *see* 17 U.S.C. § 101 (definition of "country of origin" of Berne Convention work); Berne Convention, Art. 5(4), although "country of origin" might not always be the appropriate country for purposes of choice of law concerning ownership.[11]

To whatever extent we look to the Berne Convention itself as guidance in the development of federal common law on the conflicts issue, we find nothing to alter our conclusion. The Convention does not purport to settle issues of ownership, with one exception not relevant to this case.[12] *See* Jane C. Ginsburg, *Ownership of Electronic Rights and the Private International Law of Copyright,* 22

formalities of United States copyright law, contains an explicit subsection vesting ownership of a restored work "in the author or initial rightholder of the work *as determined by the law of the source country of the work.*" 17 U.S.C. § 104A(b) (emphasis added); *see id.* § 104A(h)(8) (defining "source country").

11. In deciding that the law of the country of origin determines the ownership of copyright, we consider only initial ownership, and have no occasion to consider choice of law issues concerning assignments of rights.

12. The Berne Convention expressly provides that "[o]wnership of copyright in a cinematographic work shall be a matter for legislation in the country

where protection is claimed." Berne Convention, Art. 14 *bis* (2)(a). With respect to other works, this provision could be understood to have any of three meanings. First, it could carry a negative implication that for other works, ownership is not to be determined by legislation in the country where protection is claimed. Second, it could be thought of as an explicit assertion for films of a general principle already applicable to other works. Third, it could be a specific provision for films that was adopted without an intention to imply anything about other works. In the absence of any indication that either the first or second meanings were intended, we prefer the third understanding.

Colum.–VLA J.L. & Arts 165, 167–68 (1998) (The Berne Convention "provides that the law of the country where protection is claimed defines what rights are protected, the scope of the protection, and the available remedies; the treaty does not supply a choice of law rule for determining ownership.") (footnote concerning Art. 14 *bis* (2)(a) omitted).

Selection of Russian law to determine copyright ownership is, however, subject to one procedural qualification. Under United States law, an owner (including one determined according to foreign law) may sue for infringement in a United States court only if it meets the standing test of 17 U.S.C. § 501(b), which accords standing only to the legal or beneficial owner of an "exclusive right."

Conflicts rule for infringement issues. On infringement issues, the governing conflicts principle is usually *lex loci delicti,* the doctrine generally applicable to torts. *See Lauritzen v. Larsen,* 345 U.S. 571, 583, 73 S.Ct. 921, 97 L.Ed. 1254 (1953). We have implicitly adopted that approach to infringement claims, applying United States copyright law to a work that was unprotected in its country of origin. *See Hasbro Bradley, Inc. v. Sparkle Toys, Inc.,* 780 F.2d 189, 192–93 (2d Cir.1985). In the pending case, the place of the tort is plainly the United States. To whatever extent *lex loci delicti* is to be considered only one part of a broader "interest" approach, *see Carbotrade S.p.A. v. Bureau Veritas,* 99 F.3d 86, 89–90 (2d Cir.1996), United States law would still apply to infringement issues, since not only is this country the place of the tort, but also the defendant is a United States corporation.

The division of issues, for conflicts purposes, between ownership and infringement issues will not always be as easily made as the above discussion implies. If the issue is the relatively straightforward one of which of two contending parties owns a copyright, the issue is unquestionably an ownership issue, and the law of the country with the closest relationship to the work will apply to settle the ownership dispute. But in some cases, including the pending one, the issue is not simply who owns the copyright but also what is the nature of the ownership interest. Yet as a court considers the nature of an ownership interest, there is some risk that it will too readily shift the inquiry over to the issue of whether an alleged copy has infringed the asserted copyright. Whether a copy infringes depends in part on the scope of the interest of the copyright owner. Nevertheless, though the issues are related, the nature of a copyright interest is an issue distinct from the issue of whether the copyright has been infringed. *See, e.g., Kregos v. Associated Press,* 937 F.2d 700, 709–10 (2d Cir.1991) (pointing out that although work survives summary judgment on issue of copyrightability of compilation, scope of protection against claim of infringement might be limited). The pending case is one that requires consideration not simply of who owns an interest, but, as to the newspapers, the nature of the interest that is owned.

II.   Determination of Ownership Rights under Russian Law

Since United States law permits suit only by owners of "an exclusive right under a copyright," 17 U.S.C. § 501(b), we must first determine whether any of the plaintiffs own an exclusive right. That issue of ownership, as we have indicated, is to be determined by Russian law.

Determination of a foreign country's law is an issue of law. * * *

Under Article 14 of the Russian Copyright Law, Itar–Tass is the owner of the copyright interests in the articles written by its employees. However, Article 14(4) excludes newspapers from the Russian version of the work-for-hire doctrine. The newspaper plaintiffs, therefore, must locate their ownership rights, if any, in some other source of law. They rely on Article 11. The District Court upheld their position, apparently recognizing in the newspaper publishers "exclusive" rights *to the articles,* even though, by virtue of Article 11(2), the reporters also retained "exclusive" rights to these articles.

Having considered all of the views presented by the expert witnesses, we conclude that the defendants' experts are far more persuasive as to the meaning of Article 11. In the first place, once Article 14 of the Russian Copyright Law explicitly denies newspapers the benefit of a work-for-hire doctrine, which, if available, would accord them rights to individual articles written by their employees, it is highly unlikely that Article 11 would confer on newspapers the very right that Article 14 has denied them. Moreover, Article 11 has an entirely reasonable scope if confined, as its caption suggests, to defining the "Copyright of Compilers of Collections and Other Works." That article accords compilers copyright "in the selection and arrangement of subject matter that he has made insofar as that selection or arrangement is the result of a creative effort of compilation." Russian Copyright Law, Art. 11(1). Article 11(2) accords a publisher of compilations the right to exploit such works, including the right to insist on having their names mentioned, while expressly reserving to "authors of the works included" in compilations the "exclusive rights to exploit their works independently of the publication of the whole work." *Id.* Art. 11(2). As the defendants' experts testified, Article 11 lets *authors* of newspaper articles sue for infringement of their rights in the text of their articles, and lets *newspaper publishers* sue for wholesale copying of all of the newspaper or for copying any portions of the newspaper that embody their selection, arrangement, and presentation of articles (including headlines)—copying that infringes their ownership interest in the compilation.

Newcity's contrary interpretation, according publishers (and reporters) exclusive rights to the text of articles, draws entirely unwarranted significance from the shift of the phrase "as a whole" from the first to the second paragraph of Article 11(2). One would not expect drafters of the revised Article 11(2) to accomplish a major broadening of the rights of newspaper publishers simply by shifting the placement of this phrase. Moreover, the drafter of the revision testified that the shift was a matter of grammar, and not of any substance. Furthermore, Newcity's interpretation rests on the untenable premise that both the publisher of a newspaper and the author of an article have exclusive rights to the same article. Under his interpretation, as he acknowledged, the publisher could grant a license to a third party to publish an article, the "exclusive" rights to which are held by the author. That unlikely result cannot be accepted in the absence of clear statutory language authorizing it.[13]

* * *

Nor can the District Court's conclusion be supported by its observation that extensive copying of newspapers will ensue unless newspapers are permitted to secure redress for the copying of individual articles. In the first place, copying of articles may always be prevented at the behest of the authors of the articles or their assignees. Second, the newspapers may well be entitled to prevent copying of the protectable elements of their compilations. Lastly, even if authors lack sufficient economic incentive to bring individual suits, as the District Court apprehended, Russian copyright law authorizes the creation of organizations "for the collective administration of the economic rights of authors ... in cases where the individual exercise thereof is hampered by difficulties of a practical nature." Russian Copyright Law, Art. 44(1). Indeed, UJR, the reporters' organization, may well be able in this litigation to protect the rights of the reporters whose articles were copied by *Kurier*.

Relief. Our disagreement with the District Court's interpretation of Article 11 does not mean, however, that the defendants may continue copying with impunity. In the first place, Itar–Tass, as a press agency, is within the scope of Article 14, and, unlike the excluded newspapers, enjoys the benefit of the Russian version of the work-for-hire doctrine. Itar–Tass is therefore entitled to injunc-

---

13. Newcity sought to analogize the exclusive rights that he believed were held by both the newspaper and the author to the rights held jointly by co-authors. Russian copyright law, however, like similar provisions elsewhere, recognizes jointly held rights in "a work that is the product of the joint creative work of two or more persons." Russian Copyright Law, Art. 10(1). In the absence of either joint authorship or contractual arrangements, it would be most unusual to have exclusive rights held by anyone other than the author.

tive relief to prevent unauthorized copying of its articles and to damages for such copying, and the judgment is affirmed as to this plaintiff.

Furthermore, the newspaper plaintiffs, though not entitled to relief for the copying of the text of the articles they published, may well be entitled to injunctive relief and damages if they can show that *Kurier* infringed the publishers' ownership interests in the newspaper compilations. Because the District Court upheld the newspapers' right to relief for copying the text of the articles, it had no occasion to consider what relief the newspapers might be entitled to by reason of *Kurier*'s copying of the newspapers' creative efforts in the selection, arrangement, or display of the articles. Since *Kurier*'s photocopying reproduced not only the text of articles but also headlines and graphic materials as they originally appeared in the plaintiffs' publication, it is likely that on remand the newspaper plaintiffs will be able to obtain some form of injunctive relief and some damages. On these infringement issues, as we have indicated, United States law will apply.

* * *

Conclusion

Accordingly, we affirm the judgment to the extent that it granted relief to Itar–Tass, we reverse to the extent that the judgment granted relief to the other plaintiffs, and we remand for further proceedings. No costs.

Notes

1. In Peer Int'l Corp. v. Termidor Music Publishers Ltd, 2003 E.M.L.R. 34 (CA (Civ. Div.)), an English court addressed the ownership of exclusive licenses of the English copyrights in certain musical works that had been created in Cuba by Cuban nationals and licensed to a United Kingdom company between the 1930s and the 1950s. After the Cuban revolution, the Cuban government invalidated all prior licensing agreements unless approved by the government. However, the court declared this law to be confiscatory, and refused to apply it to exclusive licenses that were "located" in the United Kingdom. It treated these licenses as a form of property, and held that their situs was in the United Kingdom. *Id.* at para. 65.

The same principle was later applied by a United States court, in Films by Jove, Inc. v. Berov, 341 F.Supp.2d 199 (E.D.N.Y. 2004), which held that the situs of an exclusive film distribution right was the United States, because (1) the distribution rights pertained only to the United States, and (2) the licensee was domiciled in the United States. *Id.* at 210. Accordingly, the court refused to give effect to the Russian

Federation's attempt to expropriate the American distributor's interest in the copyrighted films.

2.   Unlike the United States, many countries (especially those which provide strong moral rights protection) do not have a general policy of recognizing employers or commissioning parties as "authors" of copyrighted works, although they may be copyright owners, either presumptively by statute, or by express assignment. In such countries, the author must be a natural person, subject to limited exceptions. This is consistent with the policy of recognizing that natural persons have inalienable moral rights in their works of authorship, but that they are free to assign or license the patrimonial (*i.e.,* economic exploitation) rights in those works.

For example, as illustrated in the *Nejila X.* case discussed in Chapter 2, French law generally recognizes the employee as the author of a copyrightable work created within the course of employment, and as the owner of both the moral rights and the patrimonial rights in that work. The only exceptions are for collective works (L.113–5) and software (Art. L.113–9), and in the case of software the exception applies only to the patrimonial right and to a few of the moral rights (Art. L.121–7). Although French law does not contain a work-made-for-hire provision, either for employers or commissioning parties, implied assignments of an author's economic rights are possible (although infrequently found), except with respect to publishing, public performance, or audiovisual production contracts, which must be in writing (Art. L.131–2).

Japan, by contrast, ascribes authorship to an employer when (i) the work is created based on the initiative of the employer; (ii) the work is created by an employee as a part of his duties; (iii) the work is made public under the name of the employer (except for computer programs); *and* (iv) there is no contrary stipulation in the contract of employment (Art. 15) However, this general rule does not apply to cinematographic works, as illustrated by the *Maker of a Documentary Film* case, in Part 3.D. below.

In the United Kingdom, the employee is generally considered to be the author of the work, but in the case of literary, artistic, musical or dramatic works created within the course of employment, the employer is the initial copyright owner, subject to any agreement to the contrary (Sec. 11(2)).

Even those countries that vest initial copyright ownership in the employer, such as Japan and the United Kingdom, frequently do not follow the United States approach of extending this rule to many commissioned (*i.e.,* non-employee) works, except in the case of sound recordings, motion pictures, and, in some cases, photographs (which, in contrast, generally do not qualify as commissioned works made for hire in the U.S.).

In the case of neighboring rights—that is, exclusive rights in sound recordings and broadcasts—many countries do not even apply the concept or terminology of authorship. For example, French law provides that "the natural or legal person who takes the initiative and responsibility for the initial fixation of a sequence of sounds shall be deemed the *phonogram producer*," (Art. L.213–1) (emphasis added), then identifies the specific rights that belong to the "producer."

C. JOINT WORKS

BECKINGHAM v. HODGENS

England and Wales Court of Appeal, Civil Division, 2003
[2003] EWCA Civ 143

Parker L.J:

[In the decision appealed from, the trial court held that claimant Beckingham (a session musician professionally known as "Bobby Valentino") was a joint author in the song "Young at Heart" (referred to here as the "Work"), and that, accordingly, he was entitled to proceed against defendant Hodgens for a share of the royalties derived from exploitation of the Work. The trial judge held that Valentino had initially given Hodgens a gratuitous implied license to exploit the Work, but later revoked that license, after which Hodgens' continued exploitation of the Work entitled Valentino to a 50 percent share of the royalties.]

* * *

The factual background

The factual background is set out in detail in the judge's careful and lucid judgment. For present purposes, only a brief summary is required.

In 1984 Mr. Valentino (who was then aged about 23) was a professional fiddle player. Although he was not a member of The Bluebells (the leader of which was Mr. Hodgens), he was hired as a session musician at a recording session held at Red Bus Studios in London in February 1984, at which the re-recording of The Bluebells' version of the song "Young at Heart" was completed. In the action he claims that at that session he not merely performed but wrote the violin part which features in the introduction to the song, consisting of four bars (repeated three times during the song), without any significant input from anyone else; and that his contribution in writing the violin part was such as to render him a joint author of the music ("the Work") and hence a joint owner of the copyright in it. That claim is denied by Mr. Hodgens, who claims to have written all the music (including the violin part) himself. Mr. Hodgens alleges that at the recording session Mr. Valentino merely followed instructions in relation to the violin part given by him. In the result, as already noted, the judge found in favour of Mr. Valentino on this issue and upheld his copyright claim. Subject only to permission being granted to appeal on the s.11(3) issue, therefore, there is now no possibility of appeal against that part of the judge's order whereby it is declared that Mr. Valentino is a joint author and hence a joint copyright owner of "the Work". Nor is there any separate appeal against the quantification of his interest in the copyright at 50 per cent.

The background facts in relation to the estoppel issue are as follows. Following its release in mid–1984 The Bluebells' version of the song (incorporating the disputed violin part), achieved a degree of commercial success, reaching number 8 in the charts. At that time, Mr. Valentino made no claim to be a joint author of the music. Indeed, his own evidence was that he told Mr. Hodgens in around 1984 that he had taken advice as to whether he should make such a claim but had decided not to do so.

In 1986 The Bluebells disbanded.

In 1993 The Bluebells' version of the song was (adventitiously so far as the parties were concerned) used as backing in a Volkswagen commercial. This caused a substantial resurgence in its popularity, as a result of which it reappeared in the charts and was at No.1 for a number of weeks. Its success was such that the group re-formed for the purpose of performing it on a number of occasions on the television programme "Top of the Pops".

Following this resurgence of popularity, Mr. Valentino, for the first time, claimed a share of future royalties on the basis that he was a joint author of the music. Mr. Valentino's evidence was that he made this claim in March 1993; Mr. Hodgens' evidence was that he did not do so until November 1997 at the earliest.

The judgment

The section 11(3) issue

Section 11(3) provides as follows:

In this Act 'work of joint authorship' means a work produced by the collaboration of two or more authors in which the contribution of each author is not separate from the contribution of the other author or authors.

The judge therefore had to consider, in the context of Mr. Valentino's claim, whether the requirements of the subsection were met in the instant case. * * * On the facts, the judge concluded that Mr. Valentino had collaborated in the creation of "the Work" (*i.e.*, the music); that he had made a significant contribution to it; and that his contribution was not "separate" within the meaning of the subsection. Mr. Hodgens does not challenge these conclusions.

The judge then addressed a submission made by Mr. Philip Engelman (appearing for Mr. Hodgens, as he does before us) to the effect that the subsection imposes a further requirement, *viz.* the requirement of an intention as to joint authorship (as the judge put it in para. [47] of the judgment, "a joint intention to create a joint work"). The judge rejected this contention, and Mr. Engelman now seeks permission to appeal against that rejection.

The judge addressed the s.11(3) issue in paras. [47] to [50] of the judgment, as follows:

47. Mr. Engelman argued that there is, in law, a fourth requirement before a work can be regarded as a work of joint authorship, namely a joint intention to create a joint work. In support he relied principally on a decision of Mr. Justice Cohen in the Supreme Court of British Columbia in Darryl Neudorf v. Nettwerk Productions Ltd [2000] R.P.C. 935. After an extensive review of authority in Canada, the United States and England, Cohen J. said at 962–3:

> In the result I find that the test for joint authorship that should be applied to the facts in the instant case is as follows:
>
> (i) Did the plaintiff contribute significant original expression to the songs? If yes,
>
> (ii) Did each of the plaintiff and Ms. McLachlan intend that their contributions be merged into a unitary whole? If yes,
>
> (iii) Did each of the plaintiff and Ms. McLachlan intend the other to be a joint author of the song?

48. I am afraid that, for my part, I cannot see any basis in the English cases, or in the statutory definition which I am bound to apply, for the importation of this third requirement. Plainly, for there to be a collaboration at all, the parties must have a common design to produce the work. Those authors who reach the threshold of a 'significant and original' contribution in furtherance of that common design should, in my view, be entitled to call themselves a co-author. Any other test introduces undesirable problems of proof for which I can see no basis in the Act.

49. Applying those principles to the facts as I have found them in the present case, I hold that The Bluebells' version was created by a collaboration between Mr. Hodgens and Mr. Valentino in furtherance of a common design. Whilst accepting that it was ultimately a question of fact and degree for the Court, both sides called expert evidence on the question of whether the violin part made a significant and original contri-

bution to The Bluebells' version of Young at Heart. Both experts thought the violin riff memorable and catchy. Mr. Chandler, a musicologist and copyright consultant called by the Claimant, thought the violin part more memorable than anything else in the song. Mr. Protheroe, the expert called by Mr. Hodgens, was inclined to accord the chorus rather more importance, yet nevertheless described the violin part as a reasonably striking feature of the work. In the end the dispute between them came down to whether the violin part made its contribution largely or wholly because of its prominence at the beginning of the work.

50. Having heard the piece played, and reflected on the evidence given, I conclude that the violin part does make a significant and original contribution of the right kind of skill and labour to The Bluebells' version of the song. Thus Mr. Valentino is a joint author of the copyright in that work.

[The trial court then rejected the defendant's estoppel defense, and held that Valentino had validly revoked the implied gratuitous license to Hodgens in 1993.]

* * *

Conclusions

* * *

The section 11(3) issue

I reject the submission that s.11(3) requires, as one of the elements of joint authorship, the existence of a common intention as to joint authorship. I do so for essentially the reasons which the judge gave.

In the first place, I agree with the judge that there is nothing in the express wording of s.11(3) which warrants the imposition of such a requirement. The only requirements for a "work of joint authorship" expressed in s.11(3) are that the authors should have collaborated and that their contributions should not be "separate".

As *Levy v. Rutley* makes clear, these requirements will not be met unless there has been "joint labouring in furtherance of a common design" (see *ibid.* p.529, *per* Keating J.). But the "common design" in that context is not an intention that there should be joint authorship. What Keating J. was describing, as I read his judgment, was the process of jointly creating the work in question: as the judge in the instant case put it in para. [48] of the judgment, a "common design to produce the work". So much is clear, in my judgment, from the passage in Keating J.'s judgment which follows his reference to "common design", where he says:

"I fail to discover any evidence that there was any co-operation of the two in the design of this piece [a play], or in its execution, or in any improvements either in the plot or the general structure..... If the plaintiff and the author had agreed together to rearrange the plot, and so to produce a more attractive piece out of the original materials, possibly that might have made them joint authors of the whole. So, if two persons undertake jointly to write a play, agreeing in the general outline and design, and sharing the labour of working it out, each would be contributing to the whole production, and they might be said to be joint authors of it. But, to constitute joint authorship, there must be a common design. Nothing of the sort appears here. The plaintiff made mere additions to a complete piece, which did not in themselves amount to a dramatic piece, but were intended only to make the play more attractive to the audience."

As to the Canadian case of *Darryl Neudorf*, on which Mr. Engelman naturally relies strongly, I agree with the judge that there is no basis in the English cases for importing the requirement of an intention as to joint authorship. In *Darryl Neudorf*, Cohen J. followed the United States case of Childress v. Taylor 945 F.2d 500. At p.962 of the report of *Darryl Neudorf*, Cohen J. said this:

"... the creation of the intent to co-author requirement in Childress v. Taylor happened despite the statutory definition of joint authorship ..., not because of it. The court looked beyond the language of the section and moved on to review policy considerations in the application of the section. In particular, the court could not accept that Congress intended to extend joint authorship to, for example, editors and researchers. It was for this reason that the court created the intent to co-author requirement."

In my judgment, the judge in the instant case was clearly right to confine his consideration to the language of s.11(3) and not to look beyond the section into the uncertain realms of policy. So doing, he plainly reached the correct conclusion.

I would accordingly refuse permission to appeal on the s.11(3) issue, confirming my earlier refusal of permission on the papers.

[The Court of Appeal also upheld the trial court's rejection of the defendant's estoppel argument as well as its conclusion that Valentino had revoked the implied gratuitous license to Hodgens in 1993, thus entitling Valentino to collect his share of the royalties for subsequent exploitations of the Work.]

Notes

1. *Beckingham* applied the definition of a "work of joint authorship" from the 1956 U.K. Copyright Law. The current definition is the same, except that the word "distinct" replaces "separate." Copyright, Designs, and Patents Act 1988, c.48, sec. 10(1). A recent decision approving *Beckingham*'s rejection of the requirement of mutual intent to share authorship concludes (in dictum) that the same analysis should apply under the current statute. Fisher v. Brooker, [2007] F.S.R. 12 (High Court of Justice, Chancery Div., 2006), *aff'd in relevant part*, [2008] F.S.R. 26 (Court of Appeal 2008).

2. The Canadian case referenced in *Beckingham* is Neudorf v. Nettwerk Prods. Ltd., 71 B.C.L.R. (3d) 290, 1999 CarswellBC 2774 (British Columbia Supreme Court 1999), which involved a musical collaboration between Sara McLachlan and another musician. Although the British Columbia court relied heavily on English case law regarding joint authorship, it ultimately decided to adopt the Second Circuit's *Childress v. Taylor* requirement of mutual intent to share authorship, and rejected the putative joint author's claim. Noting the similarity between the statutory definitions of joint authorship in Canada and the U.S., the court concluded that "creation of the intent to co-author requirement in *Childress v. Taylor* happened despite the statutory definition of joint authorship in s. 101, not because of it." *Id.* at para. [94]. The Canadian copyright statutes define a "work of joint authorship" as:

> a work produced by the collaboration of two or more authors in which the contribution of one author is not distinct from the contribution of the other author or authors[.]

Copyright Act, R.S.C. 1985, c. C–42, sec. 2.

3. In addition to the question of who qualifies as a joint author, jurisdictions also differ as to the legal consequences of joint authorship. In some countries, these consequences have been addressed in detail by statutes and case law; in other countries, there may be significant gaps in the existing authorities, leaving room for future judicial interpretation.

Under United Kingdom common law, the consent of all joint authors is needed for any exploitation of the work, whether by a third party or by one of the joint authors. However, a single joint author may sue an infringer without the participation of the other joint authors.

Under Art. 8 of the German copyright statutes, economic exploitation rights belong jointly to the joint authors, and alterations require their joint consent. However, a joint author "may not unreasonably refuse his consent to the publication, exploitation or alteration of the work." Each can individually sue infringers, subject to a duty to share the payment among all of the joint authors. Any proceeds from the exploitation of the work "shall accrue to the joint authors in proportion to the extent of their respective contributions to the work unless otherwise agreed between them."

Article L.113–3 of the French Intellectual Property Code states that joint authors "shall exercise their rights by common accord"; disagreements will be resolved by the courts. Where the contribution of each of the joint authors is "of a different kind," each may, unless otherwise agreed, separately exploit his own personal contribution "without, however, prejudicing the exploitation of the common work."

Because of differences such as these, exploiting a jointly authored work outside of the United States often requires a different kind of licensing arrangement than would be required for a purely domestic exploitation of the same work.

4.   The complexities of joint authorship have prompted many countries to develop special rules for collaborative works such as sound recordings and motion pictures. Motion pictures are discussed in the next section. In the case of sound recordings, the producer is typically considered the sole author of a sound recording (or "phonogram"). (*E.g.,* United Kingdom, Art. 9(2); Ireland, Art. 21(a); India 2(d)(*v*)). Because sound recordings are typically protected by neighboring rights rather than traditional copyright (or "authors' rights"), no moral rights attach to sound recordings; thus, there is no need to distinguish between authorship and initial copyright ownership. Some countries do not even use the term "author" with respect to sound recordings. The French statutes, for example, define a phonogram producer as "the natural or legal person who takes the initiative and responsibility for the initial fixation of a sequence of sounds shall be deemed the phonogram producer," and then assign specific rights to the phonogram producer. (Arts. L.213–1, L.214–1 to L.214–5).

D.   CINEMATOGRAPHIC WORKS

Many countries treat cinematographic works as a special category with respect to questions of authorship and initial copyright ownership. To a great degree, this reflects the tension between two goals: (1) recognizing contributions to motion pictures as highly creative and collaborative works that reflect the individual artistic sensibilities of their multiple creators, and (2) facilitating commercial exploitation of motion pictures. In countries where film production involves smaller budgets that are heavily subsidized by public funds (for example, in much of continental Europe), the first of these goals tends to be primary. In countries where film budgets are larger and depend more on private capital (such as the United Kingdom and, of course, the United States) the need to successfully commercialize a motion picture means that the second goal may be of equal or greater importance.

The European Union has imposed only one constraint on the freedom of member states to prescribe who should be considered the author(s) of a motion picture. Article 2(1) of the Directive 93/98/EEC on Copyright Term of Protection provides: "The principal director of a cinematographic or audiovisual work shall be considered as its author or one of its authors. Member states shall be free to designate other co-authors." Before the Directive was issued in 1993, the law of the United Kingdom designated a film's producer as its sole author. United Kingdom 1988 Act, Art. 9(2)(b)(prior to 1996 amendment). After the Directive, the United Kingdom was forced to amend its law, which now provides that the producer and the principal director are joint authors, and thus jointly own the initial copyright in the film; it also adds films to the list of works with respect to which employers are deemed to own the copyright in employee-created works. *Id.* Arts. 9(2)(ab), 10(1A), 11(2) (as amended by Art. 18 of the Copyright and Related Rights Regulations 1996).

In Chapter 4, the case of *Turner Entertainment Co. v. Huston* (concerning the moral rights of film directors) illustrates the importance, under French law, given to recognizing the inalienable moral rights of the creative contributors to a motion picture, even when they are bound by work-made-for-hire agreements executed in the United States.

In addition to France, other countries that recognize moral rights in motion pictures (a list which includes most Berne signatories) will typically distinguish between the parties entitled to moral rights protection and those entitled to ownership of the economic rights. Thus, many countries ascribe authorship to one or more of the natural persons who make creative contributions to a motion picture, but also employ various mechanisms to vest ownership of the film's economic exploitation rights in one party—typically, the producer. The purpose of this arrangement is to avoid the legal complexities of joint authorship, which could interfere with the marketability of the motion picture.

France provides a specific enumerated list of the presumptive joint authors of a motion picture. Art. L.113–7 provides:

> Authorship of an audiovisual work shall belong to the natural person or persons who have carried out the intellectual creation of the work.

> Unless proved otherwise, the following are presumed to be the joint authors of an audiovisual work made in collaboration:

> 1°.   the author of the script;

> 2°.   the author of the adaptation;

> 3°.   the author of the dialogue;

> 4°.   the author of the musical compositions, with or without words, specially composed for the work;

5°. the director.

If an audiovisual work is adapted from a preexisting work or script which is still protected, the authors of the original work shall be assimilated to the authors of the new work.

Even in France, however, the statutes create a presumption that the authors of a film assign their patrimonial rights to the producer:

Contracts binding the producer and the authors of an audiovisual work, other than the author of a musical composition with or without words, shall imply, unless otherwise stipulated * * * assignment to the producer of the exclusive exploitation rights in the audiovisual work.

Art. L.132–24. The producer is defined as the "natural or legal person who takes the initiative and responsibility for making the work." Art. L.132–23.

In the absence of specific statutory authority, some countries may assign ownership of the economic rights in a motion picture to the producer as a matter of judicial interpretation, as illustrated in the following case.

MAKER OF A DOCUMENTARY FILM*
Intellectual Property High Court (Japan), 2006
Fourth Division

Case No. 2005(Ne) No.10076

Summary of the Judgment:

In this case, with respect to the documentary film of a music group's final concert which was directed by Plaintiff X, the representative person of Plaintiff Company, and was shot by Plaintiff Company (hereinafter referred to as the "Work"), the plaintiffs allege that the DVDs, etc. manufactured and sold by Defendant Company infringe Plaintiff Company's copyright (right of reproduction and right of adaptation) as well as Plaintiff X's moral rights of authorship (right to maintain integrity and right to indicate name), and they seek an injunction against Defendant Company's reproduction and distribution of the DVDs, etc., payment of damages, and publication of an apology.

The court of the first instance made a judgment ordering Defendant Company to stop reproduction and distribution of the DVDs, etc. and pay damages. Both parties filed appeals against this judgment.

* Translation provided courtesy of the
Institute of Intellectual Property, Tokyo.

This court, as the court of the first instance had, recognized Plaintiff X as the author of the Work and Plaintiff Company as the copyright holder of the Work, but found Plaintiff Company to have assigned its copyright to a third party. Based on these findings, this court quashed the judgment of the first instance with regard to the part relating to Plaintiff Company, and dismissed Plaintiff Company's claim (the court maintained the judgment of the first instance with regard to the part related to Plaintiff X).

The court's findings regarding the author and copyright holder of the Work are as follows.

1. Author of the Work

Article 16 of the Copyright Act provides as follows: "The authorship of a cinematographic work shall be attributed to those who, by taking charge of producing, directing, filming, art direction, etc., have creatively contributed to the creation of such cinematographic work as a whole. . . ."

It is true that the Work was made under the circumstances where a number of people were involved in the project without making any particular agreement, and the relationships between such people seemed complicated and tangled. However, comprehensively taking into consideration Plaintiff X's role in making the Work, namely, taking part in the entire process of making the Work from planning to completion, serving as the director of the Work, making decisions on highly creative parts of the Work including inclusion shots of the ardent fan group and interviews with fans, and giving directions for all operations in shooting and editing, it is appropriate to recognize Plaintiff X as the only person "who has creatively contributed to the creation of the Work as a whole."

2. Ownership of the copyright in the Work

In light of the language of the provision of Article 2, item 10 of the Copyright Act and the purpose of the provision of Article 29, para.1 of the same Act, the term "maker of a cinematographic work" should be construed to mean the person who has the intention of making the cinematographic work and has legal rights and obligations in the making of a cinematographic work, and who, for this reason, makes economic profit from and disbursements for making the work.

In this case, we can find that it is Plaintiff Company that has the intention of making the cinematographic work and has legal rights and obligations in the making of the cinematographic work, and that for this reason, makes economic profit from and disbursements for making the work.

3.   Assignment of the copyright

For holding the final concert, the company in charge of the management of the music group made all arrangements and bore all expenses, and the representative person of the management company, E, took charge of the producer for the concert as a whole. Therefore, it is generally difficult to believe that E would have authorized Plaintiff X to shoot the final concert, if it is supposed that the copyright in the work recording the concert would not belong to E or the management company. Plaintiff Company, after finishing making the Work, made no assertion as the copyright holder, except that it assigned the right to exclusively broadcast the Work on television to a television station and received 1.5 million yen as a value for the television broadcast right. The predecessor company of Defendant Company paid the charges to Plaintiff Company for shooting the final concert and received the delivery of the master tape of the Work from Plaintiff X.

Taking into consideration all of these circumstances, it can be found that although Plaintiff Company should be regarded as the maker of the Work and as the original copyright holder of the Work, it also should be regarded that the copyright was assigned to E afterwards.

Notes

1.   If this film had not been a documentary, might the court have recognized more than one "author" of the film? Would this have affected its decision as to copyright ownership?

2.   How might this court address a joint authorship claim by the film's cinematographer?

3.   Like most Berne signatories, Japan recognizes the moral rights of the author of a motion picture. Who would be entitled to assert moral rights in this documentary film?

4.   How would the question of assignment in this case have been analyzed under United States copyright law?

E.   GOVERNMENT COPYRIGHT

In many countries, the national government owns the copyright in works created by its officers and employees, and/or commissioned works created under its direction or control. Some countries also assert copyright ownership in their traditional music and folklore.

The United Kingdom recognizes both Crown Copyright (Art. 163) and Parliamentary Copyright (Art. 165). The government's copyright even extends to Bills and Acts of Parliament (Arts. 164,

166). The duration of protection is from 50 to 125 years, depending on the nature of the work.

Crown copyright is also recognized, to varying degrees, by Canada, Australia, New Zealand, and India (which does not use the term "Crown"). In Australia, a 2005 report by the Copyright Law Review Committee concluded that Crown Copyright should be sharply curtailed. Australia's law became the subject of renewed controversy when the government of Victoria invoked Crown Copyright in its refusal to release data pertaining to the tragic "Black Saturday" bushfires of February 2009.

In an effort to assert some degree of intellectual property protection for their traditional works of art, music, and literature, many countries have enacted legislation granting their governments copyright authority over such works. This practice is especially favored by developing countries. Due to the nature of folklore, its copyright protection, where recognized, is perpetual.

In some cases, the scope of exclusive rights in folklore is the same as for newly created works. For example, Article 22(5) of the 1998 Copyright Act in Barbados provides:

> In respect of folklore, that is to say, all literary and artistic works that
>
> a. constitute a basic element of the traditional and cultural heritage of Barbados;
>
> b. were created in Barbados by various groups of the community; and
>
> c. survive from generation to generation,
>
> the rights of the author vest in the Crown to the same extent as if the Crown had been the original creator of the folklore.

In contrast, Nigeria's copyright law (Arts. 28–29) specifies the scope of permissible use of folklore:

28. (1) Expressions of folklore are protected against—

(a) reproduction;

(b) communication to the public by performance, broadcasting, distribution by cable or other means;

(c) adaptation, translation and other transformations,

when such expressions are made either for commercial purposes or outside their traditional or customary context.

(2) The right conferred in subsection (1) of this section shall not include the right to control—

(a) the doing of any of the acts by way of fair dealing for private and domestic use, subject to the condition that, if the use is public, it shall be accompanied by an acknowledgement of the title of the work and its sources;

(b) the utilisation for purposes of education;

(c) utilisation by way of illustration in an original work of the author:

provided that the extent of such utilisation is compatible with fair practice;

(d) the borrowing of expressions of folklore for creating an original work of the author:

(e) the incidental utilisation [of] expressions of folklore.

(3) In all printed publications, and in connection with any communications to the public, of any identifiable expression of folklore, its source shall be indicated in an appropriate manner, and in conformity with fair practice, by mentioning the community or place from where the expression utilised has been derived.

(4) The rights to authorise acts referred to in subsection (1) of this section shall vest in the Nigeria Copyright Council.

(5) For the purposes of this section, "folklore" means a group-oriented and tradition-based creation of groups or individuals reflecting the expectation of the community as an inadequate expression of its cultural and social identity, its standards and values as transmitted orally, by imitation or by other means including—

(a) folklore, folk poetry, and folk riddles;

(b) folk songs and instrumental folk music;

(c) folk dances and folk plays;

(d) productions of folk art in particular, drawings, paintings, carvings, sculptures, pottery, terracotta, mosaic, woodwork, metalwork, handicrafts, costumes, indigenous textiles.

29. A person who, without the consent of the Nigeria Copyright Council, uses an expression of folklore in a manner not permitted by section 28 of this Act shall be in breach of statutory duty and be liable to the council in damages, injunctions and any other remedies as the court may deem fit to award in the circumstances.

F. TERM OF PROTECTION

For most copyrightable works, Article 7 of the Berne Convention requires copyright protection to endure, at a minimum, for the life of the author plus 50 years. However, the minimum term for cinematographic works and anonymous or pseudonymous works is 50 years, and the minimum term for photographic works and works of applied art is 25 years. Signatory countries are free to provide longer terms of protection. The European Union, for example, has adopted a life-plus–70 term for most works. The 1996 WIPO Copyright Treaty eliminates the special 25–year term for photographic works; thus, WIPO signatories must apply Berne's life-plus–50 term to these works as well.

With respect to cinematographic or audiovisual works, the European Union term of protection is 70 years from the death of the last survivor out of the following group, regardless of whether they are considered co-authors: the principal director, the author of the screenplay, the author of the dialogue, and the composer of music specifically created for use in the film. In contrast, the rights of the film *producer* expire after 50 years. The minimum term for photographic works is life-plus–70; and for anonymous and pseudonymous works, the term is 70 years from publication. (Directive 2006/116/EC).

Signatories to the TRIPS Agreement are bound by the duration provisions of Berne. However, under Article 12 of TRIPS, if the copyright in a work is not based on the life of a natural person, the minimum term is 50 years, except in the case of photographic works and works of applied art.

Berne signatories which protect sound recordings under a neighboring rights regime rather than a copyright regime typically do not apply Berne's life-plus–50 term to sound recordings. Under both the Rome and Geneva Conventions pertaining to phonograms, the minimum term of protection for phonogram producers is 20 years from fixation. Under Art. 17 of the WIPO Performances and Phonograms Treaty, however, as well as Art. 14 of TRIPS, the minimum term is 50 years. In the European Union, the term is also 50 years (Directive 2006/116/EC), although proposed legislation would extend this to 70 years.

Like the rights of phonogram producers, the rights of broadcasters and phonogram performers are not governed by the Berne Convention because they are considered to be neighboring rights. Art. 14 of the Rome Convention sets only a 20–year minimum for performers and broadcasters. For performers, however, longer terms are required by several other agreements. Both the WIPO

Performances and Phonograms Treaty (Art. 17) and Article 14 of TRIPS set a 50–year minimum for phonogram performers. Under Directive 2006/116/EC, phonogram performers in the EU receive 50 years of protection (although this term would become 70 years under the newly proposed legislation).

G. ASSIGNMENTS

1. ECONOMIC RIGHTS

There is wide variation in the laws governing assignments of the economic rights in a copyrighted work. At one extreme, German law precludes *inter vivos* copyright assignments altogether, because it adopts a monistic view of authors' rights under which the author's personality right and economic right are inseparable; because personality rights are unassignable, it follows that author's rights are unassignable, although they are inheritable. Urheberrechtsgesetz (UrhG), Arts. 28–29. German law permits a wide variety of licensing arrangements, UrhG, Art. 31, but authors have an unwaivable right to require revision of unconscionable licenses during the first 10 years. UrhG, Art. 36. No writing is required, except in the case of exploitation licenses covering future unspecified works; these agreements are also subject to an unwaivable termination right. UrhG, Art. 40. Authors may also revoke exclusive exploitation licenses in the event of non-exercise by the licensee, UrhG, Art. 41, or if the licensed work no longer reflects the author's "conviction," in which case the author must compensate the licensee for the revocation, UrhG, Art. 42. (This provision reflects the moral right of "withdrawal," discussed in Chapter 4.)

Although French law permits assignments of the author's exploitation rights, the rules governing these assignments are detailed and, in general, highly restrictive. While there is no general requirement of a signed writing, all public performance, publishing, and audiovisual production contracts must be in writing (Art. L.131–2), and an assignment of audiovisual adaptation rights must be in writing and separate from any print publication agreement (Art. L.131–3). Even where the statutes do not expressly require a written instrument, each assigned right must be separately identified in the agreement, and the field of exploitation must be specified with respect to the scope, purpose, place, and duration of the exploitation (Art. L.131–3). Thus, as a practical matter, it is difficult to enforce an assignment without a written instrument. In addition, the author must receive royalties based on exploitation revenues; lump sum payments are permitted only under specified circumstances (Art. L.131–4). An assignment clause addressing unforeseeable forms of exploitation must be explicit, and must entitle the author to remuneration correlated to profits (Art. L.131–

5). Additional rules govern a contract that gives a publisher first preference for an author's future works (Art. L.132–4). A copyright may be assigned partially or in its entirety, (Art. L.131–4); however, a total transfer of all rights in future works is not permitted (Art. L.131–1). There are no specific provisions governing exclusive licenses.

In the United Kingdom, copyright assignments are subject to fewer restrictions. However, all copyright assignments and exclusive licenses require a signed writing (Secs. 90, 92). Copyrights may be assigned partially or in their entirety (Sec. 90), and assignments pertaining to future works are permitted (Sec. 91).

As illustrated in the *Maker of a Documentary Film* case from Japan's Intellectual Property High Court, *supra*, Japanese law generally permits implied assignments of copyright. However, despite the absence of a writing requirement, any transfer of adaptation rights must be explicit (Art. 61(2)).

2. MORAL RIGHTS

In contrast to economic exploitation rights, moral rights are not assignable. Article 6bis of the Berne Convention specifies that moral rights remain with the author even after the transfer of the author's economic rights. (Note, however, that Article 6bis is not incorporated in the TRIPS provisions of the WTO Agreement.). The WIPO Performances and Phonograms Treaty has a similar provision for the moral rights of performers (Art. 5). Accordingly, most copyright regimes treat the moral rights of authors as inalienable, and many provide the same treatment for performers. In France, the author's moral right is perpetual (Art. L.121–1). However, the Berne Convention requires only that the moral right last until the expiration of the economic right, and it permits derogation for countries that, at the time of their accession to the Convention, protected moral rights only for the life of the author.

Chapter 4

EXCLUSIVE RIGHTS

A. INTRODUCTION

Exclusive rights in works of authorship—the subject matter of traditional copyright—generally fall into two categories: economic rights (also known as "patrimonial" rights) and moral rights. In most countries, an author's economic rights are treated as a form of property, while the author's moral rights are treated as personal rights. This means that moral rights are inalienable, while economic rights can usually be assigned and licensed. Economic and/or moral rights in works of authorship are addressed in the Berne Convention, the WIPO Copyright Treaty, the TRIPS Agreement, and European Union directives. In general, the economic rights include reproduction, public distribution (sometimes including rental and/or lending rights), adaptation, and public performance and display. The moral rights include the rights of attribution and integrity (both of which are required by the Berne Convention), the right of first publication, and, in some countries, the right to withdraw a work from circulation.

In addition to the economic and moral rights associated with traditional copyright, many countries also recognize "neighboring rights," which encompass the rights of phonogram performers, phonogram producers, and broadcasters. Neighboring rights are addressed in the Rome and Geneva conventions pertaining to phonograms, the WIPO Performances and Phonograms Treaty, TRIPS, and European Union directives.

B. MORAL RIGHTS

In contrast to the United States, where economic interests are the central focus of copyright protection, in authors' rights regimes (such as those of continental Europe) moral rights generally receive strong protection.

Article 6bis of the Berne Convention sets forth a minimum standard for moral rights protection:

(1) Independently of the author's economic rights, and even after the transfer of the said rights, the author shall have the right to claim authorship of the work and to object to any distortion, mutilation or other modification of, or other derogatory action in relation to, the said work, which would be prejudicial to his honor or reputation.

(2) The rights granted to the author in accordance with the preceding paragraph shall, after his death, be maintained, at least until the expiry of the economic rights, and shall be exercisable by the persons or institutions authorized by the legislation of the country where protection is claimed. However, those countries whose legislation, at the moment of their ratification of or accession to this Act, does not provide for the protection after the death of the author of all the rights set out in the preceding paragraph may provide that some of these rights may, after his death, cease to be maintained.

(3) The means of redress for safeguarding the rights granted by this Article shall be governed by the legislation of the country where protection is claimed.

Because the Berne Convention contains no enforcement provisions, the question whether the United States complies with Article 6bis is largely academic. Although the remainder of the Berne Convention is incorporated by reference in the TRIPS Agreement, the United States took pains to ensure that Article 6bis was excluded. As illustrated in the materials which follow, strong moral rights regimes can be found throughout the world.

1. MOTION PICTURE COLORIZATION

TURNER ENTERTAINMENT CO. v. HUSTON

Court of Appeal of Versailles, 1994
Chambre Civile

[When a colorized version of the black and white film "Asphalt Jungle" was broadcast on French television, one of its screenwriters, Ben Maddow, together with the heirs of the film's director John Huston, brought suit in the French courts against the television network, alleging violation of the writer's and director's moral right of integrity as recognized under French law, even though, under their work-made-for-hire contracts, neither Huston nor Maddow would have had a comparable right under U.S. law.]

* * *

I

The cinematographic work entitled "Asphalt Jungle" was produced in 1950 in the United States by the Metro Goldwyn Mayer (MGM) company, a division of Loew's, Inc. The film was shot in black and white by the late John Huston, a movie director of American nationality, at the time bound by a contract of employment to Loew's Inc. and co-author of the screenplay with Ben Maddow, bound to the same company by a contract as a salaried writer.

On 2nd May 1950, Loew's, Inc. obtained from the U.S. Copyright Office a certificate of registration of its rights to the film. This registration was duly renewed in 1977. On 26th September 1986 the benefit of this registration was transferred to the Turner Entertainment Co. by virtue of a merger with MGM, including transfer of the ownership of MGM's movie library and connected rights.

The Turner company had the movie colorized, an operation which on 20th June 1988 resulted in registration of a copyright application, and it enabled the Fifth French Television Channel (La Cinq) to announce that it would broadcast this colorized version at 8:30 p.m. on 26th June 1988.

The broadcast was objected to by John Huston's heirs, Angelica, Daniel and Walter Huston, who were subsequently joined by Mr. Ben Maddow, the Societe des Auteurs et Compositeurs Dramatiques (SACD), the Societe des Realisateurs de Films (SRF), the Syndicat Francais des Artistes Interpretes (SFA), the Federation Europeenne des Relisateurs de l'Audiovisuel (FERA), the Syndicat Francais des Realisateurs de Television CGT and the Syndicat National des Techniciens de la Production Cinematographique et de Television. They opposed the broadcast because they deemed it a violation of the author's moral right, which was aggravated in their opinion by the fact that John Huston had opposed colorization of his works during his life.

The dispute thus arising between La Cinq and the Turner Entertainment Co. (TEC) resulted in the following decisions in France:

1) An order in summary proceedings on 24th June 1988, confirmed by a judgment of the Court of Appeal of Paris on 25th June 1988, which suspended the broadcast of the colorized film as being likely to cause unacceptable and irreparable damage;

2) On 23rd November 1988 the Court of First Instance of Paris judged as follows: "Declares the action of Messrs. and Mrs. Huston and Mr. Ben Maddow and the voluntary intervention of

TEC admissible insofar as they are limited to the television broadcasting of the colorized version of the film entitled 'Asphalt Jungle'; Declares the claims of the secondary voluntary intervenors admissible; Formally takes cognizance of the fact that Societe d'Exploitation de la Cinquieme Chaine has abandoned its plans for broadcasting the colorized version of the film entitled 'Asphalt Jungle'; As necessary forbids it from broadcasting this version on television; Dismisses all other claims; Dismisses the claim of the TEC company."

In admitting the claim, this judgment relied on the Universal Copyright Convention signed in Geneva on 6th September 1952, ratified by the United States, to conclude that this convention provides citizens of member States in France with the benefit of the Law of 11th March 1957, notably Section 6, which provides that the moral right is attached to the person and is perpetual, inalienable and imprescribable. Thus it distinguished between this moral right and the economic rights held by the Turner company in the work, notably under contracts signed with John Huston and Ben Maddow.

Finally, it held that John Huston and Ben Maddow, by their art, had imbued their work with an original and personal character and that Huston achieved renown based on his use of black and white to create an atmosphere, which atmosphere would be jeopardized by colorization.

3) The Court of Appeal of Paris, appealed to by the Turner company, judged as follows on 6th July 1989:

"States that the author of the film entitled 'Asphalt Jungle' is the Turner company and that the heirs of John Huston as well as Ben Maddow have no moral right to this work shot in black and white; Notes that the colorized version of the said film is an adaptation, under U.S. law, for which the Turner company obtained a registration certificate on 20th June 1988;

States that the principle of colorization could not be objected to by the heirs of John Huston and by Ben Maddow, even if they could claim a moral right to the black and white film;

Accordingly, reversing the judgment,

Dismisses the claims of the heirs of John Huston and Ben Maddow and judges admissible but unfounded the interventions of the six legal entities supporting their claims;

Authorizes the Fifth Channel to broadcast the colorized version of the film entitled 'Asphalt Jungle,' granting the relief requested."

The judgment further required that various warning notices be provided to television viewers, with respect to the possibility of using their color control device and respect for the memory of John Huston.

In reversing the judgment against which the appeal was brought, the Court of Appeal of Paris settled the conflict of laws in favor of U.S. law, because the law of the place of first publication of the work, according to said court, granted the status of author solely to Loew's, which cannot be negated by the Berne Convention, effective from 1st March 1989, which is an instrument to harmonize relations between the member countries and which does not affect acquired rights or the consequences of contracts between producer and director. Moreover, it dismissed the argument that the French conception of international law was violated and held that the copyright in the "derivative work" granted in 1988 to the Turner company made it impossible for Messrs. and Mrs. Huston and Mr. Maddow to raise a moral rights claim.

Messrs. and Mrs. Huston and Mr. Maddow and the intervenors appealed the judgment of the Court of Appeal of Paris to the Cour de Cassation.

In a ruling dated 28th May 1991, the Cour de Cassation reversed and cancelled the entire judgment of the Court of Appeal for violating Section 1.2 of Law 64–689 of 8th July 1964 and Section 6 of the Law of 11th March 1957, stating:

> "According to the first of these provisions, the integrity of a literary or artistic work must not be violated in France, regardless of the State in whose territory the work was first published. The person who is its author, by its creation alone, enjoys the moral right stipulated in his favor by the second of the aforesaid provisions; these are laws of mandatory application."

II

The Turner Entertainment Co. duly referred the case to the Court of Appeal of Versailles, appointed as the Court of Remand, and petitioned it to reverse the judgment of the Court of First Instance of Paris, to rule that the claims of Messrs. and Mrs Huston are inadmissible or that they have in any case no grounds to claim the moral right to which they refer and, accordingly, to dismiss their case and all other intervenors. It also claims as follows:

> - In support of its argument of inadmissibility, that Messrs. and Mrs. Huston cannot claim the status of foreign author, which is reserved for the Turner company under the laws applicable at the place of creation and the contracts governed by them; that they are therefore not entitled to invoke French law, under the Geneva Convention, in order to protect themselves and exercise rights which do not belong to them;

- That it is in any event the recognized holder of the patrimonial rights of the authors and that it was therefore entitled to introduce the colorized version by applying a technique which does not alter the essence of the work.

Messrs. and Mrs. Huston and Mr. Maddow petitioned the Court of Remand to confirm the judgment of the Court of First Instance of Paris, further petitioning the court to hold that the broadcasting of the colorized version of "Asphalt Jungle" has violated their moral right, and, accordingly, to order the Turner company to pay them FRF 1,000,000 by way of damages and costs and a further FRF 100,000 under Section 700 of the New Code of Civil Procedure; thus:

- They assert that French law alone is competent to determine the status of author, as pointed out by the Cour de Cassation in a decision which stresses the importance of moral rights and requires disregard of the law that governs the contract between director and producer; and that their claim is therefore admissible;

- That black and white is the form of expression in which the authors and especially John Huston have delivered their esthetic conception to the public; that colorization therefore alters the very essence of the work, so that it is no "adaptation" at all but a "transformation" or "modification"; that, moreover, John Huston was formally opposed to this during his life.

* * *

Maitre Pierrel ex-officio petitioned the court to declare his appeal admissible and well-founded, to take formal cognizance of the fact that La Cinq, in accordance with the judgment of the Court of Appeal of Paris on 6th July 1989, broadcast the film accompanied by the court-ordered notices, to reverse the referred judgment of the Court of First Instance of Paris and to rule once again that Messrs. and Mrs. Huston and Mr. Maddow do not have status as the film's authors and that they cannot claim in France the benefit of the moral right, to hold secondarily that colorization constitutes a legal adaptation and does not violate any moral right, to dismiss the claims of the opponents and to order Messrs. and Mrs. Huston and Mr. Maddow to pay them FRF 30,000 by virtue of Section 700 of the New Code of Civil Procedure. He thus reiterated the arguments already made by the Turner company, stressing that John Huston must have known that he did not have the status of an author under the law governing the contracts he signed with the producer.

The Turner Entertainment Co. maintained its initial claims, notably on the inadmissibility of the opponents' claims, in response to which it maintains:

- That it is the settled rule in private international law that a situation is governed by the law of the place where it occurs; that, therefore, the status of author of an art work is the status recognized in the country where the work has been created, *i.e.*, in this case, the United States of America; which designates Loew's, Inc., from which the rights were transferred;

- That the Court of Remand is not bound by the judgment of the Cour de Cassation, when criticized by authoritative doctrine;

- That, in fact, the Law of 8th July 1964, incorporated as Section L 111–4 in the Code of Intellectual Property, does not apply because it supposes that the foreign State does not provide French works with adequate and effective protection, which is not the case in the United States; that the second paragraph of Section 1 of this law, which alone is referred to in the judgment of the Cour de Cassation, is not severable;

- That, lastly, the Geneva Convention does not determine the formation of rights and authorship status, for which it addresses only protection;

- That, secondarily, the Cour de Cassation did not address the violation of the moral right alleged to result from the colorization and that such a violation has not been shown.

* * *

In response, Messrs. and Mrs. Huston and Mr. Maddow argued as follows:

- That the Cour de Cassation adopted a solution which enables the authors to exercise their moral right in France; that this position complies with Section 14*bis*(2) of the Berne Convention, which provides for application of the law of the country of protection in designating the holder of the rights to a cinematographic work;

- That U.S. law only protects economic rights, wherefore the Law of 8th July 1964 remains applicable due to the lack of reciprocal agreements on the moral right;

- That, contrary to the submissions of the Turner company, colorization violates the authors' retained moral right.

They furthermore petitioned the court to take cognizance of the violation of the authors' moral right by La Cinq's broadcasting of the "colorized" film and to order Me. Pierrel ex-officio to pay them one million francs in damages and costs on this ground.

In its rejoinder, the Turner Entertainment Co. petitioned the court again to hold that Messrs. and Mrs. Huston and Mr. Maddow cannot claim the benefit of the Berne Convention and Law of 8th

July 1985, which have no retroactive application, to reject application of the Law of 8th July 1964 because U.S. law protects every attribute of copyright; to judge

- That colorization is by its nature an adaptation within the meaning of the law and to grant it the benefit of these findings;

- That ratification by the United States of the Berne Convention postdates the disputed situation by a considerable time;

- That, contrary to the ground produced by Messrs. and Mrs. Huston and Mr. Maddow, U.S. case law provides sanctions against violations of the integrity or authorship of a work, which precludes application of the Law of 8th July 1964;

- That the Law of 3rd July 1985 cannot be invoked because it is not disputed that the Turner company is the holder of the patrimonial rights, including the right to adapt the work and therefore to introduce a colorized version.

* * *

III

* * *

The Turner company first argues in opposition to Messrs. and Mrs. Huston and Mr. Maddow and the intervenors that U.S. law should be applied to determine who has the status of the film's author; it designates the producer, *i.e.*, Loew's, Inc., which obtained the copyright on 2nd May 1950 and whose rights, renewed on 2nd May 1977, were transferred to the Turner company; the action of Messrs. and Mrs. Huston and Mr. Maddow to protect rights which they have not acquired is therefore not allowable.

But the judges in the first instance correctly stressed the "very different conceptions" of U.S. and French laws, the first focusing exclusively on the protection of economic rights without referring to the creative act underlying the inalienable moral right recognized by French law, *viz.* Section 6 of the Law of 11th March 1957, the applicable law, which provides that "the author enjoys the right to respect for his name, his status, his work—this right is attached to his person—it is perpetual, inalienable and imprescribable—it is transmitted after death to the author's heirs".

John Huston and Ben Maddow, of whom it is undisputed that the first is the co-author of the screenplay and the director of the film entitled "Asphalt Jungle" and the second is the other co-author of the screenplay, as already referred to under (I–1), are in fact its authors, having created it, and whereas they are therefore, in the meaning of the aforesaid law, vested with the corresponding moral right, which is part of public law and therefore mandatorily protected.

Section 1 of Law No. 64–689 of 8th July 1964, on the application of the principle of reciprocity with respect to copyright, provides as follows:

[1] Subject to the provisions of the international conventions to which France is a party, if it is determined, after consultation with the Minister of Foreign Affairs, that a State does not provide adequate and effective protection for works disclosed for the first time in France, irrespective of the form thereof, works disclosed for the first time in the territory of the said State shall not benefit from the copyright protection recognized by French law.

[2] However, the integrity or authorship of such works may not be violated.

The denial of protection to a foreign work under the reciprocity condition, as laid out in paragraph [1], can only concern its economic aspects, *i.e.* the patrimonial rights attached thereto, in that it is limited by the general mandatory rule providing for respect of an author's moral right as proclaimed without reservation in paragraph [2].

It follows that the moral rights attached to the person of the creators of the work entitled "Asphalt Jungle" could not be transferred and, therefore, the judges in the first instance correctly ruled that Messrs. and Mrs. Huston and Ben Maddow were entitled to claim recognition and protection thereof in France.

However, the Turner company, which, it is not disputed, is the holder of the author's economic rights, maintains that these rights include the right to adapt the work and therefore to colorize the film entitled "Asphalt Jungle," arguing that it cannot be maintained that this denatures the work; Me. Pierrel, ex-officio, makes the same argument, submitting that the colorized version of the film is merely an adaptation of the original black-and-white version which is left intact and is therefore not affected.

However, "colorization" is a technique based on the use of computer and laser and it makes it possible, after transferring the original black-and-white tape onto a videographic media, to give color to a film which did not originally have color; the application of this process is in no event to be considered an adaptation, which is defined as "an original work both in its expression and in its composition," even if it borrows formal elements from the pre-existing work; colorization, far from meeting these criteria, in fact merely consists in modifying the work by adding an element that was hitherto alien to the creator's aesthetic conception.

The judges in first instance in the present case have precisely pointed out that the aesthetic conception which earned John Huston his great fame is based on the interplay of black and white, which enabled him to create an atmosphere in pursuit of which he directed the actor and selected the backdrops; moreover, he expressed himself clearly about his film entitled "The Maltese Falcon" when he stated, "I wanted to shoot it in black and white like a sculptor chooses to work in clay, to pour his work in bronze, to sculpt in marble".

In 1950, even though color film technique was already widespread and thus another option was available, the film entitled "ASPHALT JUNGLE" was shot in black and white, pursuant to a deliberate aesthetic choice, consistent with the technique which its authors considered best suited to the character of the work.

Therefore, the film's colorization, without authorization and control by the authors or their heirs, amounted to violation of the creative activity of its makers, even if it was likely to satisfy the wishes of a certain segment of the public for obvious commercial reasons; the use of this process without the agreement of Messrs. and Mrs. Huston and Ben Maddow infringed the moral right of the authors as mandatorily protected under French law; Messrs. and Mrs. Huston and Ben Maddow have therefore good grounds to petition the court for reparation of their injury at the hands of the Turner company, and they will therefore be allotted FRF 400,000 by way of damages and costs for the damage done; moreover, the judges in first instance correctly recognized their right to demand that La Cinq SA be forbidden to broadcast the modified version of the film entitled "Asphalt Jungle."

It is established that, contrary to the order of the Court of First Instance, La Cinq SA broadcast the colorized version of the film entitled "Asphalt Jungle" pursuant to the judgment by the Court of Appeal of Paris, quashed by the Cour de Cassation on the conditions reiterated under (I–5); this broadcast was also a direct and definite violation of the moral right whose protection was demanded by Messrs. and Mrs. Huston and Ben Maddow, who are also entitled to demand reparation on this count; the Court awards them the sum of FRF 200,000 in reversing the decision below.

* * *

Notes

1. The *Turner* court holds that a colorized film is not an "adaptation" under French copyright law, because an adaptation is " 'an original work both in its expression and in its composition,' even if it borrows formal elements from the pre-existing work," whereas colorization

"merely consists in modifying the work by adding an element thus far not part of the creator's aesthetic conception." Why does the court draw this distinction? Is it relevant that Huston deliberately eschewed the use of color in this film?

2. In 2005, an Italian court held that Italian network TV Internazionale (TeleMontecarlo) violated the moral rights of director Fred Zinneman (whose rights were asserted by his son after the father's 1997 death) in 1996 and 1997 when it broadcast a colorized version of his 1944 black and white film "The Seventh Cross." The court found that Zinneman chose to make his film in black and white, even though color technology was available at the time, and that colorization violated his artistic integrity; accordingly, the court enjoined further broadcasts, and ordered the station to pay damages and destroy its colorized copies.

3. In the United Kingdom, where the rights of paternity and integrity were not enacted until 1988, these rights do not apply to literary, artistic, musical, or dramatic works whose authors died before 1988, or to films made before 1988.

2. EDITING FOR COMMERCIALS

CLAES ERIKSSON ET AL. v. TV 4*

Supreme Court of Sweden
Case No. T2117–06 (March 18, 2008)

[Film directors Claes Eriksson and Vilgot Sjoman brought suit against Swedish television network TV4, alleging that their moral rights were violated when TV4 inserted commercial breaks into the television broadcasts of their films. Both the District Court and the Court of Appeals ruled in favor of the directors, and TV4 appealed.]

* * *

OPINION OF THE COURT

In the Supreme Court, the parties have cited the same circumstances as in the Court of Appeal. The Supreme Court has held the main proceedings. The hearing in the Court of Appeal with Claes Eriksson, Vilgot Sjöman and Mats Örbrink, and the hearing at the District Court with Kjell-Åke Andersson, Kjell Grede and Astrid Söderbergh Widding have been presented through playback of the tape recordings. The Supreme Court reviewed the films in question—Claes Eriksson's "The Shark who knew too much" and Vilgot Sjöman's "Alfred"—through playback of video recordings including the advertising inserts.

In § 3 paragraph 2 of the Act on copyright for literary and artistic works (the Copyright Act), it is prescribed that a work may

---

* Translated by Johan Laestadius.
Copyright permission by KLYS, Sweden.

not be changed so that the author's literary or artistic reputation or individuality are damaged. Neither may the work be made available to the general public in such a form or in such a context that is in the stated way injurious to the author. According to the third part of this section of the Act, the author can concede his right with binding effect only insofar as it concerns an application of the work limited in type and scope. From § 54 paragraph 3 of the Copyright Act, it follows that anyone who willfully or negligently undertakes actions which constitute infringement of copyright, shall compensate the author or his assignee for losses, suffering or other detriment ensuing from that action.

The dispute concerns the interruptions for advertisements, which occurred when TV4 transmitted both the films. The parties dispute whether the interruption constitutes an infringement of the author's moral rights, whether any concession of this right was granted, and whether TV4 acted negligently.

TV4 has asserted that the advertising interruption during broadcasts occurred in conformity with the legislation and practice based on the so-called TV Directive, the Council Directive 89/552/EEC of 3rd October 1989, concerning co-ordination of certain conditions stipulated in the laws of the member states, and other conditions concerning implementation of broadcasting activity for television, amended by the European Parliament and Council Directive 97/36/EC. In Sweden, the question of advertising interruptions in the radio and TV legislation is governed, insofar as is now in question, as amended in 2002, on the basis of the TV Directive in its amended wording. According to Ch. 7 § 8 of this Act, adverts in TV broadcasts must be transmitted between programmes, but, according to § 7(a), they may under certain conditions also be broadcast during such content as feature films, but only in such a way, according to § 7, that—with consideration for natural breaks and the broadcasting length and nature of the programme—the integrity and value of the programme or the rights of the copyright holder are not violated. From the preparatory work [Ed. note: legislative history] on the amendments to the law, it is evident that the aims were matters of competition and consumer policy, more specifically to overcome the competitive disadvantages for Swedish programme companies relative to foreign ones, to which the regulations then in force led, and at the same time reduce the disruptions that commercial TV advertising breaks involve for the public. In the preparatory works it is emphasized that the change in law does not affect the copyright regulations, and that an injurious change or an interruption to a film * * * will require the rights holder's consent. Before the change, the position was that the programme could not be interrupted by advertising broadcasts; they could however be transmitted in longer breaks within sports programmes, in breaks within programmes structured around performances and with events where breaks occurred for the public as well, and between segments of programmes consisting of finished-off parts; in feature films no advertising interruptions were allowed.

The examination of whether an action taken in connection with a film being shown on TV violates the author's moral rights must therefore take place without regard to the public legislative regulations in the radio and TV legislation.

TV4 has stated that advertising breaks do not mean that the interrupted film has been changed within the meaning of § 3 paragraph 2 of the Copyright Act.

What is typical of a film work is that the creative elements of a feature film are reflected in the progression, narrative, and atmosphere created by the interplay of images and sound in a certain pattern. Advertising interspersions break into the progress of the feature film and into its atmosphere. A feature film that is shown with advertising breaks must therefore by this very fact be considered as having been altered, in the sense meant in § 3 paragraph 2 of the Copyright Act. * * *.

The next question is whether the change is injurious to the author's reputation or his individuality. In the Authorial Rights Committee Report, among other things the following statement is made concerning the condition in § 3 paragraph 2: In assessing to what extent the changes undertaken can be considered as injurious to the author, the case must be seen from the latter's point of view, although otherwise an objective yardstick is to be applied. The author is also entitled to protection against changes which, even though not detrimental to his reputation in the eyes of others, constitute an assault on the integrity of the work and violate the affection that he, as the artist, harbours for the work he has created. The assessment must be made from the starting point of the conditions within the type of art one is dealing with, and with due consideration for the circumstances of the particular case. Also, seemingly insignificant changes can misrepresent the work. The requirements are not as strict with respect to literary or musical works of lower value, although even here the author should be protected against more serious interference. The purpose of the action taken is also significant. One should also take into consideration whether the reproduction claims to present the work in its original form, or whether it is self-evident that the work is not being reproduced in original form. In the legislative proposal, the head of the department agreed in essence with the committee's statement. Concerning protection for the author's distinctiveness, it is stated that one should also keep in mind processes which—even

though they may not perhaps damage the author's reputation—
nevertheless are injurious to his personality as expressed in his
work. This statement still holds true in law.

As stated in the district court's ruling, TV4 inserted interruptions for advertisements when showing the two feature films, in
two instances in Claes Eriksson's "The Shark who knew too much"
and in three instances in Vilgot Sjöman's "Alfred". Each interruption is introduced with a vignette with musical signature and
including the word "Advertisement" (Reklam), and a voice saying
that "the feature film continues in a moment", and the interruption then finishes with a vignette with music and the words "The
feature film now continues". On one occasion the vignettes got
mixed up. Each interruption, lasting about five minutes, contained
about ten advertising slots for goods and services directed at
consumers. The interruptions occurred in connection with scene
changes or a change in the narrative of the film. The advertising
interruption was at a somewhat higher sound level than the feature
film.

Claes Eriksson has declared that he considers the advertising
breaks to be injurious because extraneous images and sound come
into his film without his permission and disturb his carefully
considered length and rhythm, and that the advertisements' messages contrast starkly with the moral of the film and its satirical
description of a hysterical pursuit of money. Vilgot Sjöman stressed
that his film has a sort of dreamy, hesitant pace, which is in conflict
with the noisy and disjointed advertising inserts, and that the film
is enacted in a Swedish and European 19th century speech environment, which he went to very great pains to recreate.

The judgment on whether the advertising interruption in a
feature film violates the author's reputation or personality must be
made on the basis of the criteria stated above. This means that the
TV viewers' perception of the advertising interruption as disruptive
must not be taken into consideration. The interest of viewers is
considered to be met through the mechanism of public legislation.

The starting point concerns the nature of the artistic work in
question. It is apparent from the expert evidence presented, such as
Claes Eriksson's and Vilgot Sjöman's information, that it is characteristic of film works that the creative work—including production,
direction and cutting—aims at an overall experience, which leads
the audience to participate in the narrative of the film in time and
space.

The fictitious time period in which the film takes place is
complex and unique for each film. Interruptions to a feature film
mean that the intended overall experience is broken up, and the
audience risks losing the thread of the narrative or missing allu-

sions forwards or backwards in the narrative. Spatially, an interruption means a change from the film's environment to other environments and moods created by the commercials. Even when the advertising is placed in between scenes or at a change of setting, the director's intended interplay between the film's different scenes is broken through the insertion of completely different settings and occurrences. Interruptions for advertisements also mean that the film's actual length is prolonged for the audience; the length of the film is not an insignificant part of the work.

In reaching judgment, the nature and significance of the work should also be considered from an artistic point of view. A feature film—whether a comedy or a tragedy in its aim—in the form of a long film must be regarded as more sensitive to encroachment than a film of the nature of a short story or an episode, consisting of mutually independent, complete parts that are not necessarily intended to be seen in connection with one another, or a film of a non-narrative genre, such as an instructional or training film. Irrespective of the artistic level, ambition and propensities of a feature film, the occurrence of commercials normally means that the continuity and dramatic nature of the film is interrupted, and that the extraneous film sequences inserted into the work are bound to harm the author's distinctive nature.

The purpose of the interruption must also be considered. The advertising interruption occurs for commercial purposes and the intention is to draw the audience's attention away from the film to the advertisement. The interests that lie behind the advertising interruptions are, as the court of appeal found, not the type that can objectively be considered as acceptable incursions into the author's interest in preventing his work from being presented in a way injurious to his intellectual rights.

For the reasons stated by the lower courts, the advertising interruptions in the films concerned in this case are considered to constitute a violation of the author's distinctive nature, contrary to the condition in § 3 paragraph two of the Copyright Act. The Supreme Court considers on the other hand, like the other courts, that the interruption does not violate Claes Eriksson's or Vilgot Sjöman's literary or artistic reputation.

The Supreme Court confirms the judgment of the courts below that Claes Eriksson and Vilgot Sjöman have not conceded their moral rights as far as the interruption to the films is concerned, and that the infringement has occurred through negligence. The Court of Appeal's ruling is therefore confirmed.

Notes

1.   How and why does the court distinguish between the author's right to his "distinctive nature" and his right to preserve his artistic reputation?

2.   *Moral rights waivers*: Although moral rights, where they exist, are always inalienable, countries vary widely on the question of whether, and under what circumstances, they can be waived. In much of continental Europe, waivers are generally prohibited, although there are occasional exceptions. In contrast, waivers are commonplace in the United Kingdom and Ireland. In the United Kingdom, Section 87 of the Copyright, Designs and Patents Act 1988 provides:

> (1) It is not an infringement of any of the rights conferred by this Chapter to do any act to which the person entitled to the right has consented.

> (2) Any of those rights may be waived by instrument in writing signed by the person giving up the right.

> (3) A waiver—

>> (a) may relate to a specific work, to works of a specified description or to works generally, and may relate to existing or future works, and

>> (b) may be conditional or unconditional and may be expressed to be subject to revocation;

>> and if made in favour of the owner or prospective owner of the copyright in the work or works to which it relates, it shall be presumed to extend to his licensees and successors in title unless a contrary intention is expressed.

> (4) Nothing in this Chapter shall be construed as excluding the operation of the general law of contract or estoppel in relation to an informal waiver or other transaction in relation to any of the rights mentioned in subsection (1).

3.   MORAL RIGHTS AND CULTURAL HERITAGE

SEHGAL v. UNION OF INDIA

High Court of Delhi at New Delhi, 2005

[2005] F.S.R. 39

Pradeep Nandrajog J.:

Copyright is one of the three main branches of the traditional law of intellectual property, along with patent law and trade mark law. Overshadowed historically by the economic worth of patents and trade marks, the plaintiff who believes that there can be no beauty without a soul, has brought the present action, hoping that the soul (copyright) is given its due place and recognition in the history of law.

The Cinderella (Copyright) of the family of intellectual property, long pushed into the chimney, seeks, in the present proceedings, to endow herself with the gift of the fairy godmother—the magical pumpkin coach and the mice footmen.

The plaintiff's pleadings takes one back to the year 1957. A peep behind the pleadings would take us back to the early fifties.

India was a nascent democracy. The world was divided into two camps: the American camp and the Soviet Russian camp. Pt. Jawahar Lal Nehru, the first Prime Minister of this country, a man of vision, realised that to be non-aligned was the best policy. India, under the leadership of Pt. Jawahar Lal Nehru, was a pioneer of the non-aligned movement. Fledgling India was asserting itself in the community of nations. International delegations were frequenting the territory of India. Conferences had to be held. Large numbers of delegates had to be accommodated. A building was conceived to be the hub of international and national conferences. It was named *"Vigyan Bhawan"*. * * *

The brick, mortar and concrete structure named *"Vigyan Bhawan"* may have been an architectural feat, imbibing the science of construction, but the building was too lifeless. It needed a soul.

What better soul could a building have other than being endowed with the cultural heritage of India. After all, Vigyan Bhawan was conceived to house international conferences and ought, therefore, to have reflected India's cultural heritage. [Accordingly, the plaintiff, Amar Nath Sehgal, was commissioned to create a work of art to decorate the building.]

* * *

The plaintiff readily agreed to the offer contained in this letter, as it was indeed a matter of honour to accomplish the task. Research and untiring work, spanning over half a decade produced a piece of art—a bronze mural sculpture—manifesting itself having 140ft span and 40ft sweep on one of the wall's of Vigyan Bhawan. The wall was no ordinary wall, as it was the lobby of Vigyan Bhawan, *i.e.* the entrance. The mural was a delicate balance between cultural and material aspects in national perspective and science of rural and modern India being its theme.

The mural continued to occupy its place of pride at the lobby of Vigyan Bhawan till it was pulled down and consigned to the store room of the Union of India in the year 1979. This act of destruction of the mural was without the permission, consent or authorisation of the plaintiff.

According to the plaintiff, the mural acquired the status of a national treasure, representing the essential part of Indian art heritage. According to the plaintiff, the mural became an important part of India's cultural heritage.

Unfortunately for the plaintiff, the motivating force behind the mural, late Pt. Jawahar Lal Nehru, was no longer in the world of the living and those in charge of the country had little concern for the cultural heritage of the country. * * *

The plaintiff ran from pillar to post. No positive action was taken. The mural created by the plaintiff was no longer available for viewing by the public of India. The mural having been put in the godown [*i.e.*, warehouse] of the Government of India, the plaintiff was left with no alternative, but to knock at the door of the Court. Taking the shelter of s.57 of the Copyright Act, 1957, the present suit was filed praying for a declaration that the plaintiff's special rights under s.57 of the Copyright Act, 1957 were violated by the defendants, for which the defendants should tender an apology. A permanent injunction was prayed for to restrain the defendants from further distorting, mutilating or damaging the plaintiff's mural. Damages in the sum of Rs.50 lacs towards compensation for humiliation, injury, insult and loss of plaintiff's reputation were prayed for. Lastly, a decree for delivery-up directing the defendants to return to the plaintiff the mural for restoration at the cost of defendants was sought.

* * *

The Union of India defended the suit by urging that it was the owner of the mural and had a right to consign the same to a store room. The plaintiff was stated to have [been] paid the price for the work. The defence of limitation was also set up. It was averred that the mural was removed in the year 1979 and the suit being filed in the year 1992, *i.e.*, after 13 years from the date of the offending act, was barred by limitation.

The following issues were framed on April 1, 2003:

1) Whether the suit is barred by limitation?

2) Whether the plaintiff has rights under s.57 of the Copyright Act, 1957 in the impugned work although the copyright in the same has been vested to the defendant?

3) Has the defendant violated the plaintiff's rights under s.57 of the said Act?

4) Whether the plaintiff has suffered any damage?

5) Relief.

* * *

[The court decided the first issue in the plaintiff's favor, holding that the suit was filed within the limitations period.]

Issue No.2 and 3

* * *

The evidence on record clearly brings out the celebrity status of eminence enjoyed by the plaintiff in the field of art and culture. What would be the relevance thereof and in what manner it influences the copyright law in India takes me to the core area of the problem[:] The moral rights of an author as flowing from s.57 of the Copyright Act, 1957, and legal consequences thereof.

In the material world, laws are geared to protect the right to equitable remuneration. But life is beyond the material. It is temporal as well. Many of us believe in the soul. Moral rights of the author are the soul of his works. The author has a right to preserve, protect and nurture his creations through his moral rights.

When an author creates a work of art or a literary work, it is possible to conceive of many rights which may flow. The first and foremost right which comes to one's mind is the *"Paternity Right"* in the work, *i.e.* the right to have his name on the work. It may also be called the *"identification right"* or *"attribution right"*. The second right which one thinks of is the right to disseminate his work, *i.e.* the *"divulgation or dissemination right"*. It would embrace the economic right to sell the work for valuable consideration. Linked to the paternity right, a third right, being the right to maintain purity in the work, can be thought of. There can be no purity without integrity. It may be a matter of opinion, but certainly, treatment of a work which is derogatory to the reputation of the author, or in some way degrades the work as conceived by the author, can be objected to by the author. This would be the moral right of *"integrity"*. Lastly, one can conceive of a right to withdraw from publication one's work, if author feels that due to passage of time and changed opinion it is advisable to withdraw the work. This would be the authors right to *"retraction"*.

Except for the "divulgation or dissemination right" which perhaps is guided by commercial considerations, the other three rights originate from the fact that *the creative individual is uniquely invested with the power and mystique of original genius, creating a privileged relationship between a creative author and his work*. As I understand it, this is the source of the last three rights noted * * * above and, therefore, could be captioned under the banner *"The Author's Moral Rights"*.

The community of nations set the International Standards for moral rights protection of the author under the *"Berne Convention For the Protection of Literary & Artistic Works"*. Since its inception in 1886, the Berne Convention has been the primary instrument of

International Copyright Law. Article 6bis of the Berne Convention enjoins the members of the Berne Union to provide legal recognition for the moral rights of attribution and integrity in a work in which copyright exits. Article 6bis of Berne Convention reads:

"(1) Independently of the author's economic rights, and even after the transfer of the said rights, the author shall have the right to claim authorship of the work and to object to any distortion, mutilation or other modification of, or other derogatory action in relation to, the said work, which would be prejudicial to his honour or reputation.

(2) The rights granted to the author in accordance with the preceding paragraph shall, after his death, be maintained, at least until the expiry of the economic rights, and shall be exercisable by the persons or institutions authorised by the legislation of the country where protection is claimed. However, those countries whose legislation, at the moment of their ratification of or accession to this Act, does not provide for the protection after the death of the author of all the rights set out in the preceding paragraph may provide that some of these rights may, after his death, cease to be maintained.

(3) The means of redress for safeguarding the rights granted by this Article shall be governed by the legislation of the country where protection is claimed."

* * *

Under Art.6bis of the Berne Convention, the moral right of integrity enables the author to seek appropriate legal remedies if the moral right of attribution and integrity in his work is violated. The moral rights set out in the Berne Convention are significant because they continue to be vested in the author even after he has parted with his economic rights in his work.

The right of the author under Art.6bis of the Berne Convention provides that an author may *"object to any distortion, mutilation or modification"* of his work which is deemed to be *"prejudicial to his honour or reputation"*.

As formulated in the Berne Convention, vindication of moral rights, being hedged with the precondition of proof of negative impact on the author's reputation, somewhat restricts the span and sweep of the moral right. It is argued by some that where a work is destroyed, since it no longer exists and cannot therefore be viewed by anyone, where is the occasion for prejudice to the author's reputation? *Per contra*, it could be argued, as indeed was the submission made by Shri Praveen Anand, learned counsel for the plaintiff, that destruction of a work can prejudice an author's reputation by reducing the volume of his creative corpus. The proponents of the narrow view argue that derogatory treatment of a creative work would mean deletion to, distortion, mutilation or modification to, or use of the work in a setting which is entirely inappropriate. The opponents of the narrow view would argue that deletion to, or mutilation is after all *"a treatment of a work"* and so is *"destruction"*. It is the extreme and ultimate form of mutilation. They argue that mutilation is nothing but destruction so as to render the work imperfect.

The plaintiff, Amar Nath Sehgal, propounds the wider view. The Union of India urges to the contrary.

While granting interim relief to the plaintiff, Jaspal Singh J. observed that s.57 of the Copyright Act, 1957 would be the key to open the door of the dispute raised in the present suit. Section 57 as originally enacted reads as under:

57. Author's special rights

(1) Independently of the author's copyright, and even after the assignment either wholly or partially of the said copyright, the author of a work shall have the right to claim the authorship of the work as well as the right to restrain, or claim damages in respect of—

(a) any distortion, mutilation or other modification of the said work; or

(b) any other action in relation to the said work which would be prejudicial to his honour or reputation.

(2) The right conferred upon an author of a work by sub-section (1), other than the right to claim authorship of the work, may be exercised by the legal representatives of the author.

The words *"prejudicial to his honour or reputation"* found place in subcl.(b) of subs.(1) of s.57. The legislature thought that the existing provisions, whereby even distortion, mutilation and modification of the work which are not prejudicial to the author's honour or reputation would violate the author's special rights may have anomalous unintended consequences and were, incidentally, in excess of the requirement of Berne Convention. The section was amended to read:

57. Author's special rights

(1) independently of the author's copyright, and even after the assignment either wholly or partially of the said copyright, the author of a work shall have the right—

(a) to claim the authorship of the work; and

(b) to restrain, or claim damages in respect of any distortion, mutilation, modification or other act in relation to the said work which is done before the expiration of the term of copyright if such distortion, mutilation, modification or other act would be prejudicial to his honour or reputation.

Provided that the author shall not have any right to restrain or claim damages in respect of any adaptation of a computer programme to which clause (aa) of subs Section (1) of Section 52 applies.

Explanation—Failure to display a work or to display it to the satisfaction of the author shall not be deemed to be an infringement of the rights conferred by this section.

(2) The right conferred upon an author of a work by subsection (1), other than the right to claim authorship of the work, may be exercised by the legal representatives of the author."

Copyright law in India was thus brought at par with the Berne Convention. In conformity with the Berne Convention, s.57 of the Copyright Act 1957 protects the author's right of paternity as also the right of integrity. Distortion, mutilation or modification if established to be prejudicial to the author's reputation or honour are actionable.

Shri Praveen Anand urged that an action under s.57 need not be restricted to injunction or damages. The action could well be to preserve the ethos of the work. As noted above, he urged that mutilation would also mean destruction.

The mural sculpture decorating Vigyan Bhawan, is the result of plaintiff's creative effort. It has not only enhanced plaintiff's celebrity, but has also attained the status of a modern national treasure of India.

Authorship is a matter of fact. It is history. Knowledge about authorship not only identifies the creator, it also identifies his contribution to national culture. It also makes possible to understand the course of cultural development in a country. Linked to each other, one flowing out from the other, *right of integrity* ultimately contributes to the overall integrity of the cultural domain of a nation. The language of s.57 does not exclude the right of integrity in relation to cultural heritage. The cultural heritage would include the artist whose creativity and ingenuity is amongst the valuable cultural resources of a nation. Through the telescope of s.57 it is possible to legally protect the cultural heritage of India through the moral rights of the artist.

As observed by Jaspal Singh J. in his interim order, India is *"rightly proud of its creativity and ingenuity"*. Artists play an important social role by contributing to cultural heritage thereby also elucidating history.

Why do patents and copyrights go into the public domain after a lapse of time? (duration governed by municipal legislation). The answer is simple. Intellectual property and knowledge are interconnected. Intellectual property embodies traditional thought and knowledge with value addition. Thus, physical destruction or loss of intellectual property has far reaching social consequence. Knowledge which has grown with it is also lost.

As opined by Mira T. Sundara Rajan in "Moral Rights and the Protection of Cultural Heritage" in the *International Journal of Cultural Property*, (2001), Vol.10, no.1, pp.79–94:

> "The rights of attribution and integrity are particularly apposite to the cultural domain. Apart from the interests of individual authors in maintaining their standing and reputation, these moral rights are closely linked to a public interest in the maintenance of historical truth and cultural knowledge. Moral rights also promote the development of a social attitude of respect toward individual creativity. While authors must accept the responsibilities which accompany the privileges of creative work, it is incumbent upon both the public and the state to acknowledge the value of artists' contributions to cultural heritage."

[The court took note that, in recent years, the Government of India had formally articulated the goal of preserving and promoting India's art, cultural, and heritage. It then noted that India had become a signatory to several international agreements designed to protect and preserve cultural property.]

* * *

It has to be noted that as originally enacted, s.57 of the Copyright Act 1957 was very widely worded because of the fact that the words *"would be prejudicial to his honour or reputation"* which found mention in subcl.(b) of subs.(1) of s.57 were not qualifying subcl.(a) of subs.(1) of s.57. Further, the words *"any other action"* which found mention in subcl.(b) implied that the action could be other than a claim for damages or a claim for injunction. Post amendment, as the section stands effective from May 10, 1995, the legislature has restricted the right of the author to claim damages or to seek an order of restraint. Further, proof of prejudice to the author's honour or reputation has been made the *sine qua non* for claiming damages.

However, the various declarations by the international community in the conventions noted above, lift the moral rights in works of art if the same acquire the status of cultural heritage of a nation. India is a signatory to the conventions and it would be the obligation of the State to honour its declarations.

There would therefore be urgent need to interpret s.57 of the Copyright Act 1957 in its wider amplitude to include destruction of a work of art, being the extreme form of mutilation, since by reducing the volume of the author's creative corpus it affects his reputation prejudicially as being actionable under said section. Further, in relation to the work of an author, subject to the work attaining the status of a modern national treasure, the right would include an action to protect the integrity of the work in relation to the cultural heritage of the nation.

Under orders passed by this Court, the physical condition of the mural in question was directed to be reported. Shri B.C.Sanyal, an artist of international repute, and Professor P.N.Mago reported that various parts were missing. Their report reveals a massive destruction of the mural. Ms. Kapila Vatsyayan, Academic Director, Indira Gandhi National Center for the Arts reported that she was pained to see an outstanding artistic composition dismembered in fragments which could not be put together even in part.

In view of the evidence on record, Ms. Jyoti Singh, learned counsel for the defendants, did not even attempt to urge that the destruction and damage to the mural was debatable.

Issues No.2 and 3 are accordingly decided in favour of the plaintiff and against the defendants. It is held that the plaintiff has a cause to maintain an action under s.57 of the Copyright Act 1957 notwithstanding that the copyright in the mural stands vested in the defendants. It is further held that the defendants have not only violated the plaintiff's moral right of integrity in the mural but have also violated the integrity of the work in relation to the cultural heritage of the nation.

Issues 4 and 5

At the hearing held on February 14, 2005, Shri Praveen Anand, learned counsel for the plaintiff, prayed for a decree directing the defendants to return to the plaintiff the remnants of the mural with a further declaration that the defendants would have no right in the same and also a declaration that the plaintiff would have a right to recreate the mural at any other place anywhere in the world including the right to sell the same. Alternatively, damages were sought.

I am of the opinion that the mural, whatever be its form today, is too precious to be reduced to scrap and languish in the warehouse of the Government of India. It is only the plaintiff who has a right to recreate his work and, therefore, has a right to receive the broken up mural. The plaintiff also has a right to be compensated for loss of reputation, honour and mental injury due to the offending acts of the defendants.

Suit is accordingly decreed in favour of the plaintiff and against the defendants as under:

(a) A mandatory injunction directing the defendants to return to the plaintiff the remnants of the mural within 2 weeks from today;

(b) Declaration is granted in favour of the plaintiff and against the defendants that all rights in the mural shall henceforth vest in the plaintiff and the defendants would have no right whatsoever in the mural;

(c) Declaration is granted in favour of the plaintiff that he would have an absolute right to recreate the mural at any place and would have the right to sell the same;

(d) Damages in the sum of Rs.5 lacs are awarded in favour of the plaintiff and against the defendants. * * *

* * *

Notes

1. France, like India, recognizes all four of the moral rights: integrity, paternity (attribution), divulgation, and withdrawal. The divulgation right is the right to decide when and under what circumstances a work will be published. The withdrawal right permits the author to withdraw a work from circulation, even after it has been published. If the author exercises this right under French law, however, he or she is required to compensate the assignee from whom the publication rights have been withdrawn. (Art. L.121–4). The withdrawal right is not required by the Berne Convention, but it is recognized in a number of other countries that have strong moral rights protection. In Germany, where it is called the "right of revocation for changed conviction," the law imposes a similar requirement to compensate the party from whom the exploitation right is withdrawn. (UrhG, Art. 42). In both France and Germany, if the author ever decides to re-release the work, the author must offer the publication opportunity to the party from whom the rights were previously withdrawn.

2. Whereas the policies underlying moral rights protection in continental Europe emphasize the personal rights of the author, *Sehgal* suggests that cultural heritage considerations provide an alternative foundation for these rights. Which of these approaches best explains the Visual Artists Rights Act in the United States?

C.   RENTAL AND LENDING RIGHTS

In some countries, including European Union members, authors and/or copyright owners enjoy a broader array of rental rights than in the United States, and in some cases they possess a lending right as well.

The WIPO Copyright Treaty provides that the authors of computer programs, cinematographic works, and works embodied in phonograms "shall enjoy the exclusive right of authorizing commercial rental to the public of the originals or copies of their works." Art. 7(1). However, the treaty allows for several exceptions. It exempts rentals of computer programs "where the program itself is not the essential object of the rental" (for example, where a computer program is a component of another device, such as an automobile). Art 7(2)(i). It also provides that rental rights for cinematographic works are not required "unless such commercial rental has led to widespread copying of such works materially impairing the exclusive right of reproduction." Art. 7(2)(ii). Finally, with respect to works embodied in phonograms, Art. 7(3) allows any signatory country which, as of April 15, 1994, had already adopted a system of equitable remuneration for authors with respect to their rental rights, to maintain that system, "provided that the commercial rental of works embodied in phonograms is not giving rise to the material impairment of the exclusive right of reproduction of authors."

The WIPO Performances and Phonograms Treaty, in turn, provides a rental right to performers with respect to "their performances fixed in phonograms." Art. 9. It, too, permits signatories to continue their equitable remuneration systems subject to the "material impairment" proviso. This rental right does not apply to performers in cinematographic works.

Article 11 of the TRIPS Agreement establishes rental rights only for computer programs and cinematographic works, and only for "authors and their successors in title." As under the WIPO Copyright Treaty, computer programs are exempt where the program is not the "essential object" of the rental. With respect to cinematographic works, rental rights are mandatory only if commercial rental of such works "has led to widespread copying of such works which is materially impairing the exclusive right of reproduction."

In the European Union, rental and lending rights were first mandated in 1992, in Directive 92/100/EEC. A challenge to that Directive was upheld in 1998, in the *Metronome Musik* opinion reproduced below. In 2006, the original Directive was repealed and replaced by an updated version, 2006/115/EC, the key provisions of which are set forth below. Shortly before the new Directive took effect, the European Court of Justice issued two opinions addressing claims that Portugal had failed to comply with the terms of the 1992 Directive. These decisions—one concerning rental rights, and the other concerning lending rights—are reproduced below. Although they construe the 1992 Directive, the substance of the 2006 Directive is essentially the same.

METRONOME MUSIK GMBH v. MUSIC POINT HOKAMP GMBH

European Court of Justice, 1998
Case C–200/96

By order of 18 April 1996, received at the Court on 13 June 1996, the Landgericht (Regional Court) Cologne, referred to the Court of Justice for a preliminary ruling under Article 177 of the EC Treaty a question on the validity of Article 1(1) of Council Directive 92/100/EEC of 19 November 1992 on rental right and lending right and on certain rights related to copyright in the field of intellectual property.

That question was raised in proceedings between Metronome Musik GmbH (hereinafter "Metronome"), which produces sound recordings, including compact discs, and Music Point Hokamp GmbH (hereinafter "Hokamp"), whose business includes the rental of compact discs.

Article 1(1) of the Directive requires the Member States to provide a right to authorise or prohibit the rental and lending of originals and copies of copyright works, and other subject-matter. Pursuant to Article 1(4), those rights are not to be exhausted by any sale or other act of distribution. Finally, under Article 2(1), the exclusive right to authorise or prohibit rental and lending is to belong to the author in respect of the original and copies of his work, to the performer in respect of fixations of his performance, to the phonogram producer in respect of his phonograms and to the producer of the first fixation of a film in respect of the original and copies of his film.

Under Article 9 of the Directive, without prejudice to the specific provisions concerning the lending and rental right, and those of Article 1(4) in particular, the distribution right, which is the exclusive right to make any of the abovementioned objects available to the public by sale or otherwise, is not to be exhausted except where the first sale in the Community of that object is made by the rightholder or with his consent.

Finally, Article 13, which is concerned with the applicability of the Directive in time, allows the Member States, under paragraph 3, to provide that rightholders are deemed to have given their authorisation to the rental of an object made available to third parties or acquired before 1 July 1994, the date by which the Directive was to be implemented.

In Germany, the obligations imposed by the Directive were put into effect by the Law of 23 June 1995, which amended the Urheberrechtsgesetz of 9 September 1965 (Copyright Law, hereinafter "the UrhG"). In particular, that Law removed rental from the category of "subsequent distribution", which is lawful where the original of the work or copies thereof has been put into circulation with the consent of the holder of the distribution right.

On the basis of the new provisions of the UrhG, Metronome, which produced the compact disc "Planet Punk", recorded by the group "Die Arzte" and issued on 15 September 1995, sought an interlocutory injunction from the Landgericht Koln against Hokamp to restrain it from renting out the compact disc.

On 4 December 1995, that court granted an interim order restraining the defendant from offering that compact disc for rental or renting it out in Germany.

Hokamp applied to have that order set aside, contending that the abovementioned provisions of the Directive and those of the UrhG implementing it were contrary to the fundamental rights guaranteed by Community law and by constitutional law, in particular the freedom to pursue a trade or profession.

In those proceedings, the Landgericht Koln entertained doubts as to the validity of the introduction of an exclusive rental right, which would in particular adversely affect the exercise of a business activity hitherto pursued without restriction. Consequently, the national court decided to refer the following question to the Court of Justice for a preliminary ruling:

> Is the introduction of an exclusive rental right, contrary to the principle of the exhaustion of distribution rights, by Article 1(1) of Council Directive 92/100/EEC of 19 November 1992 on rental right and lending right and on certain rights related to copyright in the field of intellectual property compatible with Community law, in particular Community fundamental rights?

Metronome, the German, French, Italian and United Kingdom Governments, the Council and the Commission consider that the Directive is valid. They maintain, essentially, that the exclusive rental right, which moreover is provided for in international conventions to which the Community and the Member States are parties, reflects objectives of general interest in the field of intellectual property and does not impair the substance of the right to pursue a trade or profession.

Hokamp contends, however, that the introduction of such a right by the Directive must be regarded as void since it encroaches upon the fundamental rights of undertakings which operate rental businesses, including the right freely to pursue a trade or activity, and because it distorts competition in the Member States in which that activity was carried on independently of phonogram producers.

It is clear from the grounds of the order for reference and the wording of the question submitted that the national court is concerned that the introduction of an exclusive rental right might infringe the principle of exhaustion of distribution rights in the event of the offering for sale, by the rightholder or with his consent, of copyright works.

That principle is expressed in the settled case-law of the Court of Justice according to which, whilst Article 36 of the EC Treaty allows derogations from the fundamental principle of the free movement of goods by reason of rights recognised by national legislation in relation to the protection of industrial and commercial property, such derogations are allowed only to the extent to which they are justified by the fact that they safeguard the rights which constitute the specific subject-matter of that property. However, the exclusive right guaranteed by the legislation of a Member State on industrial and commercial property is exhausted when a product has been lawfully distributed on the market in another Member State by the actual proprietor of the right or with his consent.

However, as the Court pointed out in Case 158/86, Warner Brothers and Metronome Video v. Christiansen [1988] ECR 2605, literary and artistic works may be the subject of commercial exploitation by means other than the sale of the recordings made of them. That applies, for example, to the rental of video-cassettes, which reaches a different public from the market for their sale and constitutes an important potential source of revenue for makers of films.

In that connection, the Court observed that, by authorising the collection of royalties only on sales to private individuals and to persons hiring out video-cassettes, it is impossible to guarantee to makers of films a remuneration which reflects the number of occasions on which the video-cassettes are actually hired out and which secures for them a satisfactory share of the rental market. Laws which provide specific protection of the right to hire out video-cassettes are therefore clearly justified on grounds of the protection of industrial and commercial property pursuant to Article 36 of the Treaty.

In the same judgment, the Court also rejected the argument that a maker of a film who has offered the video-cassette of that film for sale in a Member State whose legislation confers on him no exclusive right of hiring it out must accept the consequences of his choice and the exhaustion of his right to restrain the hiring-out of that video-cassette in any other Member State. Where national legislation confers on authors a specific right to hire out video-cassettes, that right would be rendered worthless if its owner were not in a position to authorise the operations for doing so.

As the Advocate General has rightly indicated in point 14 of his Opinion, the release into circulation of a sound recording cannot therefore, by definition, render lawful other forms of exploitation of the protected work, such as rental, which are of a different nature from sale or any other lawful form of distribution. Just like the right to present a work by means of public performance, the rental right remains one of the prerogatives of the author and producer notwithstanding sale of the physical recording.

Thus, the distinction drawn in the Directive between the effects of the specific rental and lending right, referred to in Article 1, and those of the distribution right, governed by Article 9 and defined as an exclusive right to make one of the objects in question available to the public, principally by way of sale, is justified. The former is not exhausted by the sale or any other act of distribution of the object, whereas the latter may be exhausted, but only and specifically upon the first sale in the Community by the rightholder or with his consent.

The introduction by the Community legislation of an exclusive rental right cannot therefore constitute any breach of the principle of exhaustion of the distribution right, the purpose and scope of which are different.

Furthermore, according to settled case-law, the freedom to pursue a trade or profession, and likewise the right to property, form part of the general principles of Community law. However, those principles are not absolute but must be viewed in relation to their social function. Consequently, the exercise of the right to property and the freedom to pursue a trade or profession may be restricted, provided that any restrictions in fact correspond to objectives of general interest pursued by the European Community and do not constitute in relation to the aim pursued a disproportionate and intolerable interference, impairing the very substance of the rights guaranteed.

The object of the Directive is to establish harmonised legal protection in the Community for the rental and lending right and certain rights related to copyright in the field of intellectual property. According to the first three recitals in its preamble, such harmonisation is intended to eliminate differences between national laws which are liable to create barriers to trade, distort competition and impede the achievement and proper functioning of the internal market. As is stated, more specifically, in the fourth, fifth and seventh recitals in the preamble to the Directive, the rental right, which, as a result of the increasing threat of piracy, is of increasing importance to the economic and cultural development of the Community, must in particular guarantee that authors and performers can receive appropriate income and amortise the especially high and risky investments required particularly for the production of phonograms and films.

Those objectives in fact conform with the objectives of general interest pursued by the Community. It should be borne in mind, in particular, that the protection of literary and artistic property, which is a category of industrial and commercial property within the meaning of Article 36 of the Treaty, constitutes a ground of general interest which may justify restrictions on the free movement of goods. It should also be noted that the cultural development of the Community forms part of the objectives laid down by Article 128 of the EC Treaty, as amended by the Treaty on European Union, which is intended in particular to encourage artistic and literary creation.

More particularly, the inclusion, challenged by the defendant in the main proceedings, of phonogram producers among the beneficiaries of the exclusive rental right appears justified by the protection of the extremely high and risky investments which are required for the production of phonograms and are essential if authors are to go on creating new works. As the Advocate General has explained in point 26 of his Opinion, the grant of an exclusive right to producers certainly constitutes the most effective form of protection, having regard in particular to the development of new technologies and the increasing threat of piracy, which is favoured by the extreme ease with which recordings can be copied. In the absence of such a right, it is likely that the remuneration of those who invest in the creation of those products would cease to be properly guaranteed, with inevitable repercussions for the creation of new works.

Furthermore, as pointed out by most of those who have submitted observations, the obligation to establish, for the producers of phonograms and all other holders of rights in respect of phonograms, an exclusive right to authorise or prohibit the commercial rental of those products is in conformity with the combined provisions of Articles 11 and 14 of the Agreement on Trade–Related Aspects of Intellectual Property Rights ("TRIPs"), annexed to the agreement establishing the World Trade Organisation, signed in Marrakesh on 15 April 1994 and approved by Council Decision 94/800/EC of 22 December 1994 concerning the conclusion on behalf of the European Community, as regards matters within its competence, of the agreements reached in the Uruguay Round multilateral negotiations (1986–1994).

Thus, the general principle of freedom to pursue a trade or profession cannot be interpreted in isolation from the general principles relating to protection of intellectual property rights and international obligations entered into in that sphere by the Community and by the Member States. Since it does not appear that the objectives pursued could have been achieved by measures which preserved to a greater extent the entrepreneurial freedom of individuals or undertakings specialising in the commercial rental of phonograms, the consequences of introducing an exclusive rental right cannot be regarded as disproportionate and intolerable.

It must also be observed that, regardless of the transitional measures provided for in Article 13, the Directive does not have the effect of eliminating any possibility of rental. Those engaged in the business of hiring out can negotiate with rightholders in order to obtain an authorisation to hire out the objects in question or a contractual licence, on terms acceptable to both parties.

As regards the distortions of competition which the defendant in the main proceedings contends would result from the overall prohibition of rental which would be imposed by certain groups producing phonograms, it need merely be observed that, even if such distortions were proved, they would not be the direct consequence of the contested provisions, which do not necessarily have either the object or the effect of encouraging interested parties systematically to prohibit the rental of their products solely for the purpose of eliminating competitors from the rental market.

The answer to be given to the national court must therefore be that examination of the question submitted has disclosed no factor of such a nature as to affect the validity of Article 1(1) of the Directive.

* * *

On those grounds,

THE COURT,

in answer to the question referred to it by the Landgericht Koln by order of 18 April 1996, hereby rules:

Examination of the question submitted has disclosed no factor of such a kind as to affect the validity of Article 1(1) of Council Directive 92/100/EEC of 19 November 1992 on rental right and lending right and on certain rights related to copyright in the field of intellectual property.

DIRECTIVE 2006/115/EC OF THE EUROPEAN PARLIAMENT AND OF THE COUNCIL OF 12 DECEMBER 2006 ON RENTAL RIGHT AND LENDING RIGHT AND ON CERTAIN RIGHTS RELATED TO COPYRIGHT IN THE FIELD OF INTELLECTUAL PROPERTY

Chapter I: Rental and Lending Right

Article 1: Object of harmonization

1. In accordance with the provisions of this Chapter, Member States shall provide, subject to Article 6, a right to authorise or prohibit the rental and lending of originals and copies of copyright works, and other subject matter as set out in Article 3(1).

2. The rights referred to in paragraph 1 shall not be exhausted by any sale or other act of distribution of originals and copies of copyright works and other subject matter as set out in Article 3(1).

Article 2: Definitions

1. For the purposes of this Directive the following definitions shall apply:

(a) 'rental' means making available for use, for a limited period of time and for direct or indirect economic or commercial advantage;

(b) 'lending' means making available for use, for a limited period of time and not for direct or indirect economic or commercial advantage, when it is made through establishments which are accessible to the public;

(c) 'film' means a cinematographic or audiovisual work or moving images, whether or not accompanied by sound.

2. The principal director of a cinematographic or audiovisual work shall be considered as its author or one of its authors. Member States may provide for others to be considered as its co-authors.

Article 3: Rightholders and subject matter of rental and lending right

1. The exclusive right to authorise or prohibit rental and lending shall belong to the following:

(a) the author in respect of the original and copies of his work;

(b) the performer in respect of fixations of his performance;

(c) the phonogram producer in respect of his phonograms;

(d) the producer of the first fixation of a film in respect of the original and copies of his film.

2.   This Directive shall not cover rental and lending rights in relation to buildings and to works of applied art.

3.   The rights referred to in paragraph 1 may be transferred, assigned or subject to the granting of contractual licences.

4.   Without prejudice to paragraph 6, when a contract concerning film production is concluded, individually or collectively, by performers with a film producer, the performer covered by this contract shall be presumed, subject to contractual clauses to the contrary, to have transferred his rental right, subject to Article 5.

5.   Member States may provide for a similar presumption as set out in paragraph 4 with respect to authors.

6.   Member States may provide that the signing of a contract concluded between a performer and a film producer concerning the production of a film has the effect of authorising rental, provided that such contract provides for an equitable remuneration within the meaning of Article 5. Member States may also provide that this paragraph shall apply mutatis mutandis to the rights included in Chapter II.

Article 4: Rental of computer programs

This Directive shall be without prejudice to Article 4(c) of Council Directive 91/250/EEC of 14 May 1991 on the legal protection of computer programs (5).

Article 5: Unwaivable right to equitable remuneration

1.   Where an author or performer has transferred or assigned his rental right concerning a phonogram or an original or copy of a film to a phonogram or film producer, that author or performer shall retain the right to obtain an equitable remuneration for the rental.

2.   The right to obtain an equitable remuneration for rental cannot be waived by authors or performers.

3.   The administration of this right to obtain an equitable remuneration may be entrusted to collecting societies representing authors or performers.

4.   Member States may regulate whether and to what extent administration by collecting societies of the right to obtain an equitable remuneration may be imposed, as well as the question from whom this remuneration may be claimed or collected.

Article 6: Derogation from the exclusive public lending right

1.   Member States may derogate from the exclusive right provided for in Article 1 in respect of public lending, provided that at least

authors obtain a remuneration for such lending. Member States shall be free to determine this remuneration taking account of their cultural promotion objectives.

2.   Where Member States do not apply the exclusive lending right provided for in Article 1 as regards phonograms, films and computer programs, they shall introduce, at least for authors, a remuneration.

3.   Member States may exempt certain categories of establishments from the payment of the remuneration referred to in paragraphs 1 and 2.

* * *

COMMISSION OF THE EUROPEAN COMMUNITIES v. PORTUGUESE REPUBLIC

European Court of Justice, 2006

By its application, the Commission of the European Communities requests the Court to declare that:

- by creating in national law a rental right in favour of producers of videograms, the Portuguese Republic has failed to fulfil its obligations under Article 2(1) of Council Directive 92/100/EEC of 19 November 1992 on rental right and lending right and on certain rights related to copyright in the field of intellectual property * * *.

- by creating in national legislation some doubt as to who is responsible for paying the remuneration owed to artists on assignment of the rental right, the Portuguese Republic has failed to comply with Article 4 of the Directive, read in conjunction with Article 2(5) and (7) thereof.

Legal context

Community legislation

The first recital in the preamble to the Directive states:

whereas differences exist in the legal protection provided by the laws and practices of the Member States for copyright works and subject-matter of related rights protection as regards rental and lending; whereas such differences are sources of barriers to trade and distortions of competition which impede the achievement and proper functioning of the internal market.

The seventh recital in the preamble to the Directive provides:

whereas the creative and artistic work of authors and performers necessitates an adequate income as a basis for further creative and artistic work, and the investments required particularly for the production of phonograms and films are especially high and risky; whereas the possibility for securing that income and recouping that investment can only effectively be guaranteed through adequate legal protection of the rightholders concerned.

[The court then set forth the relevant provisions of the Rental and Lending Rights Directive.]

National legislation

The Directive was transposed into Portuguese law by Decree–Law No 332/97 of 27 November 1997 establishing the obligation to pay remuneration to artists who have assigned their rental right.

Article 5 of the Decree–Law provides:

1.   Where the author transfers or assigns his rental rights concerning a phonogram, a videogram or the original or a copy of a film to a phonogram or film producer, he has an inalienable right to an equitable remuneration for the rental.

2.   For the purpose of paragraph 1, the producer is responsible for paying the remuneration which, in the absence of agreement, is set by arbitration and in accordance with the law.

Article 7 of the Decree–Law provides:

1.   The distribution rights, including the right of rental and lending free of charge, is also granted to:

(a) the performer in respect of the fixation of his performance;

(b) the phonogram or videogram producer in respect of his phonograms or videograms;[1]

(c) the producer of the first fixation of a film in respect of the original and copies of his film.

2.   The rights referred to in paragraph 1 shall not be extinguished upon sale or any other act of distribution of the objects mentioned.

---

1. Under Portuguese law, a "videogram" is any electronic recording of moving images, with or without sound; the term therefore encompasses a reproduction of a cinematographic or audiovisual work, such as a DVD or videocassette. OG 235 I–A, Art. 2(1), lit. (h) (Oct. 7, 1993). A "film" is the physical embodiment of a "cinematographic work," which is itself defined as "the intellectual creation" of moving images accompanied by sounds or not accompanied by sounds, for projection in showrooms specially designed for that purpose. *Id.* Art. 2(1), lit. (a), (c). Thus, a videogram may be a copy of a cinematographic work, or it may embody some other type of audiovisual work, such as a program created for television.

3.   In addition to the provisions of paragraphs 1 and 2, the right to authorise reproduction of the original and copies of that film is also granted to the producer of the first fixation of a film.

4.   For the purposes of the present act, film is defined as a cinematographic work, audiovisual work, and any moving images, whether or not accompanied by sound.

Under Article 8 of the Decree–Law:

The conclusion of a film production contract between performers and the producer gives rise to the presumption, in the absence of a contrary provision, of assignment of the performer's rental right in favour of the producer, without prejudice to the inalienable right to equitable remuneration for the rental, in accordance with Article 2(5).

* * *

The first complaint, alleging infringement of Article 2(1) of the Directive

Arguments of the parties

The Commission argues that the provisions of Article 2(1) of the Directive do not permit, contrary to the provisions of the Decree–Law, the extension to videogram producers of the exclusive right to authorise or prohibit rental enjoyed by the producer of the first fixation of a film.

According to the Commission, the list in Article 2(1) is exhaustive and therefore it is only for the producer of the first fixation and not the producer of videograms to authorise or prohibit the rental of the original and copies of a film. That list is in no way minimal or supplementary. Only the first fixation of a film justifies specific protection by Community law. Protecting copies of a film by means of a right related to copyright is unjustified due to the absence of any "ancillary" link with the literary or artistic work.

It follows that the effect of the Decree–Law, contrary to the provisions of the Directive, is to deprive the producer of the first fixation of a film of the exercise of his exclusive right by no longer allowing him to authorise or prohibit the rental of copies of his film.

In its defence, the Portuguese Republic observes that, on the date the Decree–Law was adopted, the Code of copyright and related rights gave an identical status to producers of phonograms and videograms. In order to respect that equality and to avoid causing imbalances in the current status of the two types of producer, the legislature thus added the videogram producer to the list of proprietors of exclusive rights. It is therefore with the aim of adapting to the characteristics of its national system that the Decree–Law at issue aligns the treatment of a videogram producer with that of a phonogram producer and, accordingly, grants the videogram producer a level of protection higher than that introduced by Community law.

The Portuguese Republic argues, moreover, that the Directive itself contains an ambiguity. By using, in Article 2(1), the vague term "film", the Directive seems to amalgamate into one definition cinematographic works and works recorded on videogram. It is therefore permissible to consider that the producer of the first fixation may also be the producer of copies of a film.

Finally, that Member State argues that the Decree–Law would be contrary to the Directive only if it transpired that its aims contradicted national legislation, if the Decree–Law undermined the functioning of the internal market or if it infringed third party rights. The application of that Decree–Law has raised no concrete problem at the level of either the internal market or the national market, since no one has been deprived of the rights provided for by the directive and no complaint has been made.

Findings of the Court

At the outset, it must be stated that that first complaint gives rise to the question whether exclusive rental rights are also granted to the videogram producer.

Granting an exclusive right also to videogram producers would not simply add an extra category of rightholders to the list in Article 2(1) of the Directive, but would, on the contrary, call into question the specific exclusive rights set out in that provision.

In that respect, Article 2(1) of the Directive confers on the producer of the first fixation an exclusive right to authorise or prohibit rental and lending in respect of the original and copies of his film. It follows that, if the producer of a videogram were also granted the right to control the rental of that videogram, the right of the producer of the first fixation would manifestly no longer be exclusive.

That interpretation is confirmed by the object of the Directive, which is to establish harmonised legal protection in the Community for the rental and lending right and certain rights related to copyright in the field of intellectual property.

As is specifically apparent from the first recital in the preamble thereto, the Directive aims to eliminate the differences between the Member States in respect of the legal protection for copyright works as regards rental and lending, with the aim of reducing barriers to trade and distortions of competition. If Article 2(1) of that Directive allowed Member States freely to confer the right to authorise or prohibit the rental of videograms to different categories of persons, that aim would manifestly not be achieved.

In that respect, the Court has already held that the commercial distribution of videocassettes takes the form of sales, but also of hiring-out. The right to prohibit such hiring-out in a Member State is liable to influence trade in videocassettes in that State and hence, indirectly, to affect intra-Community trade in those products.

In addition, under the seventh recital in the preamble to the Directive, the protection of the exclusive rental rights of the producers of phonograms and films is justified on the grounds of the necessity to safeguard the recoupment of extremely high and risky investments which are required for their production and which are essential if authors are to go on creating new works.

It does not appear that the production of videograms requires such high and risky investments that they merit special protection. The Court has already recognised [in prior case law concerning phonograms] the extreme ease with which recordings could be copied. Although that statement was made in the context of sound recordings, the development of new technologies has also helped to facilitate the reproduction of picture recordings.

It follows that the Decree–Law, in so far as it provides for a rental right also in favour of videogram producers, does not comply with the Directive.

* * *

In the light of the foregoing considerations, it must be found that the complaint alleging infringement of Article 2(1) of the Directive by the Portuguese Republic must be upheld.

> *The second complaint, alleging infringement of Article*
> *4 of the Directive, read in conjunction with*
> *Article 2(5) and (7) thereof*

* * *

As regards the transfer of the rental right from the performer to the film producer, the Commission argues that the Decree–Law is confused, in so far as it can refer to two different producers, namely the producer of videograms and the producer of the first fixation of a film.

Under Article 5(2) of the Decree–Law, the producer is responsible for paying the remuneration for the rental. This gives rise to a difficulty for performers in collecting the remuneration to which they are entitled since they do not know which of the two producers is required to pay that remuneration. On that point, the Directive is clear: only the producer of the first fixation of a film can be assigned the rental right of performers and required to pay the remuneration to which they are entitled. A transposition such as that carried out by the Decree–Law is therefore intended, in actual fact, to favour the copying industry.

The Portuguese Republic disputes the allegedly confused nature of the Decree–Law. In the absence of evidence to the contrary, the Decree–Law imposes the obligation to pay remuneration on the producer of the first fixation of a film. Moreover, the ambiguity derives not only from the Decree–Law but also from the definition of the term "film" given by the Directive.

Findings of the Court

* * *

As a preliminary point, it is apparent from Article 2(5) and (7) of the Directive that the rights of performers may be presumed to be transferred or transferred by the effect of the law to a film producer. In exchange for transferring that right, Article 4 of that Directive guarantees an equitable remuneration to those performers.

Article 8 of the Decree–Law provides for the assignment of exclusive rental rights from the performer to the film "producer" without further defining that term. According to Article 5 of the Decree–Law, the film producer is responsible for paying the remuneration in respect of the assignment of the rental right relating to a videogram or the original or copy of a film. The interpretation of those two articles combined could lead to the conclusion that the producer of videograms comes within the category of film producers, who are liable for the remuneration.

In that respect, the Portuguese Republic itself admits that its Decree–Law is ambiguous.

On the other hand, although Article 4(1) of the Directive, as regards the assignment of the rental right, relates to a film producer, in actual fact it refers only to the producer of the first fixation of a film. Since videograms are not mentioned in that article, the producer of videograms does not therefore enjoy the status of film producer.

The effect, therefore, of that transposition of the Directive is a situation which may prevent performers in Portugal from collecting the remuneration to which they are entitled, in so far as it is not clear who is the producer responsible for paying the equitable remuneration provided for in Article 4 of the Directive.

In those circumstances, the complaint alleging incorrect transposition of Article 4 of the Directive, read in conjunction with Article 2(5) and (7) thereof, must be upheld.

It follows from the foregoing that, by creating in national law a rental right also in favour of producers of videograms, the Portuguese Republic has failed to fulfil its obligations under Article 2(1) of the directive and, by creating in national legislation some doubt as to who is responsible for paying the remuneration owed to artists on assignment of the rental right, the Portuguese Republic has failed to comply with Article 4 of the Directive, in conjunction with Article 2(5) and (7) thereof.

RULING

On those grounds, the Court (Third Chamber):

1. Declares that:

    - by creating in national law a rental right also in favour of producers of videograms, the Portuguese Republic has failed to fulfil its obligations under Article 2(1) of Council Directive 92/100/EEC of 19 November 1992 on rental right and lending right and on certain rights related to copyright in the field of intellectual property, as last amended by Directive 2001/29/EC of the European Parliament and of the Council of 22 May 2001 on the harmonisation of certain aspects of copyright and related rights in the information society.

    - by creating in national legislation some doubt as to who is responsible for paying the remuneration owed to perfomers on assignment of the rental right, the Portuguese Republic has failed to comply with Article 4 of Directive 92/100, as amended by Directive 2001/29, in conjunction with Article 2(5) and (7) thereof.

COMMISSION OF THE EUROPEAN COMMUNITIES v. PORTUGUESE REPUBLIC

European Court of Justice, 2006

By its application, the Commission of the European Communities asks the Court for a declaration that, by exempting all categories of public lending establishments from the obligation to pay remuneration to authors for public lending, the Portuguese Republic has failed to fulfil its obligations under Articles 1 and 5 of Council Directive 92/100/EEC of 19 November 1992 on rental right and lending right and on certain rights related to copyright in the field of intellectual property.

* * *

The Directive was transposed into the Portuguese legal system by Decree–Law No 332/97 of 27 November 1997. * * *

* * *

According to Article 6 of the Decree–Law:

1.   An author is entitled to remuneration for the public lending of the original or copies of his work.

2.   The proprietor of the establishment which makes the original or copies of the work available to the public is responsible for payment of the remuneration . . .

3.   The present Article is not applicable to public, school or university libraries, museums, public archives, public foundations and private non-profit-making institutions.

The action
Arguments of the parties

According to the Commission, Article 6(3) of the Decree–Law exempts from the obligation to pay a public lending right all State central administrative services, all bodies which are part of indirect State administration, such as public establishments and public associations, and all local administrative services and bodies. To this list can be added all private-law legal persons carrying out functions of a public nature, such as bodies providing administrative services to the public and even private schools and universities, and all private non-profit-making institutions in general. Ultimately, it amounts to exempting any public lending establishment from the obligation of payment.

Article 5(3) of the Directive provides that Member States may not exempt all categories of establishments, as the Decree–Law provides, but only certain categories. The Portuguese Republic therefore acted outside the limits imposed by the Directive and that Decree–Law purely and simply prevents attainment of the Directive's objective, which is to ensure that creative and artistic work is adequately remunerated.

The Commission refers also to the close relationship between the lending of works by public services or bodies and the rental of works by businesses. In both cases, protected works are being utilised. The difference in legal protection accorded to protected works in Member States has an effect upon the functioning of the internal market and is liable to lead to distortions of competition. The lending of works, books, phonograms and videograms represents a considerable volume of activity. People who use those works and material would not buy them and, as a result, authors and creators would suffer a loss of revenue.

The Commission adds that, in order to be able to make cultural works available to their citizens free of charge, Member States have to remunerate all those who contribute to the functioning of libraries, that is, not only the staff, but, above all, the authors of the works. Remunerating the latter is in the common interest of the Community.

In its defence, the Portuguese Republic argues that Article 5 of the Directive, in particular paragraph 3 thereof, is "a compromise text", imprecise, difficult to interpret and open to challenge as regards its meaning and scope. The drafting of that provision was also intended to be open-textured and flexible in order to take into account the levels of cultural development specific to the different Member States. Moreover, the directive does not give any indication as to the meaning of that article.

The Portuguese Republic further argues that transposition of the directive directly poses the problem of the choice of "categories of establishments" and, indirectly, the problem of whether persons who are the indirect addressees of the Directive can or cannot, and to what extent, derive benefit, in an equal or almost equal manner, from the provisions of that directive which authorise Member States to allow for exemptions from the payment of the remuneration provided for in Article 5(1) of the directive on public lending. That question relates to the issue of the conflict between Article 5(3) and the principles of equal treatment, impartiality, solidarity and social cohesion. The effect of exempting certain "categories of establishments" from payment of the public lending right would be that Portuguese citizens would not have access to, and would not be able to enjoy, intellectual works under the same conditions. Moreover, the proprietors of the rights should in principle have obtained appropriate revenue in the exercise of their rights of reproduction and distribution.

In addition, the Portuguese Republic contends that public lending is residual, as the market concerned is limited to the national territory and is of minor importance in the economic area, so that the internal market could not be affected by that situation. It is therefore possible to conclude that the objectives of cultural development are more important than the disadvantages for the internal market. That is the reason why removing those disadvantages would run counter to the principle of proportionality.

Finally, that Member State argues that, in view of the specific cultural character and different levels of development of the Member States, the adoption of a new scheme for public lending and its incorporation into the national legal systems must, under the principle of subsidiarity, remain within the sphere of competence of those Member States.

Findings of the Court

Firstly, the subject-matter of the dispute between the Commission and the Portuguese Republic is solely the question relating to the scope to be given to Article 5(3) of the Directive, according to which Member States may exempt certain "categories of establishments" from the payment of the remuneration referred to in Article 5(1).

According to settled case-law, in interpreting a provision of Community law it is necessary to consider not only its wording, but also the context in which it occurs and the objective pursued by the rules of which it is part.

As regards firstly the wording of Article 5(3) of the Directive, it should be noted that this refers to "certain categories of establishments". Therefore it clearly follows that the legislature did not intend to allow Member States to exempt all categories of establishments from payment of the remuneration referred to in Article 5(1).

Next, under Article 5(3), the Directive allows Member States to derogate, in respect of public lending, from the general obligation of remuneration of authors referred to in paragraph 1 of that article. According to settled case-law, the provisions of a Directive which derogate from a general principle established by that Directive must be strictly interpreted. 23. Moreover, Article 5(3) cannot be interpreted as allowing for total derogation from that obligation of remuneration, since the effect of such an interpretation would be to render Article 5(1) meaningless and thus deprive that provision of all effectiveness.

Finally, the main objective of the Directive, as can be seen more precisely from the seventh recital, is to guarantee that authors and performers receive appropriate income and recoup the especially high and risky investments required particularly for the production of phonograms and films.

It follows that the fact of exempting all categories of establishments which engage in such lending from the obligation laid down in Article 5(1) of the directive would deprive authors of remuneration with which they could recoup their investments, with inevitable repercussions for the creation of new works. In those circumstances, a transposition of the directive that resulted in such an exemption for all categories of establishments would go directly against the objective of that directive.

The Portuguese Republic does not in effect dispute that the transposition of the Directive effected by the Decree–Law results in exempting all the categories of establishments listed in paragraph 11 of this judgment.

Accordingly, it must be acknowledged that the effect of the Portuguese legislation is to exempt all categories of public lending establishments from the obligation to pay the remuneration provided for in Article 5(1) of the directive.

To justify such a measure, that Member State puts forward various arguments, none of which, however, can be considered relevant.

Firstly, the Portuguese Republic argues that the public lending market is essentially national and not significant at an economic level. It follows that the normal functioning of the internal market cannot be affected by that situation and that, under the principle of subsidiarity, the activity of public lending should remain within the sphere of competence of the Member States.

[The Court rejected this argument, based on settled law establishing that intellectual property rights affect trade in goods and services, as well as competitive relationships, within the Community.]

Secondly, that Member State argues that the proprietors of copyrights have, in principle, already received remuneration for reproduction and distribution rights in respect of their works.

However, forms of exploitation of a protected work, such as public lending, are different in nature from sale or any other lawful form of distribution. The lending right remains one of the prerogatives of the author notwithstanding sale of the physical recording. Furthermore, the lending right is not exhausted by the sale or any other act of distribution, whereas the distribution right may be exhausted, but only and specifically upon the first sale in the Community by the rightholder or with his consent.

Thirdly, the Portuguese Republic contends that Article 5(3) of the Directive is open-textured and flexible so as to take into account the cultural development of each Member State, and the expression "certain categories of establishments" calls for a "variable geometry" style interpretation.

However, Article 5(3) of the Directive cannot, as indicated in paragraph 22 of the present judgment, be interpreted as allowing for total derogation from the obligation of remuneration laid down in Article 5(1).

Fourthly, the Portuguese Republic maintains that there is a conflict between Article 5(3) of the Directive and the principles of equal treatment, impartiality, solidarity and social cohesion. To exempt only "certain categories of establishments" from that obligation of remuneration would amount to permitting a situation in which Portuguese citizens did not have access to, and were not able to enjoy, intellectual works under the same conditions.

In that respect, the exemption of certain public lending establishments, provided for in Article 5(3) of the Directive, from the obligation to pay the remuneration referred to in Article 5(1) allows Member States, by leaving them a choice as to which establishments will be covered by the exemption, to retain discretion to decide, from among the sections of the public concerned, those for whom such an exemption will do most to facilitate access to intellectual works, whilst respecting fundamental rights and, in particular, the right to not be discriminated against.

Moreover, in the absence of sufficiently precise Community criteria in a directive to delimit the obligations thereunder, it is for the Member States to determine, in their own territory, what are the most relevant criteria for ensuring, within the limits imposed by Community law, and in particular by the directive concerned, compliance with that directive.

In that respect, it has already been held that Article 5(3) of the Directive authorises but does not oblige a Member State to exempt certain categories of establishments. Consequently, if the circumstances prevailing in the Member State in question do not enable the relevant criteria to be determined for drawing a valid distinction between categories of establishments, the obligation to pay the remuneration provided for in paragraph 1 of the article must be imposed on all the establishments concerned.

In those circumstances, the action brought by the Commission must be regarded as well founded.

As a result, it must be held that, by exempting all categories of public lending establishments from the obligation to pay remuneration to authors for public lending, the Portuguese Republic has failed to fulfil its obligations under Articles 1 and 5 of the Directive.

Ruling

On those grounds, the Court (Third Chamber) hereby:

1.   Declares that, by exempting all categories of public lending establishments from the obligation to pay remuneration to authors for public lending, the Portuguese Republic has failed to fulfil its obligations under Articles 1 and 5 of Council Directive 92/100/EEC of 19 November 1992 on rental right and lending right and on certain rights related to copyright in the field of intellectual property;

Notes

1.   The European Union has required its members to recognize rental and lending rights since 1992. In 2002, the European Commission issued a report on the status of rental and lending rights in member

countries, and this report eventually led to the adoption of the updated 2006 Rental and Lending Rights Directive. The 2002 report provides some background on the early evolution of the lending right:

> The origins of the PLR [Public Lending Right] are to be found in the early twentieth century and are closely linked to the development of public libraries. The importance of private libraries, which were "lending" books against payment or membership fees, decreased as public libraries, accessible without any payment, appeared. After World War II, the number of private libraries reduced to insignificance. Due to the fact that the increase in the number and improvement of public libraries was strongly supported by the State, the number of lent items increased considerably. This led authors to ask for remuneration for this increased use of their works. Legislators did not, however, react to this immediately but introduced progressively the PLR in form of an exclusive right or a right of remuneration for authors.

> The PLR was first introduced in the Scandinavian countries, (Denmark (1946) Sweden (1955), Finland (1961)), followed by the Netherlands (1971), Germany (1972) and the United Kingdom (1979/1982). Germany was the only country in which the PLR was integrated into copyright legislation whereas in the other Member States it was introduced in separate legislation. The provisions in these countries differed in several respects (rightholders, media and types of libraries concerned). In Belgium, the PLR was part of the distribution right. In Greece, France and Luxembourg, authors theoretically enjoyed an exclusive PLR based on the "droit de destination". In Spain, an exclusive distribution right existed; however, the right was apparently not exercised in practice. In Portugal, the law could be interpreted in various ways: no PLR or an exclusive right forming part of a broad distribution right. In Ireland and Italy, there was neither an exclusive PLR nor a right to remuneration for public lending.

Report from the Commission to the Council, the European Parliament and the Economic and Social Committee on the Public Lending Right in the European Union (2002).

2. Even though the 1992 Directive mandated lending rights in all EU countries, the EU had to initiate legal proceedings against numerous Member states for being slow to adopt lending rights legislation, for enacting overbroad exemptions, or for failing to ensure that authors received remuneration. In addition to Portugal, the European Court of Justice issued adverse rulings against against Ireland, Spain, Italy, and Luxembourg.

3. Public lending rights have been enacted in at least 30 countries to date, including Canada, Australia, and New Zealand, even though they are not mandated by any international agreements outside the EU.

4.   The International Federation of Library Associations and Institutions (IFLA) has issued a policy statement opposing public lending rights. What are some policy arguments for and against these rights?

5.   Countries that have enacted public lending rights may or may not permit foreign authors to share in the remuneration scheme. Within the EU, Community law forbids discrimination against authors from other Member states, but it does not require that remuneration be paid to authors from outside the EU. Several countries (Austria, Germany, the Netherlands) make payments to authors from other countries that recognize lending rights and provide reciprocity. Many other countries exclude foreign authors from the remuneration scheme; alternatively, they may apply the public lending scheme only to works written in their national language. In Canada, where most books held by libraries are by foreign authors, lending rights payments are made only to citizens and permanent residents of Canada. Consider whether any of these forms of discrimination may violate the "national treatment" rule of Article 5 of the Berne Convention, which provides:

> (1) Authors shall enjoy, in respect of works for which they are protected under this Convention, in countries of the Union other than the country of origin, the rights which their respective laws do now or may hereafter grant to their nationals, as well as the rights specially granted by this Convention.

* * *

> (3) Protection in the country of origin is governed by domestic law. However, when the author is not a national of the country of origin of the work for which he is protected under this Convention, he shall enjoy in that country the same rights as national authors.

6.   There is significant variation in the types of works, and the types of authors, covered by the public lending right. Some schemes are limited to books, some are limited to fiction books, some include only certain types of nonfiction books, and others apply higher rates to fiction than to nonfiction. In some countries, the lending right applies not only to books but to sound recordings, audiovisual media, and even works of art. Some schemes include translators, editors, illustrators, photographers, adapters, and even publishers.

7.   The existence of a public lending remuneration scheme requires a mechanism for collecting and remitting the remuneration to authors. There are two main methods for determining remuneration—by how often a work is loaned, or by how many copies of the work are held by lending institutions. Libraries collect this data, and provide it to the agency that administers the remuneration system. The payments themselves come from a fund provided by the government. The administering agency then disburses these funds to eligible authors, who must register in order to participate in the system.

D. EXHAUSTION OF RIGHTS

Neither the TRIPS provisions of the WTO Agreement nor international copyright treaties limit the freedom of individual nations to determine their own rules for determining when the "first sale" of a copy of a work exhausts the copyright owner's distribution right with respect to that copy. Article 6 of TRIPS provides that "nothing in this Agreement shall be used to address the issue of the exhaustion of intellectual property rights." Article 6(2) of the WIPO Copyright Treaty, which addresses the author's exclusive distribution right, states:

> Nothing in this Treaty shall affect the freedom of Contracting Parties to determine the conditions, if any, under which the exhaustion of the right in paragraph (1) applies after the first sale or other transfer of ownership of the original or a copy of the work with the authorization of the author.

To similar effect is Article 8(2) of the WIPO Performances and Phonograms Treaty, addressing performers' exclusive distribution right in fixations of their performances in phonograms.

Not all nations have adopted clear rules governing exhaustion of copyright, but those that have established such rules typically provide for national or regional exhaustion, allowing copyright owners to restrict or prevent the parallel importation of copies of their works, as is the case in the United States. This is consistent with the concept of copyright as a territorial right. National exhaustion is illustrated by the *Polo/Lauren* case below.

As illustrated by the *Laserdisken* case in Part D.2. below, the European Union has implemented a rule of Community-wide exhaustion. In contrast, Australia and New Zealand have each, to varying degrees, lifted their restrictions on parallel importation, thus venturing into controversial regimes of international exhaustion.

1. NATIONAL EXHAUSTION

POLO/LAUREN COMPANY LP v. ZILIANI HOLDINGS PTY LTD

Federal Court of Australia, 2008
New South Wales District Registry

The Court (Black CJ, Jacobson and Perram JJ):

Introduction

[Respondent Ziliani Holdings purchased genuine Polo Ralph Lauren garments at a discount in the United States and imported them into Australia for sale through its retail outlets. Most of the garments bore appellant's well-known polo player logo, in which the appellant owns the copyright. Because Ziliani's importation did not violate trademark law, appellant brought this claim for copyright infringement under section 37 (infringing importation) and 38 (infringing sale) of the 1968 Copyright Act, which prohibit importation of a copyrighted work without the copyright owner's consent. Appellant now appeals from the trial judge's holding that there was no copyright infringement.]

* * *

Issues

In this Court there were two issues between the parties. They were:

> (a) The Label Issue: Although it is an infringement of copyright to import a copyright work for sale without the permission of the copyright owner, that principle is subject to exceptions. If the copyright work is a label which is incorporated into the surface of an article then s 44C of the Act deems there to be no infringement by importation and sale. The first issue is, therefore, whether the Logo is a "label" incorporated into the surface of the garments. If it is, as Ziliani contended, then there can be no infringement of Polo/Lauren's copyright.

> (b) [Discussion of the second issue is omitted.]

* * *

First issue: Is the Logo a label?

Section 44C provides:

> 44C Copyright subsisting in accessories etc. to imported articles

> (1) The copyright in a work a copy of which is, or is on, or embodied in, a non-infringing accessory to an article is not infringed by importing the accessory with the article.

> . . .

> (2) Section 38 does not apply to a copy of a work, being a copy that is, or is on, or embodied in, a non-infringing accessory to an article, if the importation of the accessory is not an infringement of copyright in the work.

The word "accessory" is defined in s. 10 as follows:

> accessory, in relation to an article, means one or more of the following:

(a) a label affixed to, displayed on, incorporated into the surface of, or accompanying, the article;

(b) the packaging or container in which the article is packaged or contained;

(c) a label affixed to, displayed on, incorporated into the surface of, or accompanying, the packaging or container in which the article is packaged or contained;

(d) a written instruction, warranty or other information provided with the article;

(e) a record embodying an instructional sound recording, or a copy of an instructional cinematograph film, provided with the article;

but does not include any label, packaging or container on which the olympic symbol (within the meaning of the Olympic Insignia Protection Act 1987) is reproduced.

The effect of these provisions is that importation of an article bearing a label does not infringe any copyright in the label.

As developed by the parties, this issue involved four distinct questions. These were first, whether the trial judge had concluded, erroneously, that swing tags and internal tags were not within the notion of a label; secondly, whether the concept of a label contemplated a distinction between the label itself and the item labelled; thirdly, whether the Logo was primarily decorative or whether it performed an identifying function and, the relevance of the consumer's understanding of the nature of the label; finally, whether the primary judge erred by effectively assimilating the notion of a label with the notion of a trade mark.

* * *

First question—The relevance of swing tags and internal tags

[On the first question, the appellate court agreed with the trial judge that treating the Logo as "label" was not inconsistent with treating swing tags and internal tags as labels, since a garment can have more than one label.]

* * *

Second question—The distinction between the label and the labelled

Polo/Lauren submitted that the words "in relation to" where appearing in the definition of "accessory" in s. 10(1) of the Act meant that the label referred to in paras. (a) and (c) of that

definition necessarily connoted an association between the label
and the article labelled which maintained the conceptual distinction
between them. That interpretation was supported, so it was said, by
the use in para. (a) of the words "affixed to", "displayed on",
"incorporated into" and "accompanying". Polo/Lauren was careful
to disclaim any suggestion that the label had to be physically
separate from the article with which it was associated for, as Ziliani
correctly submitted, that would be inconsistent with the words
"incorporated into the surface". What was required, therefore, was
not physical but rather conceptual distinctiveness. Physical distinctiveness might be observed between, for example, a bottle of perfume and the fragrance contained therein or between a bottle of
liquor and the label appearing on the bottle. Conceptual distinctiveness was more elusive but, whatever its boundaries might be, it was
not present where a logo was an essential part of the article upon
which it appeared. Mr. Burley SC, in his careful and succinct
argument, submitted that the Logo was so integral and essential to
the clothing in question that neither meaningfully maintained its
identity without the other. As Mr. Burley put it, a Polo shirt
without the Logo is just not a Polo shirt.

Mr. Cobden SC submitted that this approach to the word
"label" paid too little attention to the words "incorporated into the
surface of" the article. There was, so he submitted, no escaping
from the fact that the Logo was "incorporated into the surface of"
the garments. Of course Ziliani accepted, and Polo/Lauren submitted, that not everything which was incorporated into the surface of
an article became thereby a label. It could not follow, therefore,
that just because the Logo was incorporated into the surface of the
garments in question that it was a label.

Consideration

In his poem "Among School Children", William Butler Yeats
asked "how can we know the dancer from the dance?" It seems to
us that Mr. Burley's argument that a label cannot be consubstan-
tial with the article to which it is affixed raises the same point,
albeit somewhat more prosaically. There is no doubt, we think, that
the definition of "accessory" exhibits in its language an assumption
that whatever else is comprehended by the expression "label" that
notion is distinct, albeit not necessarily in a physical sense, from
the article with which it is associated. So much is plain from the
use of expressions such as "affixed to", "displayed on" and "incorporated into the surface of". Further, that view is consistent with
the mischief at which the introduction of s. 44C was directed. That
mischief was the decision of Young J in R & A Bailey & Company
Ltd v. Boccaccio Pty Ltd (1986) 4 NSWLR 701. In that case, the
defendants were vendors in Australia of imported bottles of Baileys

Original Irish Cream upon which were affixed labels in which copyright subsisted. The local owner of that copyright sued to prevent the importation of the bottles on the ground that it was a secondary infringement of its copyright. Young J upheld this contention.

Two years later the Copyright Law Review Committee published its report "The Importation Provisions of the Copyright Act 1968". The Committee noted the *Bailey* case. It went on to say:

> The Committee is strongly of opinion that distributors of goods should not be able to control the market for their products by resorting to the subterfuge of devising a label or a package in which copyright will subsist. The purpose of copyright is to protect articles which are truly copyright articles such as books, sound recordings or films. This purpose is achieved by conferring on authors of works and makers of subject matter a bundle of exclusive rights entitling them to restrain conduct antipathetical to their incorporeal property and to sue for damages where such conduct has already been committed. If the simple expedient of affixing or attaching a label in which copyright subsists to any goods at all entitles the owner of the goods to exclude others from marketing similar goods, the sooner the practice is stopped the better it will be. However imaginatively labelled or packaged a bottle of liquor may be, the product is liquor. The same may be said of cigarettes, perfume and cosmetics. In the Committee's opinion it would be quite wrong to allow the present position to continue. Abuses which may occur can be remedied by resort to causes of action for passing-off, for breaches of s. 52 of the Trade Practices Act or for infringements of the Trade Marks Act 1955. If the Trade Marks Act requires amendment to confer adequate protection, that is a matter for consideration in a different form of inquiry.

> * * *

> In summary then the Committee recommends that ss. 37 and 38 should be repealed insofar as they apply to labelling and packaging of all goods of whatever kind.

Although Parliament did not implement the Committee's proposed solution it is plain that it regarded itself as addressing the problem identified by the Committee. So much appears from the Explanatory Memorandum accompanying the Copyright Amendment Bill 1997 (Cth) which, under the heading "Problem Identification and Specification of Regulatory Objectives" in Sch. 3, said:

In 1988 the CLRC reviewed the importation provisions of the Copyright Act. It concluded that, whatever the merits of importation rights over copyright goods, the ability to use the copyright protected material attached to or used in relation to goods that would not attract copyright protection in the market 'in their own right' to gain control over the right to import and market such goods in Australia, did not fit within the framework of a proper exercise of copyright.

Inherent, therefore, in the notion of a label is the notion that it is possible to speak of it "in its own right". We infer from that that the Committee assumed that a label had a separate existence from the article with which it was associated. For that reason, we would accept that a label and the articles with which it is associated must be conceptually distinct. The situation is analogous to, although not identical with, the requirement in trade mark law that the trade mark be distinct from the article to which it is affixed.

Accepting the need for that distinction however does not assist Polo/Lauren. Whilst there is obvious force in the proposition that the Logo is very closely associated with the garments, we do not think that the Logo and the garments are so inextricably bound up in each other's identity that they have ceased to be distinct. In that regard, it is not sufficient for present purposes to demonstrate that the Logo is an important element in, or an integral aspect of, the garments. It is only when the label and the labelled are conceptually indistinguishable that the former loses its quality as a label. However important or integral the Logo is to the garments, it and they remain distinct.

Third question—The function argument

[The court considered several dictionary definitions of the term "label."]

* * *

Polo/Lauren argued that these definitions required that a label had to have a function that usually, but not invariably, was one of identification. Polo/Lauren submitted that "[a]s a matter of language the label will have the characteristic of conveying instructions or details concerning the ownership, use or nature of the item". The Logo could not, so it was submitted, have that characteristic since it was primarily decorative. Further, Polo/Lauren submitted that the learned primary judge erred when focusing on the "practical effect" of the Logo. It was submitted that the Logo could only have the practical effect of identifying the garments as being associated with Polo/Lauren if a consumer knew that the Logo connoted a connection with Polo/Lauren. Without such knowledge, the Logo was merely a rider on a horse with a stick, symbolising nothing. Polo/Lauren posited that whether something was a label or not could not depend on the states of mind of consumers. Such a focus, it was said, was more apposite to the tort of passing off and proceedings under the Trade Practices Act 1974 (Cth).

We do not accept that the Logo is purely decorative. It also has a function. The primary judge found that "the [Logo] has considerable significance in identifying clothing as emanating from the Ralph Lauren group". Subject to the trade mark issue, which we will consider below, it is clear that the Logo, which also may be accepted as decorative, at least served the function of identifying those clothes with Polo/Lauren.

In our view, a functional test reflects the natural and ordinary meaning of the word "label" as it appears in the Act. The character of an object can be determined by its evident function and such is the case with a label. A label can have many functions—such as conveying information about the size of a garment, washing instructions or origin. At the most basic level, a label performs an "identifying" function. In the context of the Act, we would read "label" as including something that in fact identifies an object. The assessment of function is objective. It does not depend upon the putative labeller's intention or the understanding of consumers. That is not to say that these considerations will be irrelevant; rather they are factors that may very well be taken into account in determining whether something performs the function necessary for its characterisation as a label.

The Logo is conceptually distinct from clothing on which it is embroidered and it identifies clothing as "emanating from the Ralph Lauren group". We think it highly improbable that this identification is accidental or unintentional, but whatever the intention, the primary judge found the Logo in fact identifies a connection with Polo/Lauren. This functional element is sufficient to make it clear that the Logo is a label for the purpose of the Act.

Fourth question—The trade mark issue

Polo/Lauren submitted that his Honour had effectively interpreted the expression *label* to mean trade mark. This submission is correct. His Honour said:

> I am satisfied that a natural and ordinary English meaning of the word "label" includes a brand name, trade mark and the name by which a design or fashion house, and its product, such as "Polo" and "Ralph Lauren" and "Polo Ralph Lauren", is generally known.

In our view, the word "label" as it is used in the Act is intended to connote something physical, although as we have said, a label need not be physically distinct from the object labelled. A trade mark, of course, is an intangible property right; for this reason, we do not think "label" in the statutory context simply means "trade mark" in the statutory sense. Nonetheless, where a trade mark is physically manifested and incorporated into an article, as the Logo is here, the trade mark is being used to identify the article with its source. Its purpose is to label the goods; it is a label.

Trade marks cannot be used to prevent the importation of goods where the mark has been applied to the goods with the consent of the registered owner: see s 123(1) of the Trade Marks Act. The Copyright Act 1968 (Cth) is concerned only with labels in which copyright subsists. But where, as in the present case, there is copyright in a trade mark, and the trade mark is physically manifested and incorporated into an article so as to identify the article as that of the putative labeller, the copyright work is being used as a label. That was the situation in the *Bailey* case. This is the difficulty that Polo/Lauren cannot escape.

* * *

Conclusion on label issue

In those circumstances, the better view is that the Logo, as affixed to the garments in question, is a label within the meaning of the definition of "accessory" in s 10(1) of the Act. The necessary consequence of that conclusion is that the appeal must be dismissed. * * *

* * *

2. EXHAUSTION IN THE EUROPEAN UNION

LASERDISKEN APS v. KULTURMINISTERIET
European Court of Justice, 2006

[Laserdisken sold motion picture DVDs through its retail stores in Denmark. Some of the DVDs were imported from non-EU countries, including the United States. Under Danish copyright law, however, importing DVDs from outside the EU and the European Economic Area (EEA) required the consent of the copyright owner, whereas importation of lawfully made DVDs from other EU or EEA countries was freely permitted under the principles of "exhaustion of rights" and "free movement of goods."]

* * *

Judgment

This reference for a preliminary ruling concerns the interpretation and validity of Article 4(2) of Directive 2001/29/EC of the

European Parliament and of the Council of 22 May 2001 on the harmonisation of certain aspects of copyright and related rights in the information society (OJ 2001 L 167, p. 10) ("the Directive" or "Directive 2001/29").

The reference was made in the context of proceedings between Laserdisken ApS ("Laserdisken") and the Kulturministeriet (Ministry of Culture) concerning the applicability of section 19 of the Danish Law on copyright (Ophavsretslov), as amended by Law No 1051 (Lov nr. 1051, om ændring af ophavsretsloven) (Law No 1051 amending the Law on copyright) of 17 December 2002, to the import and sale in Denmark of DVDs lawfully marketed outside the European Economic Area (EEA).

Legal context

Directive 2001/29 was adopted on the basis of Articles 47(2) EC, 55 EC and 95 EC. Article 1 thereof, entitled "Scope", provides in paragraph 1 that "[t]his Directive concerns the legal protection of copyright and related rights in the framework of the internal market, with particular emphasis on the information society".

Under the title "Rights and exceptions", Chapter II of the Directive contains Articles 2 to 5. Article 2 concerns the right of reproduction, Article 3 the right of communication to the public of works and the right of making available to the public other subject-matter, Article 4 the right of distribution, whilst Article 5 concerns exceptions and limitations to the rules laid down in the preceding three articles.

Article 4 of the Directive reads as follows:

> 1. Member States shall provide for authors, in respect of the original of their works or of copies thereof, the exclusive right to authorise or prohibit any form of distribution to the public by sale or otherwise.
>
> 2. The distribution right shall not be exhausted within the Community in respect of the original or copies of the work, except where the first sale or other transfer of ownership in the Community of that object is made by the rightholder or with his consent.

Article 5(2) of the Directive provides that Member States may provide for exceptions or limitations to the reproduction right provided for in Article 2 in certain cases. Article 5(3) provides that Member States may also provide for exceptions or limitations to the rights provided for in Articles 2 and 3 in the cases listed in that paragraph.

According to Article 5(4) of the Directive, "[w]here the Member States may provide for an exception or limitation to the right of reproduction pursuant to paragraphs 2 and 3, they may provide similarly for an exception or limitation to the right of distribution as referred to in Article 4 to the extent justified by the purpose of the authorised act of reproduction".

Prior to transposition of Directive 2001/29, section 19 of the Danish Law on copyright provided that "[w]hen a copy of a work is, with the copyright holder's consent, sold or in some other manner transferred to another party, the copy may be distributed further".

Following amendment of that law by Law No 1051 of 17 December 2002, intended to transpose Directive 2001/29, section 19(1) has since read as follows:

> When a copy of a work is, with the copyright holder's consent, sold or in some other manner transferred to another party within the European Economic Area, the copy may be distributed further. As regards further distribution in the form of lending or rentals, the provision in the first sentence shall also apply to sales or other forms of transfer to other parties outside the European Economic Area.

* * *

The main proceedings and the questions referred for a preliminary ruling

Laserdisken is a commercial company which sells, *inter alia*, copies of cinematographic works to individual purchasers through its sales outlets in Denmark.

Until the end of 2002, those copies were mostly imported by the company from other Member States of the European Union but also from non-member countries. The products included special editions, such as original American editions, or editions filmed using special techniques. Another major part of the product range consisted of cinematographic works which were not or would not be available in Europe.

Having registered a significant drop in its operations following the abovementioned legislative amendment, on 19 February 2003 Laserdisken brought legal proceedings against the Kulturministeriet before the Østre Landsret (Eastern Regional Court), claiming that section 19 of the Law on copyright, as amended in the context of the transposition of Article 4(2) of Directive 2001/29, did not apply. According to Laserdisken, the new provisions of section 19 have a significant effect on its imports and sales of DVDs lawfully marketed outside the EEA.

* * *

Laserdisken [argues] that Article 4(2) of that directive infringes the international agreements which bind the Community in matters of copyright and related rights, the rules of the EC Treaty concerning the establishment of a competition policy, the principle of proportionality in connection with combating piracy and, more generally, completing the internal market, freedom of expression, the principle of equal treatment and the provisions of the Treaty concerning the Member States' cultural policy and educational policy, namely Articles 151 EC and 153 EC.

Since the abovementioned pleas in law were contested in their entirety by the Kulturministeriet, the Østre Landsret decided to stay the proceedings and to refer the following two questions to the Court for a preliminary ruling:

1. Is Article 4(2) of Directive [2001/29] invalid?

2. Does Article 4(2) of Directive [2001/29] preclude a Member State from retaining international exhaustion in its legislation?

The questions

The second question

By its second question, which it is appropriate to consider first, the national court asks whether Article 4(2) of Directive 2001/29 precludes national rules which provide that the distribution right in respect of the original or copies of a work is exhausted where the first sale or other transfer of ownership is made by the holder of that right or with his consent outside the Community.

Laserdisken and the Polish Government claim that Article 4(2) of Directive 2001/29 does not preclude a Member State from retaining such a rule of exhaustion in its legislation. The Commission of the European Communities maintains the opposite view.

Article 4(1) of Directive 2001/29 enshrines the exclusive right for authors, in respect of the original of their works or of copies thereof, to authorise or prohibit any form of distribution to the public by sale or otherwise.

Article 4(2) contains the rule pertaining to exhaustion of that right. According to that provision, the distribution right is not to be exhausted in respect of the original or copies of the work, except where the first sale or other transfer of ownership in the Community of that object is made by the rightholder or with his consent.

It follows that for the right in question to be exhausted, two conditions must be fulfilled: first, the original of a work or copies thereof must have been placed on the market by the rightholder or with his consent and, second, they must have been placed on the market in the Community.

Laserdisken and the Polish Government argue, essentially, that Article 4(2) of the Directive leaves it open to the Member States to introduce or maintain in their respective national laws a rule of exhaustion in respect of works placed on the market not only in the Community but also in non-member countries.

Such an interpretation cannot be accepted. According to the twenty-eighth recital in the preamble to Directive 2001/29, copyright protection under that directive includes the exclusive right to control distribution of the work incorporated in a tangible article. The first sale in the Community of the original of a work or copies thereof by the rightholder or with his consent exhausts the right to control resale of that object in the Community. According to the same recital, that right should not be exhausted in respect of the original of the work or of copies thereof sold by the rightholder or with his consent outside the Community.

It follows from the clear wording of Article 4(2) of Directive 2001/29, in conjunction with the twenty-eighth recital in the preamble to that directive, that that provision does not leave it open to the Member States to provide for a rule of exhaustion other than the Community-wide exhaustion rule.

That finding is supported by Article 5 of Directive 2001/29, which allows Member States to provide for exceptions or limitations to the reproduction right, the right of communication to the public of works, the right of making available to the public other subject-matter and the distribution right. Nothing in that article indicates that the exceptions or limitations authorised might relate to the rule of exhaustion laid down in Article 4(2) of Directive 2001/29 and, therefore, allow Member States to derogate from that rule.

This, moreover, is the only interpretation which is fully consistent with the purpose of Directive 2001/29 which, according to the first recital in the preamble thereto, is to ensure the functioning of the internal market. A situation in which some Member States will be able to provide for international exhaustion of distribution rights whilst others will provide only for Community-wide exhaustion of those rights will inevitably give rise to barriers to the free movement of goods and the freedom to provide services.

In the light of the foregoing, the answer to the second question must be that Article 4(2) of Directive 2001/29 is to be interpreted as precluding national rules providing for exhaustion of the distribution right in respect of the original or copies of a work placed on the market outside the Community by the rightholder or with his consent.

The first question

Laserdisken and the Polish Government propose that the answer to the question be that Directive 2001/29, and in particular

Article 4(2) thereof, are contrary to Community law. The European Parliament, the Council of the European Union and the Commission, on the other hand, contend that none of the grounds of invalidity put forward may be upheld.

[The Court first considered whether the community-wide exhaustion rule of Directive 2001/29 is consistent with the provisions of the EC Treaty which call for free competition and free movement of goods and services within the EU, and concluded that it is.]

* * *

Article 4(2) of Directive 2001/29

– Infringement of international agreements concluded by the Community on copyright and related rights

The national court does not state which agreements binding the Community might be infringed by the rule of Community-wide exhaustion of distribution rights laid down in Article 4(2) of Directive 2001/29.

* * *

[T]he fifteenth recital in the preamble to Directive 2001/29 states that the Directive implements the international obligations resulting from the adoption, in Geneva on 20 December 1996, under the auspices of the World Intellectual Property Organisation ("WIPO"), of the WIPO Copyright Treaty and the WIPO Performances and Phonograms Treaty, which treaties were approved on behalf of the Community by Council Decision 2000/278/EC of 16 March 2000.

Regarding the right of distribution, neither Article 6(2) of the WIPO Copyright Treaty nor Articles 8(2) and 12(2) of the WIPO Performances and Phonograms Treaty impose an obligation on the Community, as a contracting party, to provide for a specific rule concerning the exhaustion of that right.

It follows from the purpose of those treaties, as formulated *inter alia* in the first recitals in the preambles thereto, that they tend towards a harmonisation of the rules pertaining to copyright and related rights.

More specifically, regarding the right of distribution, the WIPO Copyright Treaty fulfils its harmonisation objective in providing for the exclusive right of authors to authorise the making available to the public of the originals of their works and copies thereof through sale or other transfer of ownership. The Treaty does not, however, affect the contracting parties' power to determine the conditions governing how exhaustion of that exclusive right may apply after the first sale. It thus allows the Community to pursue further harmonisation of national laws also in relation to the rule of exhaustion. The abovementioned provisions of the WIPO Copyright Treaty and those of Directive 2001/29 are therefore complementary, in the light of the harmonisation objective pursued.

It follows from all the above considerations that the submission that Article 4(2) of Directive 2001/29 infringes the international agreements concluded by the Community in the field of copyright and related rights cannot be upheld.

– *The Treaty rules relating to the establishment of a competition policy*

Laserdisken claims that the exhaustion rule laid down in Article 4(2) of Directive 2001/29 reinforces suppliers' control of the distribution channels, thereby adversely affecting free competition. The core of the argument put forward by the applicant in the main proceedings is that competition is generally nullified by that exhaustion rule combined with the regional encoding system for DVDs. Certain works placed on the market outside the Community are not accessible within the Community, due to that rule.

The Polish Government adds that that exhaustion rule prevents the promotion of greater competitiveness and gives holders of copyright and related rights a level of protection of their interests going beyond the purpose of such rights.

By all of their assertions, the applicant in the main proceedings and the Polish Government argue, essentially, that the exhaustion rule laid down in Article 4(2) of Directive 2001/29 prevents free competition at the global level.

It should be borne in mind that, according to Article 3(1)(g) EC, the activities of the Community are to include, as provided for in the Treaty and in accordance with the timetable set out therein, a system ensuring that competition in the internal market is not distorted. In that context, Title VI of the Treaty contains a Chapter 1, which includes Articles 81 EC to 89 EC laying down rules on competition.

In the present case, according to the first recital in the preamble to Directive 2001/29, harmonisation of the laws of the Member States on copyright and related rights contributes to the establishment of the internal market and to the institution of a system ensuring that competition in that market is not distorted.

It follows that the harmonisation achieved by that directive is also intended to ensure undistorted competition in the internal market, in accordance with Article 3(1)(g) EC.

According to the argument put forward by Laserdisken and the Polish Government, the Community legislature is obliged, in adopting Directive 2001/29, to take account of a principle of free competition at the global level, an obligation which does not follow from either Article 3(1)(g) EC or the other provisions of the Treaty.

It follows from the foregoing that the ground of invalidity based on infringement of the Treaty rules relating to the establishment of a competition policy must be rejected.

– *Infringement of the principle of proportionality*

According to Laserdisken and the Polish Government, the exhaustion rule laid down in Article 4(2) of Directive 2001/29 is not necessary for attaining the objective of an internal market without barriers and imposes on the citizens of the European Union burdens which go beyond what is necessary. That provision is, moreover, ineffective in preventing the distribution of works placed in circulation in the Community without the consent of holders of copyright and related rights.

According to settled case-law, the principle of proportionality, which is one of the general principles of Community law, requires that measures implemented through Community provisions be appropriate for attaining the objective pursued and must not go beyond what is necessary to achieve it (Case C–491/01 *British American Tobacco (Investments) and Imperial Tobacco* [2002] ECR I–11453, paragraph 122).

The applicant in the main proceedings criticises, essentially, the choice made by the Community institutions in favour of the rule of exhaustion of the right of distribution in the Community.

It is, accordingly, appropriate to consider whether the adoption of that rule constitutes a measure which is disproportionate in relation to the objectives pursued by those institutions.

It should be borne in mind that differences in the national laws governing exhaustion of the right of distribution are likely to affect directly the smooth functioning of the internal market. Accordingly, the objective of harmonisation in this area is to remove impediments to free movement.

Moreover, according to the ninth recital in the preamble to Directive 2001/29, the protection of copyright and related rights helps to ensure the maintenance and development of creativity in the interests of, *inter alia*, authors, performers, producers and consumers. The tenth recital in the preamble to the same directive states that legal protection of intellectual property rights is necessary in order to guarantee an appropriate reward for the use of works and to provide the opportunity for satisfactory returns on investment. In the same vein, the eleventh recital states that a rigorous, effective system of protection is a way of ensuring that European cultural creativity and production receive the necessary resources and of safeguarding the independence and dignity of artistic creators and performers.

In the light of the abovementioned objectives, it appears that the choice made by the Community legislature in Article 4(2) of Directive 2001/29 in favour of the rule of exhaustion in the Community is not a disproportionate measure capable of affecting the validity of that provision.

It follows from all the foregoing considerations that the argument alleging infringement of the principle of proportionality is unfounded.

* * *

– Infringement of the principle of equal treatment

Laserdisken claims that the rule of exhaustion laid down in Article 4(2) of Directive 2001/29 is capable of infringing the principle of equal treatment. It states, by way of example, that a producer and a licence holder established in a non-member country are not in the same situation as a producer and a licence holder established in the Community.

It is settled case-law that the principle of equal treatment requires that comparable situations must not be treated differently and that different situations must not be treated in the same way unless such treatment is objectively justified (*ABNA and Others*, paragraph 63 and case-law cited).

Even if the argument of the applicant in the main proceedings may be profitably put forward in the present context, it does not establish that the application of Article 4(2) of the Directive amounts to treating two comparable situations differently. There is no doubt that a producer and a licence holder established in a non-member country are not in an identical or comparable situation to that of a producer and a licence holder established in the Community. In actual fact, Laserdisken is essentially asserting that situations which are manifestly not comparable must be treated in the same way.

It follows that the argument that there has been infringement of the principle of equal treatment must be rejected.

* * *

On those grounds, the Court (Grand Chamber) hereby rules:

Consideration of the first question does not reveal any information such as to affect the validity of Article 4(2) of Directive 2001/29/EC of the European Parliament and of the Council of 22 May 2001 on the harmonisation of certain aspects of copyright and related rights in the information society.

Article 4(2) of Directive 2001/29 is to be interpreted as precluding national rules providing for exhaustion of the distribution right in respect of the original or copies of a work placed on the market outside the European Community by the rightholder or with his consent.

Notes

1. Laserdisken argued unsuccessfully that EU members should be permitted to adopt the principle of international exhaustion of rights. On what basis did the European Court of Justice reject that argument?

2. The European Directive on the Harmonization of Certain Aspects of Intellectual Property Rights in the Information Society (2001/29/EC) states, in Recital 29, that exhaustion does not arise when copies of a work are disseminated online; the Directive treats this as a "communication" of the work rather than a distribution. The United States Copyright Office agrees. *See* U.S. Copyright Office, DMCA Section 104 Report, Aug. 2001, Sec. III.B.1., pp. 78–105.

3. INTERNATIONAL EXHAUSTION

National exhaustion—that is, restrictions on parallel importation of copyrightable works—has been the norm in most common law countries.

Very few countries allow international exhaustion with respect to copyright. Japan's copyright law (Art. 26bis(2)(iv)) includes an international exhaustion provision, although it does not apply to motion pictures:

(1) The author shall have the exclusive right to offer his work (except a cinematographic work; the same shall apply hereinafter in this Article) to the public by transfer of ownership of the original or copies of the work * * *

(2) The provision of the preceding paragraph shall not apply in the case of the transfer of ownership of such original or copies of a work as falling within any of the following items.

* * *

(iv) the original or copies of a work the ownership of which has been transferred, outside this country, without prejudice to the right equivalent to that mentioned in the preceding paragraph [(1)] or by a person who has the right equivalent to that mentioned in that paragraph or with the authorization of such person.

However, the Japanese provision has not been tested in court.

In recent years, both Australia and New Zealand have liberalized their parallel import restrictions in an effort to bring lower prices to consumers.

Australia's process began with the removal of parallel import restrictions on books in 1991, although it partly reinstated them in 1998 due to objections from the nation's publishing industry. The 1998 amendment, which is still in effect, freely allows importation of lawfully made copies of books first published outside Australia, but in the case of books first published in Australia, the copyright owners can still restrict imports provided they maintain a sufficient domestic supply to satisfy consumer demand.

However, the 1998 legislation also amended the Copyright Act to permit importation and sale of sound recordings without the consent of the Australian copyright owners. The background and reasons for this amendment were described by the Federal Court of Australia as follows:

> On 30 July 1998, amendments to the Copyright Act 1968 (Cth) came into effect. They removed the previous prohibition on the importation of sound recordings without the consent of Australian copyright owners or licensees. The effect of the amendments was that Australian wholesalers and retailers of compact disc recordings (CDs), and other sound recordings, could thereafter acquire stock from other countries; but only provided the manufacture of that stock did not infringe copyright law in the source country and had been carried out with the consent of the copyright owner.

> The legislative amendments had major ramifications for the Australian record industry; retailers were no longer limited to purchasing CDs from Australian sources.

* * *

> *The legislative background*

> (i) The position before 30 July 1998

* * *

> The primary importation provisions of the Copyright Act are s. 37, which defines infringement of copyright in literary, dramatic, musical and artistic works by reference to their importation for sale and related purposes, and s. 102, which deals with subject matter other than works. Sections 38 and 103 deal with infringement by sale of, and related commercial dealings in, works including imported works. Section 132 sets out offences attracting criminal penalties. One offence is the importation of articles into Australia for the purpose of selling, etc., where the person knew, or ought reasonably to have

known, the article to be an infringing copy of a work in which copyright subsisted: see para. (d).

The 1988 report of the Copyright Law Review Committee recommended the provisions of the Copyright Act relating to parallel imports should continue, subject to qualifications which allowed, *inter alia*, importation of articles unavailable in Australia. The report recommended against criminal penalties for unauthorised parallel importation.

The report was followed in 1989 by an inquiry into book prices by the Prices Surveillance Authority. The Authority recommended the repeal of the importation provisions of the Copyright Act, save for pirate editions and the works of Australian resident authors with separate Australian publishing contracts. Thereafter the Copyright Amendment Act 1991 (Cth) amended the importation provisions of the Copyright Act to introduce what has been described as "a qualified closed market for books".

In 1990 the Prices Surveillance Authority conducted an inquiry into prices of sound recordings. It concluded that prices paid by Australian consumers were too high. The high prices were underpinned by three interrelated factors: price inelastic demand, the absence of domestic price competition and the restriction on competition arising from the importation provisions of the Copyright Act. It recommended that ss. 37, 38, 102 and 103 of the Copyright Act be repealed in relation to parallel imports from countries providing comparable levels of protection over the reproduction of musical works and sound recordings.

(ii) The 1998 amendments

In 1997 the Government introduced the Copyright Amendment Bill (No. 2) 1997 (Cth) (the Bill). This Bill was intended to amend the Copyright Act to give effect to the recommendations of the Prices Surveillance Authority. In his Second Reading Speech, the Attorney General explained the operation of the Bill thus:

> "The Bill will exempt the importation of non-pirate copies of a sound recording from infringement of copyright in either the sound recording or the works recorded on the recording. It will thereby remove the ability of copyright owners to control the market for each imported copy of a sound recording."

(Australia, House of Representatives, Debates (1997), p. 10,-972.)

The Bill was designed to achieve its effect through excluding action for unauthorised importation against "non-infringing copies" of sound recordings. A "non-infringing copy" was defined as one that had been made:

"(i) without infringing any law of the country in which it was made that protected copyright in any musical or other work used in the sound recording; and

(ii) with the consent of the producer of the original sound recording, or other person who was the copyright owner.

If the country in which the copy was made did not protect sound recordings, the law of the country where the original recording was made would be applied."

(Australia, House of Representatives, Debates (1997), pp. 10,-972–10,973.)

[The bill was passed, and took effect on July 30, 1998.]

* * *

As a result of these amendments, the Copyright Act now exempts, from its provisions relating to infringement, the importation of "non-infringing copies" of sound recordings. It does not permit the importation of pirated copies of sound recordings. Moreover, it places on the importer or seller the burden to establish, if challenged, that the imported stock is not pirated.

The Copyright Amendment Act introduced a new s. 10AA into the Copyright Act, defining "non-infringing copy" along the lines indicated above. New ss. 44D and 112D were inserted. They exempt, from the application of ss. 37, 38, 102 and 103, the importation for sale and related purposes of, and the sale of, and related commercial dealings with, non-infringing copies of sound recordings of literary, dramatic or musical works or in the sound recordings themselves. The new burden of proof provision is s. 130A, which provides:

"In an action for infringement of copyright described in section 37, 38, 102 or 103 by an act involving an article that is a copy of a sound recording, it must be presumed that the copy is not a non-infringing copy unless the defendant proves that the copy is a non-infringing copy."

Universal Music Australia Pty Ltd v. Australian Competition and Consumer Commission, [2003] FCAFC 193, paras. [1]–[18].

When the law went into effect, Australia retailers began importing some of their CDs from Indonesia to take advantage of lower pricing. However, the major record companies informed retailers that, if they took advantage of the new parallel importation law, the record companies would stop supplying them with CDs and/or withdraw other benefits such as discounts, favorable credit terms, and marketing support. The record companies also warned an Indonesian reseller that, if it continued to supply CDs to the Australian market, its allocation of CDs would be significantly reduced. However, the Australian Competition and Consumer Commission considered this conduct to be a violation of Australian's competition laws, and in 2003 the Federal Court of Australia agreed, imposing substantial fines on each of the recording companies. Universal Music Australia Pty Ltd v. Australian Competition and Consumer Commission, [2003] FCAFC 193.

In 2003, Australia expanded its international exhaustion regime to encompass computer software, allowing parallel imports of not only business software but also computer games and e-books. As of May 2009, the Australian government is considering a proposal to extend international exhaustion to books, permitting parallel importation to begin 12 months after the date of a book's first publication in Australia. As in the case of sound recordings, the government's goal has been to reduce prices paid by consumers. Each new rollback of parallel import restrictions in Australia has been controversial, but the actual impact—on consumers as well as on creators and publishers—remains unclear.

Australia's 1998 amendment was inspired by the even bolder action taken by New Zealand, which repealed all of its parallel import restrictions on copyrighted works in 1998. In response, however, the United States placed New Zealand on the Special 301 Watch List—a list of countries which the United States considers to have inadequate copyright laws. In October of 2003, New Zealand reinstated parallel import restrictions for motion pictures, banning parallel imports for the first nine months after a film's first international release, thus protecting the revenue streams of Australia's movie theatres. The 2003 statute also confirmed that the copyright owner's rental right still applied to imported copies of films and sound recordings, thus upholding the New Zealand High Court's 2001 decision to that effect in Video Ezy Int'l (NZ) Ltd v. Roadshow Ent. (NZ) Ltd, [2002] 1 N.Z.L.R. 855. The United States removed New Zealand from the Watch List in 2003. The 2003 amendments were scheduled to expire in 2008, at which time the New Zealand government was to review their impact and determine whether they should continue in effect. Based on recommendations in a 2008 cabinet report, the nine-month importation ban on motion pictures has been renewed for another five-year period, and

New Zealand continues to allow unrestricted importation of other copyrighted works.

E. RESALE RIGHTS

DIRECTIVE 2001/84/EC OF THE EUROPEAN PARLIAMENT AND OF THE COUNCIL OF 27 SEPTEMBER 2001 ON THE RESALE RIGHT FOR THE BENEFIT OF THE AUTHOR OF AN ORIGINAL WORK OF ART

THE EUROPEAN PARLIAMENT AND THE COUNCIL OF THE EUROPEAN UNION,

* * *

Whereas:

(1) In the field of copyright, the resale right is an unassignable and inalienable right, enjoyed by the author of an original work of graphic or plastic art, to an economic interest in successive sales of the work concerned.

(2) The resale right is a right of a productive character which enables the author/artist to receive consideration for successive transfers of the work. The subject-matter of the resale right is the physical work, namely the medium in which the protected work is incorporated.

(3) The resale right is intended to ensure that authors of graphic and plastic works of art share in the economic success of their original works of art. It helps to redress the balance between the economic situation of authors of graphic and plastic works of art and that of other creators who benefit from successive exploitations of their works.

(4) The resale right forms an integral part of copyright and is an essential prerogative for authors. The imposition of such a right in all Member States meets the need for providing creators with an adequate and standard level of protection.

(5) Under Article 151(4) of the Treaty the Community is to take cultural aspects into account in its action under other provisions of the Treaty.

(6) The Berne Convention for the Protection of Literary and Artistic Works provides that the resale right is available only if legislation in the country to which the author belongs so permits. The right is therefore optional and subject to the rule of reciprocity. It follows from the case-law of the Court of Justice of the European Communities on the application of the principle of nondiscrimina-

tion laid down in Article 12 of the Treaty, as shown in the judgment of 20 October 1993 in Joined Cases C–92/92 and C–326/92 Phil Collins and Others, that domestic provisions containing reciprocity clauses cannot be relied upon in order to deny nationals of other Member States rights conferred on national authors. The application of such clauses in the Community context runs counter to the principle of equal treatment resulting from the prohibition of any discrimination on grounds of nationality.

(7) The process of internationalisation of the Community market in modern and contemporary art, which is now being speeded up by the effects of the new economy, in a regulatory context in which few States outside the EU recognise the resale right, makes it essential for the European Community, in the external sphere, to open negotiations with a view to making Article 14b of the Berne Convention compulsory.

(8) The fact that this international market exists, combined with the lack of a resale right in several Member States and the current disparity as regards national systems which recognise that right, make it essential to lay down transitional provisions as regards both entry into force and the substantive regulation of the right, which will preserve the competitiveness of the European market.

(9) The resale right is currently provided for by the domestic legislation of a majority of Member States. Such laws, where they exist, display certain differences, notably as regards the works covered, those entitled to receive royalties, the rate applied, the transactions subject to payment of a royalty, and the basis on which these are calculated. The application or non-application of such a right has a significant impact on the competitive environment within the internal market, since the existence or absence of an obligation to pay on the basis of the resale right is an element which must be taken into account by each individual wishing to sell a work of art. This right is therefore a factor which contributes to the creation of distortions of competition as well as displacement of sales within the Community.

* * *

(17) Pursuant to Council Directive 93/98/EEC of 29 October 1993 harmonising the term of protection of copyright and certain related rights, the term of copyright runs for 70 years after the author's death. The same period should be laid down for the resale right. Consequently, only the originals of works of modern and contemporary art may fall within the scope of the resale right. * * *

(18) The scope of the resale right should be extended to all acts of resale, with the exception of those effected directly between persons acting in their private capacity without the participation of an art

market professional. This right should not extend to acts of resale by persons acting in their private capacity to museums which are not for profit and which are open to the public. * * *

(19) It should be made clear that the harmonisation brought about by this Directive does not apply to original manuscripts of writers and composers.

(20) Effective rules should be laid down based on experience already gained at national level with the resale right. It is appropriate to calculate the royalty as a percentage of the sale price and not of the increase in value of works whose original value has increased.

(21) The categories of works of art subject to the resale right should be harmonised.

(22) The non-application of royalties below the minimum threshold may help to avoid disproportionately high collection and administration costs compared with the profit for the artist. However, in accordance with the principle of subsidiarity, the Member States should be allowed to establish national thresholds lower than the Community threshold, so as to promote the interests of new artists. Given the small amounts involved, this derogation is not likely to have a significant effect on the proper functioning of the internal market.

(23) The rates set by the different Member States for the application of the resale right vary considerably at present. The effective functioning of the internal market in works of modern and contemporary art requires the fixing of uniform rates to the widest possible extent.

(24) It is desirable to establish, with the intention of reconciling the various interests involved in the market for original works of art, a system consisting of a tapering scale of rates for several price bands. It is important to reduce the risk of sales relocating and of the circumvention of the Community rules on the resale right.

* * *

(29) Enjoyment of the resale right should be restricted to Community nationals as well as to foreign authors whose countries afford such protection to authors who are nationals of Member States. A Member State should have the option of extending enjoyment of this right to foreign authors who have their habitual residence in that Member State.

* * *

HAVE ADOPTED THIS DIRECTIVE:

CHAPTER I: SCOPE

Article 1: Subject matter of the resale right

1.   Member States shall provide, for the benefit of the author of an original work of art, a resale right, to be defined as an inalienable right, which cannot be waived, even in advance, to receive a royalty based on the sale price obtained for any resale of the work, subsequent to the first transfer of the work by the author.

2.   The right referred to in paragraph 1 shall apply to all acts of resale involving as sellers, buyers or intermediaries art market professionals, such as salesrooms, art galleries and, in general, any dealers in works of art.

3.   Member States may provide that the right referred to in paragraph 1 shall not apply to acts of resale where the seller has acquired the work directly from the author less than three years before that resale and where the resale price does not exceed EUR 10,000.00.

4.   The royalty shall be payable by the seller. Member States may provide that one of the natural or legal persons referred to in paragraph 2 other than the seller shall alone be liable or shall share liability with the seller for payment of the royalty.

Article 2: Works of art to which the resale right relates

1.   For the purposes of this Directive, "original work of art" means works of graphic or plastic art such as pictures, collages, paintings, drawings, engravings, prints, lithographs, sculptures, tapestries, ceramics, glassware and photographs, provided they are made by the artist himself or are copies considered to be original works of art.

2.   Copies of works of art covered by this Directive, which have been made in limited numbers by the artist himself or under his authority, shall be considered to be original works of art for the purposes of this Directive. Such copies will normally have been numbered, signed or otherwise duly authorised by the artist.

CHAPTER II: PARTICULAR PROVISIONS

Article 3: Threshold

1.   It shall be for the Member States to set a minimum sale price from which the sales referred to in Article 1 shall be subject to resale right.

2.   This minimum sale price may not under any circumstances exceed EUR 3,000.00.

Article 4: Rates

1. The royalty provided for in Article 1 shall be set at the following rates:

> (a) 4% for the portion of the sale price up to EUR 50,000;
>
> (b) 3% for the portion of the sale price from EUR 50,000.01 to EUR 200,000;
>
> (c) 1% for the portion of the sale price from EUR 200,000.01 to EUR 350,000;
>
> (d) 0.5% for the portion of the sale price from EUR 350,000.01 to EUR 500,000;
>
> (e) 0.25% for the portion of the sale price exceeding EUR 500,000.

However, the total amount of the royalty may not exceed EUR 12,500.

* * *

Article 6: Persons entitled to receive royalties

1. The royalty provided for under Article 1 shall be payable to the author of the work and, subject to Article 8(2), after his death to those entitled under him/her.

2. Member States may provide for compulsory or optional collective management of the royalty provided for under Article 1.

Article 7: Third-country nationals entitled to receive royalties

1. Member States shall provide that authors who are nationals of third countries and, subject to Article 8(2), their successors in title shall enjoy the resale right in accordance with this Directive and the legislation of the Member State concerned only if legislation in the country of which the author or his/her successor in title is a national permits resale right protection in that country for authors from the Member States and their successors in title.

2. On the basis of information provided by the Member States, the Commission shall publish as soon as possible an indicative list of those third countries which fulfil the condition set out in paragraph 1. This list shall be kept up to date.

3. Any Member State may treat authors who are not nationals of a Member State but who have their habitual residence in that Member State in the same way as its own nationals for the purpose of resale right protection.

Article 8: Term of protection of the resale right

1. The term of protection of the resale right shall correspond to that laid down in Article 1 of Directive 93/98/EEC [which estab-

lishes the European Union's copyright term as the life of the author plus 70 years].

* * *

Notes

1. Typically an advocate of strong authors' rights, France enacted its first resale royalty (or *droit de suite*) statute in the 1920s. In the decades that followed, several other European nations followed suit, although even after the 2006 deadline had passed for implementing the Resale Rights Directive into their domestic laws, some EU nations had still not complied.

Based on the experience in France and Germany, it appears that resale royalties have provided a much greater benefit to the heirs of deceased artists than to living artists. It has been estimated that 70% of the resale royalties collected in France have gone to the heirs of the same six or seven artists, including Picasso and Matisse.

2. The resale right has been a "tough sell" outside of Europe. Why might this be?

F. PUBLIC PERFORMANCE RIGHTS

UNITED STATES—SECTION 110(5) OF THE US COPYRIGHT ACT

World Trade Organization
Report of the Panel, June 15, 2000

I. Introduction

On 26 January 1999, the European Communities and their member States (hereafter referred to as the European Communities) requested consultations with the United States under Article 4 of the Understanding on Rules and Procedures Governing the Settlement of Disputes ("DSU") and Article 64.1 of the Agreement on Trade–Related Aspects of Intellectual Property Rights ("TRIPS Agreement") regarding Section 110(5) of the United States Copyright Act as amended by the "Fairness in Music Licensing Act" enacted on 27 October 1998.

The European Communities and the United States held consultations on 2 March 1999, but failed to reach a mutually satisfactory solution. On 15 April 1999, the European Communities requested the establishment of a panel under Article 6 of the DSU and Article 64.1 of the TRIPS Agreement.

* * *

II. Factual aspects

The dispute concerns Section 110(5) of the U.S. Copyright Act of 1976, as amended by the Fairness in Music Licensing Act of 1998 ("the 1998 Amendment"), which entered into force on 26 January 1999. The provisions of Section 110(5) place limitations on the exclusive rights provided to owners of copyright in Section 106 of the Copyright Act in respect of certain performances and displays.

* * *

* * * [T]he homestyle exemption was originally intended to apply to performances of all types of works. However, given that the present subparagraph (B) applies to "a performance or display of a nondramatic musical work", the parties agree, by way of an *a contrario* interpretation, that the effect of the introductory phrase "except as provided in subparagraph (B)", that was added to the text in subparagraph (A), is that it narrows down the application of subparagraph (A) to works other than "nondramatic musical works".

The Panel notes that it is the common understanding of the parties that the expression "nondramatic musical works" in subparagraph (B) excludes from its application the communication of music that is part of an opera, operetta, musical or other similar dramatic work when performed in a dramatic context. All other musical works are covered by that expression, including individual songs taken from dramatic works when performed outside of any dramatic context. Subparagraph (B) would, therefore, apply for example to an individual song taken from a musical and played on the radio. Consequently, the operation of subparagraph (A) is limited to such musical works as are not covered by subparagraph (B), for example a communication of a broadcast of a dramatic rendition of the music written for an opera.

* * *

VI. Findings

* * *

D. *Substantive Aspects of the Dispute*

1. **General considerations about the exclusive rights concerned and limitations thereto**

(a) **Exclusive rights implicated by the EC claims**

Articles 9–13 of Section 1 of Part II of the TRIPS Agreement entitled "Copyright and Related Rights" deal with the substantive standards of copyright protection. Article 9.1 of the TRIPS Agreement obliges WTO Members to comply with Articles 1–21 of the Berne Convention (1971) (with the exception of Article 6*bis* on moral rights and the rights derived therefrom) and the Appendix thereto. The European Communities alleges that subparagraphs (A) and (B) of Section 110(5) are inconsistent primarily with Article

11*bis*(1)(iii) but also with Article 11(1)(ii) of the Berne Convention (1971) as incorporated into the TRIPS Agreement.

We note that through their incorporation, the substantive rules of the Berne Convention (1971), including the provisions of its Articles 11*bis*(1)(iii) and 11(1)(ii), have become part of the TRIPS Agreement and as provisions of that Agreement have to be read as applying to WTO Members.

(i) Article 11bis of the Berne Convention (1971)

The provision of particular relevance for this dispute is Article 11*bis*(1)(iii). Article 11*bis*(1) provides:

"Authors of literary and artistic works shall enjoy the exclusive right of authorizing:

(i) the broadcasting of their works or the communication thereof to the public by any other means of wireless diffusion of signs, sounds or images;

(ii) any communication to the public by wire or by re-broadcasting of the broadcast of the work, when this communication is made by an organization other than the original one;

(iii) the public communication by loudspeaker or any other analogous instrument transmitting, by signs, sounds or images, the broadcast of the work."

In the light of Article 2 of the Berne Convention (1971), "artistic" works in the meaning of Article 11*bis*(1) include nondramatic and other musical works. Each of the subparagraphs of Article 11*bis*(1) confers a separate exclusive right; exploitation of a work in a manner covered by any of these subparagraphs requires an authorization by the right holder. For example, the communication to the public of a broadcast creates an additional audience and the right holder is given control over, and may expect remuneration from, this new public performance of his or her work.

The right provided under subparagraph (i) of Article 11*bis*(1) is to authorize the broadcasting of a work and the communication thereof to the public by any other means of wireless diffusion of signs, sounds or images. It applies to both radio and television broadcasts. Subparagraph (ii) concerns the subsequent use of this emission; the authors' exclusive right covers any communication to the public by wire or by rebroadcasting of the broadcast of the work, when the communication is made by an organization other than the original one.

Subparagraph (iii) provides an exclusive right to authorize the public communication of the broadcast of the work by loudspeaker, on a television screen, or by other similar means. Such communication involves a new public performance of a work contained in a broadcast, which requires a licence from the right holder. For the purposes of this dispute, the claims raised by the European Communities under Article 11*bis*(1) are limited to subparagraph (iii).

(ii) Article 11 of the Berne Convention (1971)

Of relevance to this dispute are also the exclusive rights conferred by Article 11(1)(ii) of the Berne Convention (1971). Article 11(1) provides:

> "Authors of dramatic, dramatico-musical and musical works shall enjoy the exclusive right of authorizing:
>
> (i) the public performance of their works, including such public performance by any means or process;
>
> (ii) any communication to the public of the performance of their works."

As in the case of Article 11*bis*(1) of the Berne Convention (1971), which concerns broadcasting to the public and communication of a broadcast to the public, the exclusive rights conferred by Article 11 cover *public* performance; private performance does not require authorization. Public performance includes performance by any means or process, such as performance by means of recordings (*e.g.*, CDs, cassettes and videos). It also includes communication to the public of a performance of the work. The claims raised by the European Communities under Article 11(1) of the Berne Convention (1971) are limited to its subparagraph (ii).

Regarding the relationship between Articles 11 and 11*bis*, we note that the rights conferred in Article 11(1)(ii) concern the communication to the public of performances of works in general. Article 11*bis*(1)(iii) is a specific rule conferring exclusive rights concerning the public communication by loudspeaker or any other analogous instrument transmitting, by signs, sounds or images, the broadcast of a work.

As set out in section III above, the European Communities raises claims against Section 110(5) primarily under Article 11*bis*(1)(iii), which covers the communication to the public of a broadcast which has been transmitted at some point by [electromagnetic] waves. But the EC claims also relate to Article 11(1)(ii) to the extent that a communication to the public concerns situations where the entire transmission has been by wire.

We share the understanding of the parties that a communication to the public by loudspeaker of a performance of a work transmitted by means other than [electromagnetic] waves is covered by the exclusive rights conferred by Article 11(1) of the Berne Convention (1971). Moreover, we note that both parties consider that it is the third exclusive right under Article 11*bis*(1)(iii)—*i.e.*, the author's right to authorize the public communication of a broadcast of a work by loudspeaker or any other analogous instrument—which is primarily concerned in this dispute. But we also note that there is no disagreement between the parties that both subparagraphs (A) and (B) of Section 110(5) implicate both Articles 11*bis*(1)(iii) and 11(1)(ii)—albeit to a varying extent.

Both provisions, *i.e.*, Articles 11*bis*(1)(iii) and 11(1)(ii) of the Berne Convention (1971) are implicated only if there is a *public* element to the broadcasting or communication operation. We note that it is undisputed between the parties that playing radio or television music by establishments covered by Section 110(5) involves a communication that is available to the *public* in the sense of Articles 11*bis*(1)(iii) and 11(1)(ii) of the Berne Convention (1971). We share this view of the parties.

As noted above, the United States acknowledges that subparagraphs (A) and (B) of Section 110(5) implicate Articles 11*bis*(1)(iii) and 11(1)(ii) of the Berne Convention (1971). Consequently, the core question before this Panel is which of the exceptions under the TRIPS Agreement invoked are relevant to this dispute and whether the conditions for their invocation are met so as to justify the exemptions under subparagraphs (A) and (B) of Section 110(5) of the U.S. Copyright Act.

(b) Limitations and exceptions

(i) Introduction

A major issue in this dispute is the interpretation and application to the facts of this case of Article 13 of the TRIPS Agreement. The U.S. defense is firmly based upon it. * * *

Article 13 of the TRIPS Agreement, entitled "Limitations and Exceptions", is the general exception clause applicable to exclusive rights of the holders of copyright. It provides:

> "Members shall confine limitations or exceptions to exclusive rights to certain special cases which do not conflict with a normal exploitation of the work and do not unreasonably prejudice the legitimate interests of the right holder."

* * *

2. The three criteria test under Article 13 of the TRIPS Agreement

(a) General introduction

Article 13 of the TRIPS Agreement requires that limitations and exceptions to exclusive rights (1) be confined to certain special cases, (2) do not conflict with a normal exploitation of the work, and (3) do not unreasonably prejudice the legitimate interests of the right holder. The principle of effective treaty interpretation requires us to give a distinct meaning to each of the three conditions and to avoid a reading that could reduce any of the conditions to "redundancy or inutility." The three conditions apply on a cumulative basis, each being a separate and independent requirement that must be satisfied. Failure to comply with any one of the three conditions results in the Article 13 exception being disallowed. * * *

* * *

(b) "Certain special cases"

(i) General interpretative analysis

* * *

In the case at hand, in order to determine whether subparagraphs (B) and (A) of Section 110(5) are confined to "certain special cases", we first examine whether the exceptions have been clearly defined. Second, we ascertain whether the exemptions are narrow in scope, *inter alia*, with respect to their reach. In that respect, we take into account what percentage of eating and drinking establishments and retail establishments may benefit from the business exemption under subparagraph (B), and in turn what percentage of establishments may take advantage of the homestyle exemption under subparagraph (A). On a subsidiary basis, we consider whether it is possible to draw inferences about the reach of the business and homestyle exemptions from the stated policy purposes underlying these exemptions according to the statements made during the U.S. legislative process.

(ii) The business exemption of subparagraph (B)

* * *

It appears that the European Communities does not dispute the fact that subparagraph (B) is clearly defined in respect of the size limits of establishments and the type of equipment that may be used by establishments above the applicable limits. The primary bone of contention between the parties is whether the business exemption, given its scope and reach, can be considered as a "special" case within the meaning of the first condition of Article 13.

The Congressional Research Service ("CRS") estimated in 1995 the percentage of the U.S. eating and drinking establishments and retail establishments that would have fallen at that time below the size limits of 3,500 square feet and 1,500 square feet respectively. Its study found that:

    (d) 65.2 per cent of all eating establishments;

    (e) 71.8 per cent of all drinking establishments; and

    (f) 27 per cent of all retail establishments

would have fallen below these size limits.

The United States confirms these figures as far as eating and drinking establishments are concerned.

We note that this study was made in 1995 using the size limit of 3,500 square feet for eating and drinking establishments, and the size limit of 1,500 square feet for retail establishments, while the size limits under subparagraph (B) now are 3,750 square feet for eating and drinking establishments and 2,000 square feet for retail establishments. Therefore, in our view, it is safe to assume that the actual percentage of establishments which may fall within the finally enacted business exemption in the Fairness in Music Licensing Act of 1998 is higher than the above percentages.

* * *

We note that, according to its preparatory works, Article 11*bis*(iii) of the Berne Convention (1971) was intended to provide right holders with a right to authorize the use of their works in the types of establishments covered by the exemption contained in Section 110(5)(B). Specifically, the preparatory works for the 1948 Brussels Conference indicate that the establishments that were intended to be covered were places "above all, where people meet: in the cinema, in restaurants, in tea rooms, railway carriages...." The preparatory works also refer to places such as factories, shops and offices. We fail to see how a law that exempts a major part of the users that were specifically intended to be covered by the provisions of Article 11*bis*(1)(iii) could be considered as a *special* case in the sense of the first condition of Article 13 of the TRIPS Agreement.

We are aware that eating, drinking and retail establishments are not the only potential users of music covered by the exclusive rights conferred under Articles 11*bis*(1)(iii) and 11(1)(ii) of the Berne Convention (1971). The United States has mentioned, *inter alia*, conventions, fairs and sporting events as other potential users of performances of works in the meaning of the above Articles. However, we believe that these examples of other potential users do not detract from the fact that eating, drinking and retail establishments are among the major groups of potential users of the works in the ways that are covered by the above-mentioned Articles.

The factual information presented to us indicates that a substantial majority of eating and drinking establishments and close to half of retail establishments are covered by the exemption contained in subparagraph (B) of Section 110(5) of the U.S. Copyright Act. Therefore, we conclude that the exemption does not qualify as a "certain special case" in the meaning of the first condition of Article 13.

* * *

(iii) The homestyle exemption of subparagraph (A)

We examine now whether the homestyle exemption in subparagraph (A), in the form in which it is currently in force in the United States, is a "certain special case" in the meaning of the first condition of Article 13 of the TRIPS Agreement.

The United States submits that the exemption of subparagraph (A) is confined to "certain special cases", because its scope is limited to the use involving a "homestyle" receiving apparatus. In the U.S. view, in the amended version of 1998 as well, this is a well-defined fact-specific standard. The essentially identical description of the homestyle exemption in the original Section 110(5) of 1976 was sufficiently clear and narrow for U.S. courts to reasonably and consistently apply the exception—including square footage limitation since the *Aiken* case—in a number of individual decisions. For the United States, the fact that judges have weighed the various factors slightly differently in making their individual decisions is simply a typical feature of a common-law system.

The European Communities contends that the criteria of the homestyle exemption in subparagraph (A) are ambiguously worded because the expression "a single receiving apparatus of a kind commonly used in private homes" is in itself imprecise and a "moving target" due to technological development. Also the variety of approaches and factors used by U.S. courts in applying the original version of the homestyle exemption are proof for the European Communities that the wording of subparagraph (A) of Section 110(5) is vague and open-ended.

Beneficiaries of the homestyle exemption

* * *

We note that the parties have submitted quantitative information on the coverage of subparagraph (A) with respect to eating, drinking and other establishments. The 1995 CRS study found that:

(a) 16 per cent of all U.S. eating establishments;

(b) 13.5 per cent of all U.S. drinking establishments; and

(c) 18 per cent of all U.S. retail establishments

were as big as or smaller than the *Aiken* restaurant (1,055 square feet of total space), and could thus benefit from the homestyle exemption. These figures are not disputed between the parties. The

United States expressly confirms these figures as far as eating and drinking establishments are concerned.

We believe that from a quantitative perspective the reach of subparagraph (A) in respect of potential users is limited to a comparably small percentage of all eating, drinking and retail establishments in the United States.

We are mindful of the above-mentioned EC argument alleging a judicial trend towards broadening the homestyle exemption of 1976 in recent years. We cannot exclude the possibility that in the future U.S. courts could establish precedents that would lead to the expansion of the scope of the currently applicable homestyle exemption as regards covered establishments. But we also note that since 1976 U.S. courts have in the vast majority of cases applied the homestyle exemption in a sufficiently consistent and clearly delineated manner. Given the sufficiently consistent and narrow application practice of the homestyle exemption of 1976, we see no need to hypothesise whether at some point in the future U.S. case law might lead to a *de facto* expansion of the homestyle exemption of 1998.

Homestyle equipment

We note that what is referred to as homestyle equipment (*i.e.,* "a single receiving apparatus of a kind commonly used in private homes") might vary between different countries, is subject to changing consumer preferences in a given country, and may evolve as a result of technological development. We thus agree in principle with the European Communities that the homestyle equipment that was used in U.S. households in 1976 (when the original homestyle exemption was enacted) is not necessarily identical to the equipment used in 1998 (when U.S. copyright legislation was amended) or at a future point in time. However, we recall that the term "*certain* special case" connotes "known and particularised, but not explicitly identified". In our view, the term "homestyle equipment" expresses the degree of clarity in definition required under Article 13's first condition. In our view, a Member is not required to identify homestyle equipment in terms of exceedingly detailed technical specifications in order to meet the standard of clarity set by the first condition. While we recognize that homestyle equipment may become technologically more sophisticated over time, we see no need to enter into speculations about potential future developments in the homestyle equipment market. At any rate, we recall that our factual determinations are invariably limited to what currently is being perceived as homestyle equipment in the U.S. market.

Musical works covered by subparagraph (A)

We have noted the common view of the parties that the addition of the introductory phrase "except as provided in subparagraph (B)" to the homestyle exemption in the 1998 Amendment should be understood by way of an *a contrario* argument as limiting the coverage of the exemption to works other than "nondramatic" musical works. As regards musical works, the currently applicable version of the homestyle exemption is thus understood to apply to the communication of music that is part of an opera, operetta, musical or other similar dramatic work when performed in a dramatic context. All other musical works are covered by the expression "nondramatic" musical works, including individual songs taken from dramatic works when performed outside any dramatic context. Subparagraph (B) would, therefore, apply for example to an individual song taken from a musical and played on the radio. Consequently, given the common view of the parties, the operation of subparagraph (A) is limited to such musical works as are not covered by subparagraph (B), for example a communication of a broadcast of a dramatic rendition of the music written for an opera, operetta, musical or other similar works.

While taking this position on the interpretation of subparagraph (A), the European Communities has, however, cautioned that U.S. courts might read a broader coverage into subparagraph (A) at a future point in time. In view of the common understanding of the parties in the current dispute, and given the EC responses to our questions about the scope of its claims, we see no need to speculate whether in the future subparagraph (A) could be interpreted by U.S. courts to cover musical works other than those considered as "dramatic".

In practice, this means that most if not virtually all music played on the radio or television is covered by subparagraph (B). Subparagraph (A) covers, in accordance with the common understanding of the parties, dramatic renditions of operas, operettas, musicals and other similar dramatic works. We consider that limiting the application of subparagraph (A) to the public communication of transmissions embodying such works, gives its provisions a quite narrow scope of application in practice.

* * *

Taking into account the specific limits imposed in subparagraph (A) and its legislative history, as well as in its considerably narrow application in the subsequent court practice on the beneficiaries of the exemption, permissible equipment and categories of works, we are of the view that the homestyle exemption in subparagraph (A) of Section 110(5) as amended in 1998 is well-defined and limited in its scope and reach. We, therefore, conclude that the exemption is confined to certain special cases within the meaning of the first condition of Article 13 of the TRIPS Agreement.

* * *

(c) "Not conflict with a normal exploitation of the work"

* * *

(ii) The business exemption of subparagraph (B)

* * *

We recall that a substantial majority of eating and drinking establishments and close to half of retail establishments are eligible to benefit from the business exemption. This constitutes a major potential source of royalties for the exercise of the exclusive rights contained in Articles 11(1)*bis*(iii) and 11(1)(ii) of the Berne Convention (1971), as demonstrated by the figures of the D & B studies referred to under our analysis of the first condition of Article 13.

We recall that subparagraph (B) of Section 110(5) exempts communication to the public of radio and television broadcasts, while the playing of musical works from CDs and tapes (or live music) is not covered by it. Given that we have not been provided with reasons other than historical ones for this distinction, we see no logical reason to differentiate between broadcast and recorded music when assessing what is a normal use of musical works.

* * *

Right holders of musical works would expect to be in a position to authorize the use of broadcasts of radio and television music by many of the establishments covered by the exemption and, as appropriate, receive compensation for the use of their works. Consequently, we cannot but conclude that an exemption of such scope as subparagraph (B) conflicts with the "normal exploitation" of the work in relation to the exclusive rights conferred by Articles 11*bis*(1)(iii) and 11(1)(ii) of the Berne Convention (1971).

In the light of these considerations, we conclude that the business exemption embodied in subparagraph (B) conflicts with a normal exploitation of the work within the meaning of the second condition of Article 13.

(iii) The homestyle exemption of subparagraph (A)

The United States argues that the homestyle exemption, even before nondramatic musical works were removed from its scope through the 1998 Amendment, was limited to the establishments that were not large enough to justify a subscription to a commercial background music service. As noted in the House Report (1976), the

United States Congress intended that this exemption would merely codify the licensing practices already in effect. The original home-style exemption of 1976 was intended to affect only those establishments that were not likely otherwise to enter into a licence, or would not have been licensed under the practices at that time. The United States contends that subparagraph (A) of the amended Section 110(5) does not conflict with the expectation of right holders concerning the normal exploitation of their works.

As regards the permissible equipment, we note that, according to the House Report (1976), the purpose of the exemption in its original form was to exempt from copyright liability "anyone who merely turns on, in a public place, an ordinary radio or television receiving apparatus of a kind commonly sold to members of the public for private use". "[The clause] would impose liability where the proprietor has a commercial 'sound system' installed or converts a standard home receiving apparatus (by augmenting it with sophisticated or extensive amplification equipment) into the equivalent of a commercial sound system." We also recall the rationale behind the homestyle exemption as expressed in the legislative history relating to its original version: "The basic rationale of this clause is that the secondary use of the transmission by turning on an ordinary receiver in public is so remote and minimal that no further liability should be imposed."

In other words, the provision is intended to define the borderline between two situations: a situation where one listens to the radio or watches the television—this is clearly not covered by the scope of copyright and, hence, outside normal exploitation of works—and a situation where one uses appropriate equipment to cause a new public performance of music contained in a broadcast or other transmission. This borderline is defined by laying emphasis on "turning on an ordinary receiver", albeit that members of the public might also hear the transmission.

As regards the beneficiaries of the homestyle exemption, we note that its legislative history reveals the intention that the exemption should affect only those establishments that were not likely otherwise to enter into a licence, or would not have been licensed under the practices at that time. As pointed out above, according to the 1995 CRS study, the number of establishments that were as big or smaller than the *Aiken* restaurant and could benefit from the homestyle exemption is limited to a comparatively small percentage of all eating, drinking and retail establishments in the United States.

The United States argues that the homestyle exemption of 1998 is even less capable of being in conflict with normal exploitation of works because its scope is now limited to works other than nondramatic musical works. While a collective licensing mechanism for nondramatic musical works exists in the United States, there is no such mechanism for "dramatic" musical works and there is little or no direct licensing by individual right holders of the establishments in question. Therefore, in the U.S. view, authors might not reasonably expect to exploit "dramatic" musical works in the normal course of events through licensing public performances or communications thereof to the establishments that may invoke subparagraph (A).

We recall that it is the common understanding of the parties that the operation of subparagraph (A) is limited, as regards musical works, to the public communication of transmissions embodying dramatic renditions of "dramatic" musical works, such as operas, operettas, musicals and other similar dramatic works. Consequently, performances of, *e.g.*, individual songs from a dramatic musical work outside a dramatic context would constitute a rendition of a nondramatic work and fall within the purview of subparagraph (B).

It is our understanding that the parties agree that the right holders do not normally license or attempt to license the public communication of transmissions embodying dramatic renditions of "dramatic" musical works in the sense of Article 11*bis*(1)(iii) and/or 11(1)(ii). We have not been provided with information about any existing licensing practices concerning the communication to the public of broadcasts of performances of dramatic works (*e.g.*, operas, operettas, musicals) by eating, drinking or retail establishments in the United States or any other country. In this respect, we fail to see how the homestyle exemption, as limited to works other than nondramatic musical works in its revised form, could acquire economic or practical importance of any considerable dimension for the right holders of musical works.

Therefore, we conclude that the homestyle exemption contained in subparagraph (A) of Section 110(5) does not conflict with a normal exploitation of works within the meaning of the second condition of Article 13.

(d) "Not unreasonably prejudice the legitimate interests of the right holder"

* * *

(ii) *The business exemption of subparagraph (B)*

[The United States and the European Communities submitted vastly different estimates of the annual economic losses experienced by right holders due to the section 110(5)(B) exemption. After examining the methodologies underlying each estimate, the Panel concluded that the United States had failed to meet its burden of proof to establish that the exemption "does not unreasonably prejudice the legitimate interests of the right holder." Accordingly, the exemption does not satisfy the third condition of Article 13 of TRIPS.]

* * *

(iii) The homestyle exemption of subparagraph (A)

* * *

We recall our discussion concerning the legislative history of the original homestyle exemption in connection with the first and second conditions of Article 13. In particular, as regards the beneficiaries of the exemption, the Conference Report (1976) elaborated on the rationale of the exemption by noting that the intent was to exempt a small commercial establishment "which was not of sufficient size to justify, as a practical matter, a subscription to a commercial background music service". We also recall the estimations on the percentages of establishments covered by the exemption. Moreover, the exemption was applicable to such establishments only if they use homestyle equipment. The House Report (1976) noted that "[the clause] would impose liability where the proprietor has a commercial 'sound system' installed or converts a standard home receiving apparatus (by augmenting it with sophisticated or extensive amplification equipment) into the equivalent of a commercial sound system." In this respect, we refer to our discussion on permissible equipment as well as the applicability of the exemption to Internet transmissions in connection with the first and second conditions of Article 13.

Furthermore, we recall the common understanding of the parties that the operation of the homestyle exemption as contained in the 1998 Amendment has been limited, as regards musical works, to the public communication of transmissions embodying dramatic renditions of "dramatic" musical works (such as operas, operettas, musicals and other similar dramatic works). We have not been presented with evidence suggesting that right holders would have licensed or attempted to license the public communication, within the meaning of Article 11(1)(ii) or 11*bis*(1)(iii) of the Berne Convention (1971), of broadcasts of performances embodying dramatic renditions of "dramatic" musical works either before the enactment of the original homestyle exemption or after the 1998 Amendment. We also fail to see how communications to the public of renditions of entire dramatic works could acquire such economic or practical importance that it could cause unreasonable prejudice to the legitimate interests of right holders.

We note that playing music by the small establishments covered by the exemption by means of homestyle apparatus has never been a significant source of revenue collection for CMOs. We recall our view that, for the purposes of assessing unreasonable prejudice to the legitimate interests of right holders, potential losses of right holders, too, are relevant. However, we have not been presented with persuasive information suggesting that such potential effects of significant economic or practical importance could occur that they would give rise to an unreasonable level of prejudice to legitimate interests of right holders. In particular, as regards the exemption as amended in 1998 to exclude from its scope nondramatic musical works, the European Communities has not explicitly claimed that the exemption would currently cause any prejudice to right holders.

In the light of the considerations above, we conclude that the homestyle exemption contained in subparagraph (A) of Section 110(5) does not cause unreasonable prejudice to the legitimate interests of the right holders within the meaning of the third condition of Article 13.

VII.   Conclusions and Recommendations

In the light of the findings * * * above, the Panel concludes that:

> (a) Subparagraph (A) of Section 110(5) of the U.S. Copyright Act meets the requirements of Article 13 of the TRIPS Agreement and is thus consistent with Articles 11*bis*(1)(iii) and 11(1)(ii) of the Berne Convention (1971) as incorporated into the TRIPS Agreement by Article 9.1 of that Agreement.

> (b) Subparagraph (B) of Section 110(5) of the U.S. Copyright Act does not meet the requirements of Article 13 of the TRIPS Agreement and is thus inconsistent with Articles 11*bis*(1)(iii) and 11(1)(ii) of the Berne Convention (1971) as incorporated into the TRIPS Agreement by Article 9.1 of that Agreement.

The Panel recommends that the Dispute Settlement Body request the United States to bring subparagraph (B) of Section 110(5) into conformity with its obligations under the TRIPS Agreement.

Notes

1.   Do you agree with the argument made by the U.S. Trade Representative in this proceeding that the 1998 amendments removed nondramatic musical works from the scope of section 110(5)(A)? If federal

courts were to reject this interpretation, how would this affect the analysis of whether section 110(5)(A) violates TRIPS?

2. The question of the appropriate trade sanction to be imposed against the U.S. for its failure to amend or repeal section 110(5)(B) is still being negotiated.

3. *Public performance rights in sound recordings*: The 1961 Rome Convention for the Protection of Performers, Producers of Phonograms and Broadcasting Organizations requires signatories to grant public performance rights to record producers and performers. This performance right falls into the "neighboring rights" category. Specifically, Article 12 of the Convention provides:

> If a phonogram published for commercial purposes, or a reproduction of such phonogram, is used directly for broadcasting or for any communication to the public, a single equitable remuneration shall be paid by the user to the performers, or to the producers of the phonograms, or to both. Domestic law may, in the absence of agreement between these parties, lay down the conditions as to the sharing of this remuneration.

The Rome Convention has 88 signatories. However, the United States is not among them. Unlike virtually every other western nation, and several Asian nations as well, the United States does not recognize a general public performance right in sound recordings. Instead, section 106(6) provides a limited public performance right that applies only to digital transmissions.

It is generally understood that, as a neighboring right, the public performance right in sound recordings is not subject to the nondiscrimination ("national treatment") provisions of the Berne Convention. The national treatment provisions of the Rome Convention apply only to its signatories. Accordingly, most nations do not extend their public performance rights to recordings made in the United States, because the United States does not reciprocate. What arguments can you think of both for and against adopting a general public performance right for sound recordings in the United States? (Legislation extending section 106(6) to terrestrial radio was under consideration as of June, 2009.)

4. *Performers' Rights*: Several international agreements recognize performers' rights in their performances. Article 7(1) of the Rome Convention, which applies to a wide variety of live and recorded performers, provides:

> 1. The protection provided for performers by this Convention shall include the possibility of preventing:
>
> (a) the broadcasting and the communication to the public, without their consent, of their performance, except where the performance used in the broadcasting or the public communication is itself already a broadcast performance or is made from a fixation;

(b) the fixation, without their consent, of their unfixed performance;

(c) the reproduction, without their consent, of a fixation of their performance:

(i) if the original fixation itself was made without their consent;

(ii) if the reproduction is made for purposes different from those for which the performers gave their consent;

(iii) if the original fixation was made in accordance with the provisions of Article 15 (permitting exceptions primarily for private use, news reporting, and research), and the reproduction is made for purposes different from those referred to in those provisions.

Similar protections are required under TRIPS (Art. 14) and the WIPO Performances and Phonograms Treaty (Arts. 6–10); Article 9 of the latter also extends rental rights to performers, but only with respect to performances fixed on phonograms. In each case, the minimum term of protection is 50 years.

In addition to the economic rights described above, the WIPO Performances and Phonograms Treaty requires protection of certain moral rights. Article 5 provides:

(1) Independently of a performer's economic rights, and even after the transfer of those rights, the performer shall, as regards his live aural performances or performances fixed in phonograms, have the right to claim to be identified as the performer of his performances, except where omission is dictated by the manner of the use of the performance, and to object to any distortion, mutilation or other modification of his performances that would be prejudicial to his reputation.

Here, too, the minimum term of protection is 50 years.

G.   CROSS–BORDER INFRINGEMENT

SOCIETY OF COMPOSERS, AUTHORS & MUSIC PUBLISHERS OF CANADA v. CANADIAN ASSN. OF INTERNET PROVIDERS

Supreme Court of Canada, 2004
2004 CarswellNat 1919
2004 SCC 45, [2004] 2 S.C.R. 427

[Canada's Society of Composers, Authors and Music Publishers ("SOCAN") sought to impose liability for royalties on Internet Service Providers located in Canada for music downloaded in Canada from Internet transmissions originating outside of Canada. The

Copyright Board held that no obligation to royalties arose from these transmissions, because an Internet communication occurs in Canada only if it originates from a server in Canada. Accordingly, a content provider was subject to the Canadian royalty only if the content was posted on a server located in Canada. The portion of the Supreme Court's opinion discussing the standards for ISP liability appears in Chapter 6. The passages reproduced below contain the court's discussion of whether Canadian copyright law applies to Internet transmissions originating overseas.]

Binnie J.:

* * *

IV. Analysis

This Court has recently described the Copyright Act as providing "a balance between promoting the public interest in the encouragement and dissemination of works of the arts and intellect and obtaining a just reward for the creator (or, more accurately, to prevent someone other than the creator from appropriating whatever benefits may be generated)". The capacity of the Internet to disseminate "works of the arts and intellect" is one of the great innovations of the information age. Its use should be facilitated rather than discouraged, but this should not be done unfairly at the expense of those who created the works of arts and intellect in the first place.

The issue of the proper balance in matters of copyright plays out against the much larger conundrum of trying to apply national laws to a fast-evolving technology that in essence respects no national boundaries. * * * It is with an eye to this broader context that the relatively precise questions raised by the Copyright Board must be considered.

A. Communication under the Copyright Act

It is an infringement for anyone to do, without the consent of the copyright owner, "anything that, by this Act, only the owner of the copyright has the right to do" (s. 27(1)), including, since the 1988 amendments, the right "to communicate the work to the public by telecommunication ... and to *authorize* any such acts" (emphasis added) (s. 3(1)(f)). In the same series of amendments, "telecommunication" was defined as "any transmission of signs, signals, writings, images or sounds or intelligence of any nature by wire, radio, visual, optical or other electromagnetic system" (s. 2). The Board ruled that a telecommunication occurs when the music is transmitted from the host server to the end user. I agree with this. The respondent says that the appellants as intermediaries participate in any such transmission of their copyrighted works, and authorize others to do so, and should therefore be required to pay compensation fixed under Tariff 22.

* * *

The Board took the view that "[t]o occur in Canada, a communication must originate from a server located in Canada on which content has been posted", except perhaps if the content provider has "the intention to communicate it specifically to recipients in Canada". In my view, with respect, this is too rigid and mechanical a test. An Internet communication that crosses one or more national boundaries "occurs" in more than one country, at a minimum the country of transmission and the country of reception. In Dow Jones & Co. v. Gutnick (High Court of Australia 2002), 194 A.L.R. 433, [2002] HCA 56, the defendant argued that the appropriate law should be that of the jurisdiction where the host server is located, but this was rejected in favour of the law of the State of reception by the High Court of Australia. To the extent the Board held that a communication that does not originate in Canada does not occur in Canada, I disagree with its decision.

At the end of the transmission, the end user has a musical work in his or her possession that was not there before. The work has, necessarily, been communicated, irrespective of its point of origin. If the communication is by virtue of the Internet, there has been a "telecommunication". To hold otherwise would not only fly in the face of the ordinary use of language but would have serious consequences in other areas of law relevant to the Internet, including Canada's ability to deal with criminal and civil liability for objectionable communications entering the country from abroad.

The word "communicate" is an ordinary English word that means to "impart" or "transmit". Communication presupposes a sender and a receiver of what is transmitted. The "communicator" is the sender, not the recipient. Thus, says SOCAN, all those entities located in Canada (other than Backbone Service Providers) who participate in the act of imparting or transmitting a copyrighted work across the Internet are guilty of infringement of the Canadian copyright. Any lesser protection, SOCAN says, would not strike an appropriate balance between the rights of copyright owners and the public interest in the encouragement and dissemination of their musical works.

* * *

C.   Application and Scope of the Copyright Act

The Federal Court of Appeal was unanimous in its conclusion that copyright infringement occurs in Canada where there is a real and substantial connection between this country and the communication at issue. * * *

I agree with the general proposition that the Board erred in holding that the only relevant connection between Canada and the communication is the location of the host server. As a matter of international law and practice, as well as the legislative reach of our Parliament, Canada's jurisdiction is not so limited.

It is a different issue, however, whether Canada intended to exercise its copyright jurisdiction to impose copyright liability on every participant in an Internet communication with "a real and substantial connection" to Canada. This second issue raises questions of statutory interpretation of the Copyright Act.

1.   Canada's Legislative Reach

While the Parliament of Canada, unlike the legislatures of the Provinces, has the legislative competence to enact laws having extraterritorial effect, it is presumed not to intend to do so, in the absence of clear words or necessary implication to the contrary. This is because "[i]n our modern world of easy travel and with the emergence of a global economic order, chaotic situations would often result if the principle of territorial jurisdiction were not, at least generally, respected".

While the notion of comity among independent nation States lacks the constitutional status it enjoys among the provinces of the Canadian federation, and does not operate as a limitation on Parliament's legislative competence, the courts nevertheless presume, in the absence of clear words to the contrary, that Parliament did not intend its legislation to receive extraterritorial application.

Copyright law respects the territorial principle, reflecting the implementation of a "web of interlinking international treaties" based on the principle of national treatment.

The applicability of our Copyright Act to communications that have international participants will depend on whether there is a sufficient connection between this country and the communication in question for Canada to apply its law consistent with the "principles of order and fairness ... that ensure security of [cross-border] transactions with justice".

* * *

Canada clearly has a significant interest in the flow of information in and out of the country. Canada regulates the reception of broadcasting signals in Canada wherever originated. Our courts and tribunals regularly take jurisdiction in matters of civil liability arising out of foreign transmissions which are received and have their impact here.

Generally speaking, this Court has recognized as a sufficient "connection" for taking jurisdiction, situations where Canada is the country of transmission or the country of reception. This jurisdictional posture is consistent with international copyright practice.

In a recent decision of the European Commission involving "simulcasting", a model reciprocal agreement approved by the Commission was based on the country-of-destination principle. The decision commented that according to the principle *"which appears to reflect the current legal situation in copyright law*, the act of communication to the public of a copyright protected work takes place *not only* in the country of origin (emission-State) but also in all the States where the signals can be *received* (reception-States)". EC, Commission Decision of 8 October 2002 relating to a proceeding under Article 81 of the EC Treaty and Article 53 of the EEA Agreement, Case No. COMP/C2/38.014 IFPI ("the Simulcasting decision").

Canada is a signatory but not yet a party to the WIPO Copyright Treaty. This treaty responded to the development of the Internet and other on-demand telecommunications technology. Article 8 provides that:

> ... authors of literary and artistic works shall enjoy the exclusive right of authorizing any communication to the public of their works, by wire or wireless means, including the making available to the public of their works in such a way that members of the public may access these works from a place and at a time individually chosen by them.

The "making available" right is generally exercised at the point of transmission. This does not deny the interest of the country of reception but avoids, as a matter of policy, a "layering" of royalty obligations in different countries that are parties to the WCT.

In 2000, the European Commission issued what is known as its E–Commerce Directive; see Directive 2000/31 EC of the European Parliament and of the Council of June 8, 2000 on certain legal aspects of information society services, in particular electronic commerce, in the Internal Market ("Directive on electronic commerce"). Its purpose was to ensure the free movement among Member States of "information society services", defined as "any service normally provided for remuneration, at a distance, by means of electronic equipment ... and at the individual request of a recipient of a service". The E–Commerce Directive preferred as a matter of policy the law of the Member State on whose territory the service provider is established. It was thought that "[i]nformation society services should be supervised at the source of the activity ... to that end, it is necessary to ensure that the competent authority provides such protection not only for the citizens of its own country but for all Community citizens". The Directive notes that the place where a service provider is established should be determined by the case law of the European Court of Justice, which holds that the proper situs is not the place where the technology is, or the place where the person accessing the service is, but rather where the service provider's centre of activities is.

Supranational organizations such as the European Commission may thus allocate responsibility among their member States whether the state of transmission or the state of reception as a matter of policy. In the absence of such regional or international arrangements, the territorial nature of copyright law must be respected.

National practice confirms that either the country of transmission or the country of reception may take jurisdiction over a "communication" linked to its territory, although whether it chooses to do so is a matter of legislative or judicial policy.

a.   The United States

At present there is authority in the United States for taking copyright jurisdiction over both the sender of the transmission out of the United States and the receiver in the United States of material from outside that country.

In N.F.L. v. PrimeTime 24 Joint Venture, 211 F.3d 10 (U.S. 2nd Cir., 2000), the U.S. defendant caused satellite transmission of NFL football games from the U.S. to Canada. The court found this to violate the NFL's U.S. copyright even though the broadcasts were being sent to the satellite and thence to Canada for Canadian viewers. The United States was the country of transmission. It was held sufficient to constitute U.S. copyright infringement that a significant step in the telecommunication had taken place in the United States (at p. 13):

> ... it is clear that PrimeTime's uplink transmission of signals captured in the United Sates is a step in the process by which NFL's protected work wends its way to a public audience. In short, PrimeTime publicly displayed or performed material in which the NFL owns the copyright. Because PrimeTime did not have authorization to make such a public performance, PrimeTime infringed the NFL's copyright.

At the same time, some U.S. courts take the view that U.S. copyright is also breached when the U.S. is the country of reception. Thus in Los Angeles News Service v. Conus Communications Co., 969 F.Supp. 579 (U.S. C.D. Cal., 1997), the plaintiff had videotaped riots that occurred in Los Angeles in connection with the Rodney King assault case. The CBC broadcast some of the footage in Canada. Inevitably, some homes in border States saw the

CBC broadcast. The plaintiff alleged breach of U.S. copyright. The CBC moved to dismiss the U.S. proceeding for lack of jurisdiction, but was unsuccessful. The court held, at pp. 583–84:

> Under the plain language of the Act, the subject footage was "displayed" on television sets within the United States within the meaning of the Copyright Act. To find otherwise would leave a substantial loophole in the copyright laws. Broadcasters could deliberately transmit potentially infringing material from locations across the U.S. borders for display in the United States without regard to the rights of copyright owners set forth in the U.S. Copyright Act.

Equally, in N.F.L. v. TVRadioNow Corp., 53 U.S.P.Q.2d 1831 (U.S. W.D. Pa., 2000), the court found that a Web site in Canada that "streamed" U.S. cable television through the Internet with worldwide availability infringed the U.S. transmission rights of the copyright owners despite the fact that the defendant was located in Canada and arguably was not in violation of Canadian copyright laws.

b. Australia

Australia has recently adopted the Copyright Amendment (Digital Agenda) Act 2000 to implement its obligations under the WIPO treaties. The definition of "communication to the public" appears to apply Australian copyright law to communications entirely within Australia, those originating within Australia and received by an end user outside Australia, and those originating outside Australia but received by an end user in Australia:

10.   Interpretation

(1) In this Act, unless the contrary intention appears

> "communicate" means make available online or electronically transmit (whether over a path, or a combination of paths, provided by a material substance or otherwise) a work or other subject-matter.

> "to the public" means to the public *within or outside* Australia. [Emphasis added.]

The definition of "to the public" seems to permit Australian copyright holders to exact royalties on both communication from Australia of material directed to overseas audiences as well as overseas communications received in Australia.

c. France

An analysis of liability in France suggests that "[c]ourts will likely assert jurisdiction not only over transmissions *from France,* but also transmissions *into France* that are alleged to cause damage" (emphasis added); see D. J. Gervais, "Transmissions of Music on the Internet: An analysis of the Copyright Laws of Canada, France, Germany, Japan, the United Kingdom, and the United States" (2001), 34 Vand. J. Transnat'l L. 1363, at p. 1376. In UEJF v. Yahoo! Inc., (Trib. Gr. Inst. Paris, May 22, 2000), the court ordered Yahoo! Inc., a U.S. based Internet company, to block access by French users to an Internet auction offering Nazi paraphernalia because [translation] "the harm is suffered in France".

Accordingly, the conclusion that Canada could exercise copyright jurisdiction in respect both of transmissions originating here and transmissions originating abroad but received here is not only consistent with our general law but with both national and international copyright practice.

This conclusion does not, of course, imply imposition of automatic copyright liability on foreign content providers whose music is telecommunicated to a Canadian end user. Whether or not a real and substantial connection exists will turn on the facts of a particular transmission. It is unnecessary to say more on this point because the Canadian copyright liability of foreign content providers is not an issue that arises for determination in this appeal, although, as stated, the Board itself intimated that where a foreign transmission is aimed at Canada, copyright liability might attach.

This conclusion also raises the spectre of imposition of copyright duties on a single telecommunication in both the State of transmission and the State of reception, but as with other fields of overlapping liability (taxation for example), the answer lies in the making of international or bilateral agreements, not in national courts straining to find some jurisdictional infirmity in either State.

* * *

Notes

1. In the 2009 *Pirate Bay* case, the operators of a file-sharing service were convicted of criminal violations of the Swedish copyright statutes. The Stockholm District Court held that copyright infringement took place in Sweden even when the parties who made works available through the file-sharing service were located outside of the country:

> The investigation into the case has revealed that some of The Pirate Bay's users, whose making available is the subject of the action, have been located outside Sweden when they made the works available to the general public.

* * *

According to the District Court, there is strong reason to regard an offence which involves the making available of something on the

Internet as having been committed in a country where the Internet user can obtain the information which has been made available, provided that the making available has legal implications in the country (*cf.* Schønning, Ophavsretsloven with commentary, 3rd edition, p. 686). This applies not least when the information—as in this case—is published in a language spoken in that country.

This suggests that all principal offences, even those committed by persons located outside Sweden, should be regarded as having been committed in Sweden. This conclusion is further reinforced by the fact that the servers (computers) hosting The Pirate Bay's website and the tracker [*i.e.*, a search and indexing engine] were located in Sweden.

Case No. B 13301–06 (Stockholm District Court, April 17, 2009). However, the court's statement that the servers were located in Sweden may be inaccurate; some media reports indicate that the servers were in the Netherlands, even though Pirate Bay's base of operation was in Sweden. Nonetheless, the opinion was upheld on appeal.

Before the Swedish decision, an Italian court in August of 2008 ordered ISPs to block access to the Pirate Bay website. In October of 2008, the Court of Bergamo reversed, holding that a foreign website could not be censored for infringement under Italian law. However, the court also acknowledged that the Pirate Bay website had received hundreds of thousands of contacts from computers within Italy, and these contacts were probably related to the acquisition of infringing content. The Court of Cassation, Italy's highest court, is expected to consider the validity of the blocking order in September of 2009. In addition, the Swedish conviction has increased the likelihood of an Italian criminal prosecution. In the meantime, Pirate Bay has agreed to be acquired, and is likely to change to a non-infringing business model.

2. In Europe, the traditional approach to cross-border transmissions is that the infringement, if any, takes place only in the country where the transmission is initiated. Although this rule was initially developed for radio broadcasts, it was applied to satellite and cable transmissions in the EU's 1993 Satellite/Cable Directive. Should the same rule apply to Internet transmissions? Or should a single transmission expose the sender to liability in every country where the transmission is received? What if an activity is non-infringing in the country of transmission (for example, because the copyright has expired or the activity constitutes fair use) but not in the country where the transmission is received? Is an international convention needed?

Chapter 5

FAIR USE

A. TREATY PROVISIONS

Some degree of fair use—also known around the world as "fair dealing," "fair quotation," and "fair practice"—is contemplated by each of the major treaties pertaining to copyright and neighboring rights. Several of these "exceptions" provisions are also the basis for the more specific statutory privileges under U.S. law, such as those contained in section 110, and for similar specific privileges in other countries.

For example, in the two WIPO treaties and the TRIPS Agreement, the relevant language allows signatories to provide limitations or exceptions in "certain special cases which do not conflict with a normal exploitation of the [work, performance, or phonogram] and do not unreasonably prejudice the legitimate interests of the [author, rightholder, performer or producer]." (TRIPS Art. 13; WIPO Performances and Phonograms Treaty Art. 16; WIPO Copyright Treaty Art. 10).

Other treaties provide as follows:

Berne Convention
Article 9
(1) Authors of literary and artistic works protected by this Convention shall have the exclusive right of authorizing the reproduction of these works, in any manner or form.

(2) It shall be a matter for legislation in the countries of the Union to permit the reproduction of such works in certain special cases, provided that such reproduction does not conflict with a normal exploitation of the work and does not unreasonably prejudice the legitimate interests of the author.

* * *

197

Article 10

(1) It shall be permissible to make quotations from a work which has already been lawfully made available to the public, provided that their making is compatible with fair practice, and their extent does not exceed that justified by the purpose, including quotations from newspaper articles and periodicals in the form of press summaries.

(2) It shall be a matter for legislation in the countries of the Union, and for special agreements existing or to be concluded between them, to permit the utilization, to the extent justified by the purpose, of literary or artistic works by way of illustration in publications, broadcasts or sound or visual recordings for teaching, provided such utilization is compatible with fair practice.

(3) Where use is made of works in accordance with the preceding paragraphs of this Article, mention shall be made of the source, and of the name of the author, if it appears thereon.

Article 10bis

(1) It shall be a matter for legislation in the countries of the Union to permit the reproduction by the press, the broadcasting or the communication to the public by wire, of articles published in newspapers or periodicals on current economic, political or religious topics, and of broadcast works of the same character, in cases in which the reproduction, broadcasting or such communication thereof is not expressly reserved. Nevertheless, the source must always be clearly indicated; the legal consequences of a breach of this obligation shall be determined by the legislation of the country where protection is claimed.

(2) It shall also be a matter for legislation in the countries of the Union to determine the conditions under which, for the purpose of reporting current events by means of photography, cinematography, broadcasting or communication to the public by wire, literary or artistic works seen or heard in the course of the event may, to the extent justified by the informatory purpose, be reproduced and made available to the public.

Rome Convention

Article 15

Permitted Exceptions: 1. Specific Limitations;

2. Equivalents with copyright

1. Any Contracting State may, in its domestic laws and regulations, provide for exceptions to the protection guaranteed by this Convention as regards:

(a) private use;

(b) use of short excerpts in connection with the reporting of current events;

(c) ephemeral fixation by a broadcasting organisation by means of its own facilities and for its own broadcasts;

(d) use solely for the purposes of teaching or scientific research.

2. Irrespective of paragraph 1 of this Article, any Contracting State may, in its domestic laws and regulations, provide for the same kinds of limitations with regard to the protection of performers, producers of phonograms and broadcasting organisations, as it provides for, in its domestic laws and regulations, in connection with the protection of copyright in literary and artistic works. However, compulsory licences may be provided for only to the extent to which they are compatible with this Convention.

Geneva Phonograms Convention

Article 6: Limitations on Protection

Any Contracting State which affords protection by means of copyright or other specific right, or protection by means of penal sanctions, may in its domestic law provide, with regard to the protection of producers of phonograms, the same kinds of limitations as are permitted with respect to the protection of authors of literary and artistic works. * * *

B.   EUROPEAN UNION DIRECTIVE

In 2001, the European Union issued Directive 2001/29/EC on the Harmonisation of Certain Aspects of Copyright and Related Rights in the Information Society. The Directive lays down broad protections for authors, performers, broadcasters, phonogram producers, and film producers, followed by a list of permissible exceptions. Those that come closest to resembling a fair use privilege are:

2. Member States may provide for exceptions or limitations to the reproduction right provided for in Article 2 in the following cases:

(a) in respect of reproductions on paper or any similar medium, effected by the use of any kind of photographic technique or by some other process having similar effects, with the exception of sheet music, provided that the rightholders receive fair compensation;

(b) in respect of reproductions on any medium made by a natural person for private use and for ends that are neither directly nor indirectly commercial, on condition that the rightholders receive fair compensation which takes account of the application or non-application of technological measures referred to in Article 6 to the work or subject-matter concerned;

(c) in respect of specific acts of reproduction made by publicly accessible libraries, educational establishments or museums, or by archives, which are not for direct or indirect economic or commercial advantage;

* * *

3.   Member States may provide for exceptions or limitations to the rights provided for in Articles 2 and 3 [the right of communication and making available to the public] in the following cases:

(a) use for the sole purpose of illustration for teaching or scientific research, as long as the source, including the author's name, is indicated, unless this turns out to be impossible and to the extent justified by the non-commercial purpose to be achieved;

* * *

(c) reproduction by the press, communication to the public or making available of published articles on current economic, political or religious topics or of broadcast works or other subject-matter of the same character, in cases where such use is not expressly reserved, and as long as the source, including the author's name, is indicated, or use of works or other subject-matter in connection with the reporting of current events, to the extent justified by the informatory purpose and as long as the source, including the author's name, is indicated, unless this turns out to be impossible;

(d) quotations for purposes such as criticism or review, provided that they relate to a work or other subject-matter which has already been lawfully made available to the public, that, unless this turns out to be impossible, the source, including the author's name, is indicated, and that their use is in accordance with fair practice, and to the extent required by the specific purpose;

(e) use for the purposes of public security or to ensure the proper performance or reporting of administrative, parliamentary or judicial proceedings;

(f) use of political speeches as well as extracts of public lectures or similar works or subject-matter to the extent justified by the informatory purpose and provided that the source, including the author's name, is indicated, except where this turns out to be impossible;

* * *

(i) incidental inclusion of a work or other subject-matter in other material;

* * *

(k) use for the purpose of caricature, parody or pastiche;

* * *

(o) use in certain other cases of minor importance where exceptions or limitations already exist under national law, provided that they only concern analogue uses and do not affect the free circulation of goods and services within the Community, without prejudice to the other exceptions and limitations contained in this Article.

* * *

5. The exceptions and limitations provided for in paragraphs 1, 2, 3 and 4 shall only be applied in certain special cases which do not conflict with a normal exploitation of the work or other subject-matter and do not unreasonably prejudice the legitimate interests of the rightholder.

C. STATUTES AND CASE LAW

Outside of the United States, fair use statutes tend to be drafted in more specific terms than section 107, and they tend to be narrower in scope. Typically, they describe specific activities that are considered to be fair use, and there is generally no "catch all" provision comparable to section 107. However, the American concept of "fair use" appears to be having an increasing influence on copyright policy in several countries, including Canada and Japan.

CCH CANADIAN LTD. v. LAW SOCIETY OF UPPER CANADA

Supreme Court of Canada, 2004
[2004] 1 S.C.R. 339, 2004 SCC 13

* * *

(3) *The Law Society and Fair Dealing*

The Great Library [of the Law Society of Upper Canada] provides a custom photocopy service. Upon receiving a request from a lawyer, law student, member of the judiciary or authorized researcher, the Great Library staff photocopies extracts from legal material within its collection and sends it to the requester. The question is whether this service falls within the fair dealing defence under s. 29 of the Copyright Act which provides: "Fair dealing for the purpose of research or private study does not infringe copyright."

(a) The Law

Before reviewing the scope of the fair dealing exception under the Copyright Act, it is important to clarify some general considerations about exceptions to copyright infringement. Procedurally, a defendant is required to prove that his or her dealing with a work has been fair; however, the fair dealing exception is perhaps more properly understood as an integral part of the Copyright Act than simply a defence. Any act falling within the fair dealing exception will not be an infringement of copyright. The fair dealing exception, like other exceptions in the Copyright Act, is a user's right. In order to maintain the proper balance between the rights of a copyright owner and users' interests, it must not be interpreted restrictively. As Professor Vaver has explained, at p. 171: "User rights are not just loopholes. Both owner rights and user rights should therefore be given the fair and balanced reading that befits remedial legislation."

As an integral part of the scheme of copyright law, the s. 29 fair dealing exception is always available. Simply put, a library can always attempt to prove that its dealings with a copyrighted work are fair under s. 29 of the Copyright Act. It is only if a library were unable to make out the fair dealing exception under s. 29 that it would need to turn to s. 30.2 of the Copyright Act to prove that it qualified for the library exemption.

In order to show that a dealing was fair under s. 29 of the Copyright Act, a defendant must prove: (1) that the dealing was for the purpose of either research or private study and (2) that it was fair.

The fair dealing exception under s. 29 is open to those who can show that their dealings with a copyrighted work were for the purpose of research or private study. "Research" must be given a large and liberal interpretation in order to ensure that users' rights are not unduly constrained. I agree with the Court of Appeal that research is not limited to non-commercial or private contexts. The Court of Appeal correctly noted that "[r]esearch for the purpose of advising clients, giving opinions, arguing cases, preparing briefs and factums is nonetheless research". Lawyers carrying on the business of law for profit are conducting research within the meaning of s. 29 of the Copyright Act.

The Copyright Act does not define what will be "fair"; whether something is fair is a question of fact and depends on the facts of each case. Lord Denning explained this eloquently in *Hubbard v. Vosper* (1971), [1972] 1 All E.R. 1023 (Eng. C.A.), at p. 1027:

> It is impossible to define what is 'fair dealing'. It must be a question of degree. You must consider first the number and extent of the quotations and extracts. Are they altogether too many and too long to be fair? Then you must consider the use made of them. If they are used as a basis for comment, criticism or review, that may be a fair dealing. If they are used to convey the same information as the author, for a rival purpose, that may be unfair. Next, you must consider the proportions. To take long extracts and attach short comments may be unfair. But, short extracts and long comments may be fair. Other considerations may come to mind also. But, after all is said and done, it must be a matter of impression. As with fair comment in the law of libel, so with fair dealing in the law of copyright. The tribunal of fact must decide.

At the Court of Appeal, Linden J.A. acknowledged that there was no set test for fairness, but outlined a series of factors that could be considered to help assess whether a dealing is fair. Drawing on the decision in *Hubbard, supra,* as well as the doctrine of fair use in the United States, he proposed that the following factors be considered in assessing whether a dealing was fair: (1) the purpose of the dealing; (2) the character of the dealing; (3) the amount of the dealing; (4) alternatives to the dealing; (5) the nature of the work; and (6) the effect of the dealing on the work. Although these considerations will not all arise in every case of fair dealing, this list of factors provides a useful analytical framework to govern determinations of fairness in future cases.

(i) The Purpose of the Dealing

In Canada, the purpose of the dealing will be fair if it is for one of the allowable purposes under the Copyright Act, namely research, private study, criticism, review or news reporting: see ss. 29, 29.1 and 29.2 of the Copyright Act. As discussed, these allowable purposes should not be given a restrictive interpretation or this could result in the undue restriction of users' rights. This said, courts should attempt to make an objective assessment of the user/defendant's real purpose or motive in using the copyrighted work. Moreover, as the Court of Appeal explained, some dealings, even if for an allowable purpose, may be more or less fair than others; research done for commercial purposes may not be as fair as research done for charitable purposes.

(ii) The Character of the Dealing

In assessing the character of a dealing, courts must examine how the works were dealt with. If multiple copies of works are being widely distributed, this will tend to be unfair. If, however, a single copy of a work is used for a specific legitimate purpose, then it may be easier to conclude that it was a fair dealing. If the copy of the work is destroyed after it is used for its specific intended purpose, this may also favour a finding of fairness. It may be relevant to consider the custom or practice in a particular trade or industry to determine whether or not the character of the dealing is fair. For example, in *Sillitoe v. McGraw Hill Book Co. (U.K.) Ltd.*, [1983] F.S.R. 545 (Eng. Ch.), the importers and distributors of "study notes" that incorporated large passages from published works attempted to claim that the copies were fair dealings because they were for the purpose of criticism. The court reviewed the ways in which copied works were customarily dealt with in literary criticism textbooks to help it conclude that the study notes were not fair dealings for the purpose of criticism.

(iii) The Amount of the Dealing

Both the amount of the dealing and importance of the work allegedly infringed should be considered in assessing fairness. If the amount taken from a work is trivial, the fair dealing analysis need not be undertaken at all because the court will have concluded that there was no copyright infringement. As the passage from *Hubbard* indicates, the quantity of the work taken will not be determinative of fairness, but it can help in the determination. It may be possible to deal fairly with a whole work. As Vaver points out, there might be no other way to criticize or review certain types of works such as photographs. The amount taken may also be more or less fair depending on the purpose. For example, for the purpose of research or private study, it may be essential to copy an entire academic article or an entire judicial decision. However, if a work of litera-ture is copied for the purpose of criticism, it will not likely be fair to include a full copy of the work in the critique.

(iv) Alternatives to the Dealing

Alternatives to dealing with the infringed work may affect the determination of fairness. If there is a non-copyrighted equivalent of the work that could have been used instead of the copyrighted work, this should be considered by the court. I agree with the Court of Appeal that it will also be useful for courts to attempt to determine whether the dealing was reasonably necessary to achieve the ultimate purpose. For example, if a criticism would be equally effective if it did not actually reproduce the copyrighted work it was criticizing, this may weigh against a finding of fairness.

(v) The Nature of the Work

The nature of the work in question should also be considered by courts assessing whether a dealing is fair. Although certainly not determinative, if a work has not been published, the dealing may be more fair in that its reproduction with acknowledgement could lead to a wider public dissemination of the work—one of the goals of copyright law. If, however, the work in question was confidential, this may tip the scales towards finding that the dealing was unfair.

(vi) Effect of the Dealing on the Work

Finally, the effect of the dealing on the work is another factor warranting consideration when courts are determining whether a dealing is fair. If the reproduced work is likely to compete with the market of the original work, this may suggest that the dealing is not fair. Although the effect of the dealing on the market of the copyright owner is an important factor, it is neither the only factor nor the most important factor that a court must consider in deciding if the dealing is fair.

To conclude, the purpose of the dealing, the character of the dealing, the amount of the dealing, the nature of the work, available alternatives to the dealing and the effect of the dealing on the work are all factors that could help determine whether or not a dealing is fair. These factors may be more or less relevant to assessing the fairness of a dealing depending on the factual context of the allegedly infringing dealing. In some contexts, there may be factors other than those listed here that may help a court decide whether the dealing was fair.

(b) Application of the law to these facts

In 1996, the Law Society implemented an "Access to the Law Policy" ("Access Policy") which governs the Great Library's custom photocopy service and sets limits on the types of requests that will be honoured:

Access to the Law Policy

The Law Society of Upper Canada, with the assistance of the resources of the Great Library, supports the administration of justice and the rule of law in the Province of Ontario. The Great Library's comprehensive catalogue of primary and secondary legal sources, in print and electronic media, is open to lawyers, articling students, the judiciary and other authorized researchers. Single copies of library materials, required for the purposes of research, review, private study and criticism, as well as use in court, tribunal and government proceedings, may be provided to users of the Great Library.

This service supports users of the Great Library who require access to legal materials while respecting the copyright of the publishers of such materials, in keeping with the fair dealing provisions in Section 27 of the Canadian Copyright Act.

Guidelines to Access

1 The Access to the Law service provides single copies for specific purposes, identified in advance to library staff.

2 The specific purposes are research, review, private study and criticism, as well as use in court, tribunal, and government proceedings. Any doubt concerning the legitimacy of the request for these purposes will be referred to the Reference Librarian.

3 The individual must identify him/herself and the purpose at the time of making the request. A request form will be completed by library staff, based on information provided by the requesting party.

4 As to the amount of copying, discretion must be used. No copies will be made for any purpose other than that specifically set out on the request form. Ordinarily, requests for a copy of one case, one article or one statutory reference will be satisfied as a matter of routine. Requests for substantial copying from secondary sources (e.g. in excess of 5% of the volume or more than two citations from one volume) will be referred to the Reference Librarian and may ultimately be refused.

5 This service is provided on a not for profit basis. The fee charged for this service is intended to cover the costs of the Law Society.

When the Access Policy was introduced, the Law Society specified that it reflected the policy that the Great Library had been following in the past; it did not change the Law Society's approach to its custom photocopy service.

At trial, the Law Society claimed that its custom photocopy service does not infringe copyright because it is a fair dealing within the meaning of s. 29 of the Copyright Act. The trial judge held that the fair dealing exception should be strictly construed. He concluded that copying for the custom photocopy service was not for the purpose of either research or study and therefore was not within the ambit of fair dealing. The Court of Appeal rejected the argument that the fair dealing exception should be interpreted restrictively. The majority held that the Law Society could rely on the purposes of its patrons to prove that its dealings were fair. The Court of Appeal concluded, however, that there was not sufficient evidence to determine whether or not the dealings were fair and, consequently, that the fair dealing exception had not been proven.

This raises a preliminary question: is it incumbent on the Law Society to adduce evidence that every patron uses the material provided for in a fair dealing manner or can the Law Society rely on its general practice to establish fair dealing? I conclude that the latter suffices. Section 29 of the Copyright Act states that "[f]air dealing for the purpose of research or private study does not infringe copyright". The language is general. "Dealing" connotes not individual acts, but a practice or system. This comports with the purpose of the fair dealing exception, which is to ensure that users are not unduly restricted in their ability to use and disseminate copyrighted works. Persons or institutions relying on the s. 29 fair dealing exception need only prove that their own dealings with copyrighted works were for the purpose of research or private study and were fair. They may do this either by showing that their own practices and policies were research-based and fair, or by showing that all individual dealings with the materials were in fact research-based and fair.

The Law Society's custom photocopying service is provided for the purpose of research, review and private study. The Law Society's Access Policy states that "[s]ingle copies of library materials, required for the purposes of research, review, private study and criticism ... may be provided to users of the Great Library". When the Great Library staff make copies of the requested cases, statutes, excerpts from legal texts and legal commentary, they do so for the purpose of research. Although the retrieval and photocopying of legal works are not research in and of themselves, they are necessary conditions of research and thus part of the research process. The reproduction of legal works is for the purpose of research in that it is an essential element of the legal research process. There is no other purpose for the copying; the Law Society does not profit from this service. Put simply, its custom photocopy service helps to ensure that legal professionals in Ontario can access the materials necessary to conduct the research required to carry on the practice of law. In sum, the Law Society's custom photocopy service is an integral part of the legal research process, an allowable purpose under s. 29 of the Copyright Act.

The evidence also establishes that the dealings were fair, having regard to the factors discussed earlier.

(i) Purpose of the Dealing

The Access Policy and its safeguards weigh in favour of finding that the dealings were fair. It specifies that individuals requesting copies must identify the purpose of the request for these requests to be honoured, and provides that concerns that a request is not for one of the legitimate purposes under the fair dealing exceptions in the Copyright Act are referred to the Reference Librarian. This policy provides reasonable safeguards that the materials are being used for the purpose of research and private study.

(ii) Character of the Dealing

The character of the Law Society's dealings with the publishers' works also supports a finding of fairness. Under the Access Policy, the Law Society provides single copies of works for the specific purposes allowed under the Copyright Act. There is no evidence that the Law Society was disseminating multiple copies of works to multiple members of the legal profession. Copying a work for the purpose of research on a specific legal topic is generally a fair dealing.

(iii) Amount of the Dealing

The Access Policy indicates that the Great Library will exercise its discretion to ensure that the amount of the dealing with copyrighted works will be reasonable. The Access Policy states that the Great Library will typically honour requests for a copy of one case, one article or one statutory reference. It further stipulates that the Reference Librarian will review requests for a copy of more than five percent of a secondary source and that, ultimately, such requests may be refused. This suggests that the Law Society's dealings with the publishers' works are fair. Although the dealings might not be fair if a specific patron of the Great Library submitted numerous requests for multiple reported judicial decisions from the same reported series over a short period of time, there is no evidence that this has occurred.

(iv) Alternatives to the Dealing

It is not apparent that there are alternatives to the custom photocopy service employed by the Great Library. As the Court of Appeal points out, the patrons of the custom photocopying service cannot reasonably be expected to always conduct their research on-site at the Great Library. Twenty per cent of the requesters live outside the Toronto area; it would be burdensome to expect them to travel to the city each time they wanted to track down a specific legal source. Moreover, because of the heavy demand for the legal collection at the Great Library, researchers are not allowed to borrow materials from the library. If researchers could not request copies of the work or make copies of the works themselves, they would be required to do all of their research and note-taking in the Great Library, something which does not seem reasonable given the volume of research that can often be required on complex legal matters.

The availability of a licence is not relevant to deciding whether a dealing has been fair. As discussed, fair dealing is an integral part of the scheme of copyright law in Canada. Any act falling within the fair dealing exception will not infringe copyright. If a copyright owner were allowed to license people to use its work and then point to a person's decision not to obtain a licence as proof that his or her dealings were not fair, this would extend the scope of the owner's monopoly over the use of his or her work in a manner that would not be consistent with the Copyright Act's balance between owner's rights and user's interests.

(v) Nature of the Work

I agree with the Court of Appeal that the nature of the works in question—judicial decisions and other works essential to legal research—suggests that the Law Society's dealings were fair. As Linden J.A. explained, at para. 159: "It is generally in the public interest that access to judicial decisions and other legal resources not be unjustifiably restrained." Moreover, the Access Policy puts reasonable limits on the Great Library's photocopy service. It does not allow all legal works to be copied regardless of the purpose to which they will be put. Requests for copies will be honoured only if the user intends to use the works for the purpose of research, private study, criticism, review or use in legal proceedings. This further supports a finding that the dealings were fair.

(vi) Effect of the Dealing on the Work

Another consideration is that no evidence was tendered to show that the market for the publishers' works had decreased as a result of these copies having been made. Although the burden of proving fair dealing lies with the Law Society, it lacked access to evidence about the effect of the dealing on the publishers' markets. If there had been evidence that the publishers' markets had been negatively affected by the Law Society's custom photocopying service, it would have been in the publishers' interest to tender it at trial. They did not do so. The only evidence of market impact is that the publishers have continued to produce new reporter series and legal publications during the period of the custom photocopy service's operation.

(vii) Conclusion

The factors discussed, considered together, suggest that the Law Society's dealings with the publishers' works through its custom photocopy service were research-based and fair. The Access Policy places appropriate limits on the type of copying that the Law Society will do. It states that not all requests will be honoured. If a request does not appear to be for the purpose of research, criticism, review or private study, the copy will not be made. If a question arises as to whether the stated purpose is legitimate, the Reference

Librarian will review the matter. The Access Policy limits the amount of work that will be copied, and the Reference Librarian reviews requests that exceed what might typically be considered reasonable and has the right to refuse to fulfill a request. On these facts, I conclude that the Law Society's dealings with the publishers' works satisfy the fair dealing defence and that the Law Society does not infringe copyright.

* * *

Notes

1. *CCH Canadian* dealt specifically with Section 29 of the Canada statutes, which states broadly that "[f]air dealing for the purpose of research or private study does not infringe copyright." The decision has been praised for introducing greater flexibility into judicial interpretations of that provision. In contrast, Canada's other two fair dealing provisions, Sections 29.1 and 29.2, are more specific:

> **29.1** Fair dealing for the purpose of criticism or review does not infringe copyright if the following are mentioned:
>
> (*a*) the source; and
>
> (*b*) if given in the source, the name of the
>
> > (i) author, in the case of a work,
> >
> > (ii) performer, in the case of a performer's performance,
> >
> > (iii) maker, in the case of a sound recording, or
> >
> > (iv) broadcaster, in the case of a communication signal.
>
> **29.2** Fair dealing for the purpose of news reporting does not infringe copyright if the following are mentioned:
>
> (*a*) the source; and
>
> (*b*) if given in the source, the name of the
>
> > (i) author, in the case of a work,
> >
> > (ii) performer, in the case of a performer's performance,
> >
> > (iii) maker, in the case of a sound recording, or
> >
> > (iv) broadcaster, in the case of a communication signal.

2. Japan is considering enacting its first general fair use statute, modeled on the U.S. approach, and may do so by the end of 2009. Until now, permissible uses of copyrighted works in Japan have been limited to a series of narrow exceptions. Consider, for example, the limited scope of Japan's "private use" exception:

> Article 30. (1) It shall be permissible for a user to reproduce by himself a work forming the subject matter of copyright (hereinafter in this Subsection referred to as a "work") for the purpose of

his personal use, family use or other similar uses within a limited circle (hereinafter referred to as "private use"), except in the case:

(i) where such reproduction is made by means of automatic reproducing machines ("automatic reproducing machine" means a machine having reproducing functions and in which all or the main parts of its reproducing devices are automatic) installed for the use by the public * * *.

Also, while quotations from published works are permitted for such purposes as research and criticism (Art. 32), it is not clear whether this would permit a work to be incorporated in a parody or other expressive work. Such an interpretation seems unlikely, because the law expressly states that none of the statutory exceptions apply to the author's moral rights of divulgation, attribution, or integrity (Art. 50).

FRASER–WOODWARD LTD v. BRITISH BROADCASTING CORPORATION

England and Wales High Court, Chancery Division, 2005
[2005] EWHC 472 (Ch)

MANN J.:

Introduction

This is an action for infringement of copyright in photographs, the copyright in which is vested in the claimant ("Fraser–Woodward"). They are all photographs of various members of the well-known Beckham family. Mr. David Beckham is a very well-known footballer, and his wife Victoria is a well-known pop singer who was formally a member of a group called the Spice Girls, in which context she was known as Posh Spice. Together and individually they have acquired celebrity status, and their private and public lives are apparently of great interest to many people. At the time of the TV programme which is at the heart of this case they had two small children, Brooklyn and Romeo (they have since had a third). The photographs in question were originally published in various tabloid newspapers. That publication was by licence. The second defendant ("Brighter") is a television production company. It used images of the newspaper pages on which the photographs were published in a programme which it made for, and which was broadcast by, the first defendant ("the BBC"). It is that use which is complained of as being an infringement of copyright. Additional damages for flagrancy are sought, partly on the grounds of the flagrancy of the alleged breaches. The principal defences of the defendants are fair dealing within s.30(1) of the Copyright, Designs and Patents Act 1988 ("the Act"), and incidental inclusion within the meaning of s.31(1) of that Act.

The Facts

The fact of the use of the photographs, the existence of copyright and its being vested in the claimant are not in dispute. I will therefore be able to deal with them relatively shortly. There is, however, a dispute as to the level of editorial control exerted by Victoria Beckham, and the state of mind of Brighter when it made the programme (going to flagrancy of breach and additional damages, and going to the fairness of dealing).

There are 14 photographs in issue in this case. At the trial they were given the names Beckham 1 to 14, and I shall continue to identify them in that way. Beckhams 1–13 were taken by Mr. Jason Fraser, a well-known photographer who has a reputation for taking photographs of celebrities for the purposes of being sold, and ultimately reproduced, in various publications. The claimant company is a company of which he is a shareholder, and it owns the rights in various photographs, which it exploits from time to time. Beckham 14 was taken by Michele Crosera, an Italian photographer with a commercial relationship with both the claimant and Mr. Fraser. He originally had the copyright in this last photograph ("Beckham 14"); he has assigned it to the claimant. All the photographs except Beckham 14 are photographs of two or more members of the Beckham family taken in apparently off-guard moments when their subjects were conducting their day-to-day activities in public. They are not formal photographs in the sense that their subjects formally sat for them; on their face they might be thought to be photographs taken on occasions not intended for photography and in circumstances in which their subjects were not intended to be photographed (though whether that is right or not is one of the points made in the television programme which reproduced them). Beckham 14 is of Mrs. Beckham by herself.

At the end of 2002 Brighter embarked on the production of the television programme in question, which was ultimately broadcast under the title "Tabloid Tales". The pleaded purpose of the programme (which was one of six in a series) was that it "intended to and did criticise and/or review tabloid journalism and the methods employed by the tabloid press and/or the celebrities featured to build and exploit a story to their advantage" (to quote the Defence in this case). The Beckham programme was broadcast on April 29, 2003 at 22.40. It was narrated by Mr. Piers Morgan, a well-known former Fleet Street tabloid editor. He opens the programme by saying:

> Tonight Tabloid Tales exposes Victoria Beckham's relationship with the press, revealing the truth, the rumours and the lies behind the headlines.

A little later on he says:

The big question is whether she is really just a canny little minx cleverly manipulating the media for her own gain, or whether the press are a bunch of tabloid vultures, preying on Victoria to sell newspapers.

The programme (which runs for a little under 40 minutes) then contains a sort of survey of press coverage of the Beckhams, and in particular Victoria Beckham, starting with her career as a member of the Spice Girls pop group and showing, or claiming to show, a developing relationship with the press. This is achieved by linking narration of Mr. Morgan, clips of interviews with various journalists and media personnel, some short contributions from Mr. Fraser himself, rather longer extracts from an interview of Victoria Beckham and her mother by Mr. Morgan, and a mixture of film clips, clips from pop videos and (most importantly for the purposes of this case) images of newspaper headlines, articles and photographs. The 14 photographs which are the subject of this action featured in this last context. Apart from one which was on screen for about four seconds, they were shown for no more than two or three seconds each, and some of them less than that. On occasions they were shown as part of a brief still image; on others the camera panned quickly across them or zoomed in relation to them.

* * *

Fair dealing and incidental use—the nature of the parties' respective cases

Before turning to the details of the use of the photographs in question it will be useful to indicate what the respective cases of the parties are on the point.

Section 30(1) is in the following terms:

30 (1). Fair dealing with a work for the purpose of criticism or review, of that or another work or of a performance of a work, does not infringe any copyright in the work provided that it is accompanied by a sufficient acknowledgement.

The criticism or review on which the defendants rely for these purposes is twofold. First, there is said to be criticism and review of the photographs themselves (or at least some of them). Secondly, their use was said to have taken place in the context of criticism or review of another work (or more appropriately, works), namely the tabloid press's coverage of celebrities. It is said that the use of the photographs was fair for the purposes of the concept of "fair dealing"—their use on screen was not over-long, and the use in the context of criticism and review was not a contrivance to justify a use whose purpose was in substance not that of criticism and review. For the claimant it was said that criticism or review, at least in the present context, had to be criticism or review of the photographs themselves, and that criticism or review had to be with some degree of particularity—a passing and unargued observation (for example, and by way of illustration, "this photograph is a bad photograph") was not sufficient to bring the act within the section. In the context of fairness of dealing, the use should not conflict with the normal exploitation of the work, or unreasonably prejudice the legitimate interests of the author. The true purpose must be genuine criticism or review, and the use must not be something else dressed up in criticism's clothing. The extent to which the work is reproduced is also said to be relevant to fair dealing—in the case of photographs, the longer the display, and the more completely the photograph is displayed, the less likely it is that the use is fair, particularly if the criticism is slight. In addition, there was insufficient acknowledgment.

* * *

[The court then described the program in detail. The theme of the program was Victoria Beckham's skill at manipulating the press. One segment dealt with Victoria's control over press coverage of her wedding. Another dealt with photographer Jason Fraser's photos of the Beckhams showing off their new haircuts and their young son. The program then suggests that Fraser, who publishes many supposedly unposed photographs of the Beckhams, in fact acts in collusion with the Beckhams to take these photographs, which are pre-arranged and staged, although they are intended to give the appearance of being "snatched" while the couple is simply going about their everyday activities in public places. The program includes an interview with Victoria Beckham, in which she admits that she occasionally arranges with a photographer to, for example, repeat an exit from a building in order to obtain a suitable photo. The next segment addresses some of her unfavorable press coverage, including an incident in which she was thought to have acquired a lip ring, which was seen as another deliberate attempt to obtain media attention. Her announcement of her second pregnancy at this point was said to be an attempt to obtain more favorable coverage, an attempt which succeeded. Once again, the candidness of Jason Fraser's supposedly "snatched" photos is questioned. The next segment deals with far-fetched media reports on a supposed plot to kidnap Victoria and her family, and suggests that these were concocted by the tabloids simply to sell papers. The program ends by suggesting that the Victoria and the media have mutually "used and abused" each other.]

The Defences

Having set out that material, I can now turn to the Defences, and I shall take fair dealing first.

Criticism and review

The first question which arises under this head is whether the use made of the photographs was for the purposes of criticism and review of the work (*i.e.* the photographs) or of another work. This raises two separate points—was there criticism or review, and if so what was the work being criticised or reviewed? In what follows, for ease of exposition I shall use the expression "other work" as if it were the expression appearing in the statute (which refers to "another work")—they do not differ materially.

The defendants' case was that the concept of criticism or review had to be interpreted liberally. Here there was criticism or review of both the photographs and of another work or works, namely the coverage of the Beckhams (and in particular Mrs. Beckham) in the tabloid press. The criticism and/or review was thus of two things—there was criticism and review of the photographs themselves (or some of them at least) and the philosophy or ideas behind them, and there was criticism and review of another work (or works), namely the tabloid press. One had to look at the programme as a whole, and not dissect it too readily into unrealistic parts, and one had to look at the programme as it would strike the reasonable viewer.

The claimant had a number of answers to this. First, so far as it was alleged that there was criticism or review of the photographs themselves, it had to be more than mere passing comment or passing reference, and in the present case there was no such thing. One pointer as to whether there is genuine criticism or review is whether the same point can be made without displaying the copyright material. Secondly, so far as criticism or review of another work was concerned, then that other work had to be a copyright work within the meaning of the Act, that is to say, a work falling within s.1 of the Act, and that other work must be identified (which it was not in the present case). Miss Michalos disputed that the other work could be general media attitude, or that references to underlying philosophy and ideas appearing in the authorities should be taken as being a reference to any such concepts other than those appearing in the actual specific work itself.

* * *

This impossibility of plotting boundaries makes it impossible to accept Miss Michalos's submission that there must be something beyond a bare comment. It is not helpful to try to introduce such limitations into the debate; at worst it is misleading, and at best is unhelpful because it will merely shift the debate to the question of whether, in its own context, the relevant remark is merely a "bare comment" or goes further and is criticism. The context is likely to be all-important.

The next point is to what I apply those concepts—what is capable of being the subject of criticism or review for the purposes of the section? The photographs, as subjects, are easy enough as a concept. However, there is more difficulty (in the present case) about criticisms of what Miss May called the philosophy and ideas underlying a work, and what (if any) other works were the subject of any criticism of review in this case.

Miss May said that, in addition to relying on criticism of the photographs themselves, she was entitled to rely on criticism or review of the philosophy or ideas underlying them. By the end of the case I do not think that there was any difference in principle between her and Miss Michalos on this. That it is correct appears from Hubbard v. Vosper [1972] 2 Q.B. 84, in which the copyright works were various works about Scientology, extracts of which appeared in the defendant's book which was critical of the cult. It was submitted that the fair dealing section applied only to criticism of the work, not of the doctrine or philosophy underlying it. Lord Denning disagreed with this submission:

> I do not think that this proviso is confined as narrowly as Mr. Pain submits. A literary work consists, not only of the literary style, but also of the thoughts underlying it, as expressed in the words. Under the defence of "fair dealing" both can be criticised. Mr. Vosper is entitled to criticise not only the literary style, but also the doctrine or philosophy of Mr. Hubbard as expounded in the books.

The same view was expressed in Time Warner Entertainments LP v. Channel Four Television Corp Plc [1994] E.M.L.R. 1 at 13 and 15, and confirmed in Pro Sieben [Media AG v. Carlton UK Television Ltd, [1999] F.S.R. 610, 621]. I agree with Miss Michalos that on analysis this is because criticising the philosophy is criticising the work. It must follow that if the review or criticism is of another work (*i.e.* a work other than the one in respect of which fair dealing is claimed) then that review or criticism can extend to, or even be confined to, the ideas and philosophy underlying that other work.
* * *

* * *

With those points established and in mind, I can now turn to the assertion of the defendants that the programme contained relevant criticism. They say that it contained criticism both of the photographs themselves (except Beckham 14) and of a certain style of tabloid journalism which amounted to criticism of the newspapers themselves and the ideas behind their reporting of celebrities. If that is a proper description of the nature of criticism then there is criticism (or review) within the meaning of s.30 in precisely the same way as there was such criticism in the *Pro Sieben* case.

Having viewed a recording of the programme, I have come to the clear conclusion that the deployment of the first 13 photographs is for the purpose of criticism or review within the meaning of s.30. I have sought to set out the shape of, and the most significant points in, the programme in the extracts referred to above. Like the programme in *Pro Sieben* (as that programme is described in the law report), "Tabloid Tales" contains frequent shots of newspapers, their mastheads and their stories, and in addition their pictures. It also contains various film clips demonstrating the public presentation of, or public appearances of, the Beckhams. They are all there to demonstrate a certain style of journalism—the coverage of celebrity—and to comment on (in the form of criticism) that style as manifested in the relevant publications (tabloid newspapers and, to a certain extent, magazines). Various points are made in the course of the programme, including important reflections on the fact that certain items are covered at all (for example, the haircuts), the extent of the coverage, the extent to which rival newspapers cover or disdain to cover matters such as Victoria Beckham's alleged eating disorder (which she denies in her interview), and the extent to which the newsworthiness of the everyday lives of these particular celebrities is capable of pushing other matters which might be thought to be more important ("war and famine") off the front page. So far as the dictionary definitions are concerned, it falls fairly and squarely within the definitions of "criticism" when applied to the ideas underlying the reporting, and to some extent to the reports themselves, though those reports are not actually cited save insofar as headlines are sometimes briefly in shot.

* * *

I do not think that this applies to Beckham 14, however. That is the small photograph appearing tucked into the sensational headline about the Beckham kidnap plot. The point of the shot in question is to show the headline. The small photograph happens to be there. While the photograph appears in the context of criticism or review of the other works, it does not appear "for the purpose" of criticism or review. Its proper place appears below when I consider it again in the context of incidental use.

Accordingly all of Beckhams 1–13 are deployed in the context of, and for the purpose of, criticism or review of the other works, that is to say, the tabloid press and magazines, and I so find. In addition, it is clear to me that in relation to most of the photographs there is also criticism of the photographs themselves. Beckham 1 first appears when the programme turns to the Beckham haircut. As it is shown there is an oral attribution of the photograph to Mr. Fraser by Mr. Morgan. After Mr. Fraser's contribution

Mr. Morgan makes his remark about how mysterious it is that Mr. Fraser manages to be in the right place at the right time, and questions where he gets his information from. The question is answered almost immediately by Mr. Wansell's saying that Mrs. Beckham can manipulate "certain photographers" and by Mr. Morton's explicit allegation that the photographs are pre-arranged and:

> It looks as though they're snatched pictures, that they're taken off guard, off duty, when all along those pictures were rehearsed and pre-arranged.

This is accompanied by Beckhams 2–5 being shown simultaneously, and Beckhams 3–5 appearing again almost immediately afterwards. It is clear that Mr. Morton is speaking about the Jason Fraser photographs. That is a clear criticism of the photographs—it is said that the photographs are not in fact as they appear, or as the subject and photographer would wish them to appear. That is a clear act of criticism of the photographs themselves, and the context in which all five are shown indicates that it applies to all five. [The court found other instances in which the program's criticism was aimed at the photographs because it conveyed the message that the photographs were staged. However, this conclusion did not apply to Beckham 14 or the third appearance of Beckham 12.] * * *

For those reasons, therefore, each of the publications of the photographs, save for the third showing of Beckham 12 and the only showing of Beckham 14 are in the context of criticism of the photographs themselves within the meaning of s.30(1).

* * *

[Miss Michalos] also submitted that a helpful indication as to whether what was taking place was criticism or review was whether the "criticism" could be done without using the copyright work. If it could then that was a strong pointer against its being criticism (though it was not determinative). I reject this submission too. It has no foundation in the statute. What the statute permits is "fair dealing" for the purposes of criticism or review. There is no requirement of necessity of use in s.30(1); there is merely a requirement of fair dealing.

Fair dealing

If use of copyright material is to fall within s.30(1) of the Act then that use must amount to "fair dealing". In considering whether the use in the present case amounted to fair dealing (and the claimant says it was not) the following guidelines are relevant:

i) It is relevant to have regard to the motives of the user (contrast the question of criticism and review where the focus is more on the actual use without, or without so much, reference to the motive—see *Pro Sieben* at 620).

ii) Whether there is fair dealing is a matter of impression.

> What amounts to fair dealing must depend on the facts of the particular case and must to a degree be a matter of impression. What is of prime importance is to consider the real objective of the party using the copyright work. Section 30 is designed to protect a critic or reviewer who may bona fide wish to use the copyright material to illustrate his review or criticism. (*Banier* at 815).

iii) If some degree of use would be fair dealing, excessive use can render the use unfair—Hyde Park Residence Ltd v. Yelland [2001] Ch. 143 at [40].

iv) In assessing whether the dealing is fair the court can have regard to the actual purpose of the work, and will be live to any pretence in the purported purpose of the work:

> ... it is necessary to have regard to the true purpose of the work. Is it a genuine piece of criticism or review, or is it something else, such as an attempt to dress up the infringement of another's copyright in the guise of criticism, and so profit unfairly from another's work? (*Time Warner, supra,* at 14).

v) In the same vein, the amount of the work used can be relevant:

> I may add, however, that the substantiality of the part reproduced is, in my view, an element which the Court will take into consideration in arriving at a conclusion whether what has been done is a fair dealing or not. To take an example, if a defendant published long and important extracts from a plaintiff's work and added to those extracts some brief criticisms upon them, I think that the Court would be very ready to arrive at the conclusion that that was not fair dealing within the section (Morton J. in Johnstone v. Bernard Jones Publications Ltd [1938] Ch. 599 at 603–4).

vi) However, this must be carefully applied in relation to photographs. It makes more sense in relation to extended literary or musical works. If one is critiquing a photograph, or using it for the purpose of criticising another work, then the nature of the medium means that any reference is likely to be by means of an inclusion of most of the work because otherwise the reference will not make much sense. This degree of care is particularly appropriate in the context of a television programme where the exposure is not as (for example) continuous or permanent as publication in printed form would be.

vii) Reproduction should not unreasonably prejudice the legitimate interests of the author or conflict with the author's normal exploitation of the work—see the Berne Copyright Convention Art. 9(2).

These factors were not seriously in dispute between the parties. Miss May said that none of them pointed towards unfairness of use or dealing, and Miss Michalos said that they did, when one looked at the actual use and at the evidence of the parties. Despite the many points that Miss Michalos made in relation to fairness, my clear view is that there was nothing unfair about the use of the photographs in this case in relation to which I have found criticism or review to have occurred (Beckhams 1–13). It was the defendants' case that the use of the photographs was genuinely for the purpose of criticism and review; that there was no hidden or ulterior motive; that manner of use was not unfair; and that the interests of the claimant were not unfairly prejudiced (if indeed they were prejudiced at all). The claimant alleged, for the reasons appearing below, that the use of the photographs was not fair in the circumstances, and put forward a number of reasons for saying this.

First, it was said that the use was not fair because the programme relied on comments by Mr. Fraser when he had refused consent to use his photographs. It was unfair to obtain those comments from someone who gave them voluntarily believing that the defendants were not going to use his works. * * * [However, this argument does not weaken the fair dealing defence, because] the unfairness has to arise in relation to the dealing with photographs—it has to go beyond some aspect of unfairness as between the parties which is not related to the use of the photographs. It principally relates to the manner and purpose of use, though it can extend to the circumstances in which the copyright material was obtained (see, *e.g. Hyde Park*, where the photographs in question had been dishonestly obtained). * * *

Next, it was said that there was excessive use of the photographs in the sense that they were substantially reproduced when that was not justified by the brief criticism of the photographs themselves. I do not consider that this criticism is justified. It is true that in every case what the programme showed was what the newspaper printed. It is also true that in many, though not all, cases what the newspaper reproduced was substantially the whole of the photograph (it was not true of Beckham 8 and Beckham 10, which were heavily cropped to reveal what the newspaper wished to use as the central subject). However, any legitimate use of a photograph for the purposes of criticism and review is likely to require display of a large part of the photograph in order to make the point that is being made. That is certainly true of the photographs in this case. Unless the photographs had been shown as printed the point made by the programme could not have been made, either in relation to the criticism of the tabloid press coverage or in relation to the particular photographs themselves. The length of display of the whole photograph has to be taken into account here too. It could not conceivably be treated as too lingering on the facts of this case. In no case was the display of any photograph longer than about three seconds, and many were shorter. And in the case of some of the longer periods the whole photograph was not shown for the entire period because the camera panned across it or zoomed into some limited part of it, thus preventing any potentially unjustifiable lingering. In some cases the exposure was so brief as to make it difficult to spot exactly which photograph was being shown—see the second uses of Beckhams 3–5, which are little more than flashes on the screen as a directorial nuance demonstrating "snapping" (perhaps with some irony). Overall I regard this criticism as unjustified. If there is such a thing as a limit defined by a criticism:exposure ratio, then this case fell easily on the "fair" side of the line.

The claimant then relied on the fact that this was a commercial use of the photographs which makes the use unfair. Miss Michalos did not go so far as to say that any commercial use was unfair, and obviously she could not sensibly do so—there is no reason why a review done for commercial purposes (which most reviews will be, since they will appear in some commercial publication) should be deprived of the use of the reviewed material when a non-commercial review would not be. However, she said that a use which had a commercial purpose would or could be unfair, and should be put in the scales when weighing up matters in order to arrive at an overall impression. As an example she relied on Associated Newspapers Group Plc v. News Group Newspapers [1986] R.P.C. 515 where one newspaper (*The Sun*) printed copyright letters passing between the late Duke and Duchess of Windsor, the exclusive rights to which had been obtained by another. At 518 Walton J. referred to a passage in *Hubbard* in which it was said to be not fair for a rival "to take copyright material and use it to his own benefit". Walton J. said:

> That seems to be exactly what has happened in the present case. There is no blinking the fact that the *Sun* is trying to attract readers by means of printing these letters or extracts from letters.

It is not clear to what extent there was any attempt at criticism or review in that case, but what I think Walton J. was seeking to say is that it is not fair if what the user of the material is actually doing is seeking to deploy the copyright material so as to derive benefit *from that deployment*. That is basically a use[] which is coloured by the motive. The motive was not to use the letters so as to criticise them (see the examples of genuine criticism given earlier on the same page of *Associated Newspapers*), but "to attract readers". There is absolutely no evidential basis on which that can be said in the present case. There was, for example, no suggestion that the programme was trailed by alerting viewers to the fact that it would contain these photographs, or even photographs of a similar nature which would have the viewers switching on to see them. Nor is it plausible that that was the motive when one looks at the programme itself. The photographs were deployed briefly at various points in the programme, amidst a lot of other visual material. There is no way in which it can sensibly be said that these photographs were somehow intended as a ratings booster, and no evidence which would begin to justify such an assertion (let alone a finding) to that effect.

The same point can be made in relation to the allied point that this was copyright infringement dressed up as criticism and review. The criticism and review were, on their face, genuine enough—I have so found above. It is not readily apparent that there was a disguise to be penetrated when one looked at the programme. Having heard about the making of the programme from Miss Williamson, there is no evidence that behind the scenes there was any attempt at dressing up either.

Next is the point that the use in the programme competes with the claimant's own commercial use of the material in such a way, and to such an extent, as to tend to render the use unfair. Mr. Fraser gave very firm evidence that he was generally reluctant to allow use of his photographs in television programmes because the more lucrative press market was "hugely diminished" by over-exposure to large TV audiences, and for that reason he would never have considered allowing the use of his exclusive photographs of the Beckhams to be included in this programme. * * *

* * *

* * * I find that on the evidence presented to me it was not proved that the exposure of the photos in the "Tabloid Tales" programme had a diminishing effect on the value of the photos of any, or any significant, amount. I accept that Mr. Fraser thought that it might, and that his fear was genuinely felt, but overall he has not made out more than his fear of the risk of damage. He has not made out any actual damage to his commercial interests, and he has not established any particular level of significant risk.

How, then, does that affect the assessment as to the fairness of the dealing? Risk to the commercial value of the copyright may go towards demonstrating or creating unfairness, but it does not follow that any damage or any risk makes any use of the material unfair. If it did then there could be no use of copyright material in criticism or review if it could be said that that use might damage the value of the material to the copyright owner. That would be inconsistent with the purpose of the section which is to balance the interests of the copyright owner and the critic. It is all a question of balance. In the present case I consider it to be clear that the level of risk of damage (whatever it may be) is not sufficiently great to mean that the use of the photographs was unfair. The exploitation of the photographs in the programme was not gratuitous or lingering, so if there was any risk of over-exposure it was kept to an acceptable minimum. So far as this factor is concerned the use of the photographs was well on the "fair" side of the fair/unfair borderline (wherever that may lie).

* * *

Last, as an aspect of "dressing up", it was alleged that the programme was not genuine criticism or review because what the programme makers in fact set out to do was to produce a light-weight piece of entertainment which was in fact a public relations exercise for Mrs. Beckham. It was even asserted that Mrs. Beckham had editorial control over the programme. Having seen the programme, and considered the evidence, I am satisfied that there is nothing in this point. Objectively speaking the programme contains criticism; I have already dealt with that above. It may or may not amount to entertainment as well, but I do not think that entertainment is necessarily inconsistent with criticism or review. If "light-weight entertainment" is intended as some sort of antithesis to criticism and review, then this programme does not fall into that category, but in truth it does not seem to me that the question of whether use is fair dealing or not can be determined by deciding what other labels can be applied to it. The real question here is whether this is a trivial programme dressed up as criticism or review so as to provide an ostensible justification for showing copyright material under some pretence, or whether it is genuinely critical and reviewing. Objectively speaking it is the latter, as I have already found, and nothing in the evidence suggests that anyone behind the scenes had any other, more sinister, intention.

If it were established that Mrs. Beckham had editorial control over the programme, then that might tend to indicate that it was not genuine criticism or review, though what would be more significant would be how she exercised it. However, it is quite clear on the evidence that she had no such thing. * * *

* * *

In the circumstances I find that the use of the photographs amounted to fair dealing for the purposes of s.30(1) of the Act.

Sufficient acknowledgment

Under s.30(1), fair dealing is only a defence:

> ... provided that it is accompanied by a sufficient acknowledgement.

It is accepted by the claimant that there was sufficient acknowledgment in relation to Beckhams 1, 6–10 and the first use of 11, but not in respect of the other use of photographs said to be covered by the fair dealing defence. I must therefore consider it in relation to those.

"Sufficient acknowledgment" is defined in s.178:

> 'sufficient acknowledgment' means an acknowledgment identifying the work in question by its title or other description, and identifying the author unless—

> (a) in the case of a published work it is published anonymously;

> (b) [immaterial on the facts of this case]

No question arises as to anonymous publication in this case, nor does any question arise in relation to an identification of the work in question. The questions that are said to arise do so in relation to the requirement to identify the author. Miss Michalos's point was that the identification of the author had to be express, and it was not sufficient for it to be implied.

There is no authority in support of Miss Michalos's submission, and it does not seem to me to accord with principle. The borderline between what is express and what is implied can get blurred anyway, and it is not a satisfactory distinction to introduce in this area of the law. What is important in principle is that there is something which can properly be seen as an identification of the author. * * *

* * *

[The court concluded that there was sufficient identification, express or implied, of Jason Fraser as the author of Beckhams 1–13 each time these photos appeared during the program.]

Conclusions on fair dealing

It follows from the above, and I find, that the defendants are entitled to the benefit of the fair dealing provisions of s.30(1) in relation to each of Beckhams 1–13.

Incidental inclusion

Section 31(1) provides:

Copyright is not infringed by its incidental inclusion in an artistic work, sound recording or broadcast.

The defendants rely on this provision as an additional or alternative defence in relation to the third appearance of Beckham 12, and the appearance of Beckham 14. Their case is that both photographs were included as an integral part of the headlines or coverage of the kidnap plot.

* * *

Accordingly, my task is to review the use of the photograph in its context and consider whether it was incidental (which must mean incidental to some other purpose) in the ordinary sense of that word.

[The court concluded that the third appearance of Beckham 12 was not incidental, because it was the focus of criticism and review during that segment of the program.]

* * *

I have reached a different conclusion in relation to Beckham 14. This is the small photograph appearing within a newspaper headline. The focus of the filmed shot in the programme is on the headline. It zooms in slightly during the four seconds it is shown, but that is obviously to create a little drama or visual interest. In the run up to this shot the story was introduced by Mr. Morgan, and there were three separate shots of headlines appearing in the *News of the World*, followed by a brief clip from a BBC News broadcast of the item. Then the relevant headline and Beckham 14 appear. I am satisfied that the headline appears as an example of another sensational headline; that is why it is there. In that context the small photograph of Mrs. Beckham is incidental—it is there because it happened to be there in the original. While it might have been there to lend interest to the original headline, its appearance in the programme shot was, in everyday terms, incidental. * * * As far as I can judge, the headline was chosen as a headline, not because it also contained a photograph of Mrs. Beckham. That conclusion is fortified by the fact that at least one of the reproductions of the *News of the World* headlines is without any photographic accompaniment—it is there for the drama of the headline, and that is true of the headline accompanying the appearance of Beckham 14.

In the circumstances I find that there was no infringement in relation to the appearance of Beckham 14 because its inclusion in the programme was incidental.

* * *

Conclusion

Accordingly I shall dismiss this claim.

Notes

1.   France, like most of Europe, utilizes specific exceptions in place of a more flexible fair use privilege. Prior to 2006, the exceptions (contained in Art. L.122–5) were limited as follows:

Once a work has been disclosed, the author may not prohibit:

1°.   private and gratuitous performances carried out exclusively within the family circle;

2°.   copies or reproductions reserved strictly for the private use of the copier and not intended for collective use, with the exception of copies of works of art to be used for purposes identical with those for which the original work was created and copies of software other than backup copies made in accordance with paragraph II of Article L.122–6–1, as well as copies or reproductions of an electronic database;

3°.   on condition that the name of the author and the source are clearly stated:

a) analyses and short quotations justified by the critical, polemic, educational, scientific or informatory nature of the work in which they are incorporated;

b) press reviews;

c) dissemination, even in their entirety, through the press or by broadcasting, as current news, of speeches intended for the public made in political, administrative, judicial or academic gatherings, as well as in public meetings of a political nature and at official ceremonies;

d) complete or partial reproductions of works of graphic or three-dimensional art intended to appear in the catalogue of a judicial sale held in France, in the form of the copies of the said catalogue made available to the public prior to the sale for the sole purpose of describing the works of art offered for sale.

A decree by the Conseil d'Etat shall determine the characteristics of the documents and the conditions governing their distribution.

4°.   parody, pastiche and caricature, observing the rules of the genre.

5°.   acts necessary to access the contents of an electronic database for the purposes of and within the limits of the use provided by contract.

In 1995, the Cour de Cassation held that the privilege of "short quotations" did not apply to a news broadcast in which an artist's mural was visible in the background. Although the artist had died in 1940, the artists' collective rights organization (SPADEM) brought suit on behalf of the artist's beneficiaries. The news story was about the restoration of the theatre, and the re-hanging of the mural panels after they had been stolen and then recovered. During the one-hour broadcast, the camera remained on the mural for 49 seconds. The Cour de Cassation upheld the court of appeal's decision that this was not a short quotation, because while the mural was visible only briefly, it was visible in its entirety. Arret de la 1ere Chambre Civile de la Court de Cassation de 4 Juillet 1995, Societe Nationale de Programes Antenne 2 v. Societe SPADEM.

In 2006, France expanded the list of exceptions in L.122–5. They now include, *inter alia*:

> The reproduction or communication to the public, in whole or in part, of a graphic, sculptural, or architectural work, in the written, audiovisual or online press, for the sole purpose of providing immediate information and in direct relation to that information, provided that the author's name is clearly indicated.
>
> The previous paragraph does not apply to works, notably photographs and illustrations, which are themselves for the purpose of providing information.
>
> Reproductions or communications to the public, which, especially in their number or format, are not in strict proportion to the exclusive purpose of the immediate information which follows or which are not directly related to it require remuneration to the authors * * *
>
> The enumerated exceptions in the present article cannot interfere with the normal exploitation of the work or unreasonably prejudice the legitimate interests of the author.

Art. L.122–5, para. 9. How would the mural case have been decided under this amendment?

In 2007, the Cour de Cassation rejected a "short quotation" defense by a French football magazine that had published an image of the FIFA trophy on its cover. Although L.122–5 permitted "analyses and short quotations justified by the critical, polemic, educational, scientific or informatory nature of the work in which they are incorporated," the court held that the use of the image was not for informational purposes because the magazine article was about football players, rather than about the trophy itself. Arret de la 1ere Chambre Civile de la Cour de Cassation de 2 Octobre 2007, No. 05–14.298. The facts of this case arose before the 2006 amendment. Would the case have come out differently if the amendment had applied?

Recall the *Marcio X* case from Chapter 2. In that case, the Cour de Cassation held that the defendants' Internet posting of photographs taken during Paris fashion shows violated the copyrights of the design houses. The Court expressly rejected the argument that the defendants' actions were protected by Article L.122–5, para. 9 of the French Intellectual Property Code. The Court held that this provision did not apply to fashion designs. As is typical of the Cour de Cassation, the Court did not explain its reasoning. Can you?

In Sarl Louis Feraud Int'l v. Viewfinder, Inc., 489 F.3d 474 (2d Cir. 2007), the Second Circuit held that, in determining whether to enforce a default judgment against the website that published the unauthorized fashion photos in the *Marcio X* case, the federal district court had to determine whether French copyright law provides the website operator with protection comparable to U.S. fair use. How should the Southern District of New York rule on this question?

2.   France's explicit exception for "parody, pastiche, and caricature" sets it apart from the vast majority of other countries that recognize fair use. However, the limiting phrase "observing the rules of the genre" leaves much room for interpretation. In an attempt to balance moral rights against free expression, the French courts have applied this exception only where the parodic work has a humorous intention, and only where the parody is clearly distinct from the work being parodied.

Spain also has an explicit parody exception. Australia added one in 2006, and New Zealand may soon follow suit.

In the United Kingdom, parodies receive no special treatment. instead, they have been evaluated under general fair use principles, with mixed results. Legislative proposals for an explicit parody exception have not borne fruit.

In the EU, Directive 2001/29/EC permits, but does not require, EU members to adopt a parody exception; thus far, few of them have done so.

In Canada, parody defenses have generally not succeeded, because courts have not perceived parodies as a form of criticism. Some observers believe that the Canadian Supreme Court's liberalized view of fair use in *CCH Canadian* (reproduced above) may lead courts to be more receptive toward parody claims. Others believe that an explicit statutory exception is needed.

Is a categorical exception for parodies permitted under international agreements?

Chapter 6

SECONDARY LIABILITY

A. LIABILITY FOR "AUTHORIZING"

CCH CANADIAN LTD. v. LAW SOCIETY OF UPPER CANADA

Supreme Court of Canada, 2004
[2004] 1 S.C.R. 339, 2004 SCC 13

The Chief Justice:

I. Introduction—The Issues To Be Determined

The appellant, the Law Society of Upper Canada, is a statutory non-profit corporation that has regulated the legal profession in Ontario since 1822. Since 1845, the Law Society has maintained and operated the Great Library at Osgoode Hall in Toronto, a reference and research library with one of the largest collections of legal materials in Canada. The Great Library provides a request-based photocopy service (the "custom photocopy service") for Law Society members, the judiciary and other authorized researchers. Under the custom photocopy service, legal materials are reproduced by Great Library staff and delivered in person, by mail or by facsimile transmission to requesters. The Law Society also maintains self-service photocopiers in the Great Library for use by its patrons.

The respondents, CCH Canadian Ltd., Thomson Canada Ltd. and Canada Law Book Inc., publish law reports and other legal materials. In 1993, the respondent publishers commenced copyright infringement actions against the Law Society, seeking a declaration of subsistence and ownership of copyright in eleven specific works and a declaration that the Law Society had infringed copyright when the Great Library reproduced a copy of each of the works. The publishers also sought a permanent injunction prohibiting the

Law Society from reproducing these eleven works as well as any other works that they published.

The Law Society denied liability and counterclaimed for a declaration that copyright is not infringed when a single copy of a reported decision, case summary, statute, regulation or a limited selection of text from a treatise is made by the Great Library staff or one of its patrons on a self-service photocopier for the purpose of research.

The key question that must be answered in this appeal is whether the Law Society has breached copyright by * * * maintaining self-service photocopiers and copies of the publishers' works in the Great Library for use by its patrons. * * *

The publishers have filed a cross-appeal in which they submit that, in addition to infringing copyright by reproducing copies of their works, the Law Society infringed copyright * * * by selling copies of the publishers' copyrighted works through its custom photocopy service. * * *

* * *

II. Analysis on Appeal

* * *

(2) *Authorization: The Self–Service Photocopiers*

(a) *The Law*

Under s. 27(1) of the Copyright Act, it is an infringement of copyright for anyone to do anything that the Act only allows owners to do, including authorizing the exercise of his or her own rights. It does not infringe copyright to authorize a person to do something that would not constitute copyright infringement. See *C.A.P.A.C. v. CTV Television Network*, [1968] S.C.R. 676 (S.C.C.), at p. 680. The publishers argue that the Law Society is liable for breach of copyright under this section because it implicitly authorized patrons of the Great Library to copy works in breach of the Copyright Act.

"Authorize" means to "sanction, approve and countenance": *Muzak Corp. v. Composers, Authors & Publishers Assn. (Canada)*, [1953] 2 S.C.R. 182 (S.C.C.), at p. 193; *de Tervagne v. Beloeil (Town)*, [1993] 3 F.C. 227 (Fed. T.D.). Countenance in the context of authorizing copyright infringement must be understood in its strongest dictionary meaning, namely, "give approval to, sanction, permit, favour, encourage". Authorization is a question of fact that depends on the circumstances of each particular case and can be inferred from acts that are less than direct and positive, including a sufficient degree of indifference: *C.B.S. Inc. v. Ames Records & Tapes*, [1981] 2 All E.R. 812 (Eng. Ch. Div.), at pp. 823–24.

However, a person does not authorize infringement by authorizing the mere use of equipment that could be used to infringe copyright. Courts should presume that a person who authorizes an activity does so only so far as it is in accordance with the law. This presumption may be rebutted if it is shown that a certain relationship or degree of control existed between the alleged authorizer and the persons who committed the copyright infringement.

(b) Application of the Law to these Facts

For several decades, the Law Society has maintained self-service photocopiers for the use of its patrons in the Great Library. The patrons' use of the machines is not monitored directly. Since the mid–1980s, the Law Society has posted the following notice above each machine:

> The copyright law of Canada governs the making of photocopies or other reproductions of copyright material. Certain copying may be an infringement of the copyright law. This library is not responsible for infringing copies made by users of these machines.

At trial, the Law Society applied for a declaration that it did not authorize copyright infringement by providing self-service photocopiers for patrons of the Great Library. No evidence was tendered that the photocopiers had been used in an infringing manner.

The trial judge declined to deal with this issue, in part because of the limited nature of the evidence on this question. The Federal Court of Appeal, relying in part on the Australian High Court decision in *Moorehouse v. University of New South Wales*, [1976] R.P.C. 151 (Australia H.C.), concluded that the Law Society implicitly sanctioned, approved or countenanced copyright infringement of the publishers' works by failing to control copying and instead merely posting a notice indicating that the Law Society was not responsible for infringing copies made by the machine's users.

With respect, I do not agree that this amounted to authorizing breach of copyright. *Moorhouse, supra*, is inconsistent with previous Canadian and British approaches to this issue. See D. Vaver, *Copyright Law* (2000), at p. 27, and McKeown, *supra*, at p. 21–108. In my view, the *Moorhouse* approach to authorization shifts the balance in copyright too far in favour of the owner's rights and unnecessarily interferes with the proper use of copyrighted works for the good of society as a whole.

Applying the criteria from *Muzak Corp., supra*, and *de Tervagne, supra*, I conclude that the Law Society's mere provision of photocopiers for the use of its patrons did not constitute authorization to use the photocopiers to breach copyright law.

First, there was no evidence that the photocopiers had been used in a manner that was not consistent with copyright law. As noted, a person does not authorize copyright infringement by authorizing the mere use of equipment (such as photocopiers) that could be used to infringe copyright. In fact, courts should presume that a person who authorizes an activity does so only so far as it is in accordance with the law. Although the Court of Appeal assumed that the photocopiers were being used to infringe copyright, I think it is equally plausible that the patrons using the machines were doing so in a lawful manner.

Second, the Court of Appeal erred in finding that the Law Society's posting of the notice constitutes an express acknowledgement that the photocopiers will be used in an illegal manner. The Law Society's posting of the notice over the photocopiers does not rebut the presumption that a person authorizes an activity only so far as it is in accordance with the law. Given that the Law Society is responsible for regulating the legal profession in Ontario, it is more logical to conclude that the notice was posted for the purpose of reminding the Great Library's patrons that copyright law governs the making of photocopies in the library.

Finally, even if there were evidence of the photocopiers having been used to infringe copyright, the Law Society lacks sufficient control over the Great Library's patrons to permit the conclusion that it sanctioned, approved or countenanced the infringement. The Law Society and Great Library patrons are not in a master-servant or employer-employee relationship such that the Law Society can be said to exercise control over the patrons who might commit infringement: see, for example, *De Tervagne, supra.* Nor does the Law Society exercise control over which works the patrons choose to copy, the patron's purposes for copying or the photocopiers themselves.

In summary, I conclude that evidence does not establish that the Law Society authorized copyright infringement by providing self-service photocopiers and copies of the respondent publishers' works for use by its patrons in the Great Library. I would allow this ground of appeal.

(3) The Law Society and Fair Dealing

[The court next analyzed the Law Society's custom photocopying practices and concluded that they satisfied the requirements for the "fair dealing" defense under section 29 of Canada's Copyright Act. This part of the opinion is reproduced in Chapter 5 above.]

* * *

(5) Conclusion on Main Appeal

I would allow the appeal and issue a declaration that the Law Society does not * * * authorize copyright infringement by maintaining a photocopier in the Great Library and posting a notice warning that it will not be responsible for any copies made in infringement of copyright.

III. Analysis on Cross–Appeal

* * *

(2) Did the Law Society infringe copyright in the publishers' works by selling copies contrary to s. 27(2) of the Copyright Act?

Under s. 27(2)(a) of the Copyright Act, it is an infringement of copyright to sell a copy of a work that the person knows or should have known infringes copyright, a practice known as secondary infringement. The majority at the Court of Appeal rejected the allegation of secondary infringement on the ground that it was not established that the Law Society knew or should have known it was dealing with infringing copies of the publishers' works. The publishers appeal this finding on cross-appeal.

At the Court of Appeal, Rothstein J.A., in his concurring judgment, properly outlined the three elements that must be proven to ground a claim for secondary infringement: (1) the copy must be the product of primary infringement; (2) the secondary infringer must have known or should have known that he or she is dealing with a product of infringement; and (3) the secondary dealing must be established; that is, there must have been a sale.

In the main appeal, I have concluded that the Law Society did not infringe copyright in reproducing the publishers' works in response to requests under its custom photocopy service. Absent primary infringement, there can be no secondary infringement. I would dismiss this ground of cross-appeal.

* * *

Notes

1. Under Canada's current copyright law, unauthorized public distribution is actionable only as a matter of secondary infringement—that is, only when the defendant knew or should have known that the copies were infringing. Should Canada enact a broader distribution right?

2. In a 2008 opinion, the Intellectual Property High Court of Japan held that a government agency was jointly liable for copyright infringement where it loaned copies of a copyrighted book to visitors to its offices and provided space for coin-operated photocopiers to make

copies of the book. The court held that the owner of the photocopying equipment was also jointly liable.

3. Does the Canada Supreme Court's ruling on "authorization" have any relevance in the Internet context? Consider the following case.

B.   ISP LIABILITY

SOCIETY OF COMPOSERS, AUTHORS & MUSIC PUBLISHERS OF CANADA v. CANADIAN ASSN. OF INTERNET PROVIDERS

Supreme Court of Canada, 2004
2004 CarswellNat 1919
2004 SCC 45, [2004] 2 S.C.R. 427

Binnie J.:

This appeal raises the difficult issue of who should compensate musical composers and artists for their Canadian copyright in music downloaded in Canada from a foreign country via the Internet. * * *

* * *

The answer to this challenge proposed by the respondent, the Society of Composers, Authors and Music Publishers of Canada ("SOCAN"), is to seek to impose liability for royalties on the various Internet Service Providers located in Canada irrespective of where the transmission originates. There is no doubt that such an imposition, from SOCAN's perspective, would provide an efficient engine of collection.

The appellants, on the other hand, representing a broad coalition of Canadian Internet Service Providers, resist. Their basic argument is that none of them, as found by the Copyright Board, regulate or are even in the usual case aware of the content of the Internet communications which they transmit. Like a telephone company, they provide the medium, but they do not control the message.

Parliament has spoken on this issue. In a 1988 amendment to the Copyright Act, R.S.C. 1985, c. C–42, it made it clear that Internet intermediaries, as such, are not to be considered parties to the infringing communication. They are service providers, not participants in the content of the communication. In light of Parliament's legislative policy, when applied to the findings of fact by the Copyright Board, I agree with the Board's conclusion that as a matter of law the appellants did not, in general, "communicate" or "authorize" the communication of musical works in Canada in violation of the respondent's copyright within the meaning of the Copyright Act.

SOCAN sought a judicial review of the Board's decision by the Federal Court of Appeal, which essentially upheld the Board's exclusion of the appellants from copyright liability where they perform a pure intermediary function. However, the court, in a 2–1 majority decision, also held that where an Internet Service Provider in Canada creates a "cache" of Internet material, even for purely technical reasons, they are no longer a mere intermediary but a communicator and thus become a participant in the copyright infringement. A contrary conclusion was reached by Sharlow J.A., dissenting in part, who agreed with the Copyright Board that to cache for the purpose of enhancing Internet economy and efficiency does not constitute infringement. I agree with the dissent on this point. To that extent, the appeal should be allowed.

The respondent's cross-appeal seeking to hold Internet intermediaries liable for copyright royalties even where serving only as a conduit should be dismissed.

I. Facts

* * *

The respondent, SOCAN is a collective society recognized under s. 2 of the Copyright Act, to administer "performing rights" in Canada including those of (1) its Canadian member composers, authors and music publishers, and (2) foreign composers, authors and music publishers whose interest is protected by a system of reciprocal agreements with counterpart societies here and in other countries. Essentially, SOCAN administers in Canada "the world repertoire of copyright protected music".

In 1995, SOCAN applied to the Copyright Board for approval of Tariff 22 applicable to Internet telecommunications of copyrighted music. Tariff 22 would require a licence and a royalty fee

> . . . to communicate to the public by telecommunication, in Canada, musical works forming part of SOCAN's repertoire, by a telecommunications service to subscribers by means of one or more computer(s) or other device that is connected to a telecommunications network where the transmission of those works can be accessed by each subscriber independently of any other person having access to the service.

Recognizing that there might be many participants in any Internet communication, the Board convened a Phase I hearing to "determine which activities on the Internet, if any, constitute a protected use targeted in the tariff".

* * *

The Copyright Board found that Internet Service Providers who "host" Web sites for others are generally neither aware of nor control the content of the files stored in memory; however, in some cases they do warn content providers not to post illegal content (*e.g.*, criminal pornography, defamatory material, copyright infringing materials, viruses, etc.), and will usually retain a master "root" password that allows them to access all the files on the server. The contract generally reserves to the host server provider the authority to periodically review for content posted in breach of their agreement and to remove such files. The existence of such means of control, and the host server provider's discretion in whether or not to exercise them, justifies the imposition of liability for a copyright licence on host servers, according to SOCAN.

* * *

A particular issue arose in respect of the appellants' use of "caching". When an end user visits a Web site, the packets of data needed to transmit the requested information will come initially from the host server where the files for this site are stored. As they pass through the hands of an Internet Service Provider, a temporary copy may be made and stored on its server. This is a cache copy. If another user wants to visit this page shortly thereafter, using the same Internet Service Provider, the information may be transmitted to the subsequent user either directly from the Web site or from what is kept in the cache copy. The practice of creating "caches" of data speeds up the transmission and lowers the cost. The subsequent end user may have no idea that it is not getting the information directly from the original Web site. Cache copies are not retained for long periods of time since, if the original files change, users will get out-of-date information. The Internet Service Provider controls the existence and duration of caches on its own facility, although in some circumstances it is open to a content provider to specify no caching, or an end user to program its browser to insist on content from the original Web site.

SOCAN argued that where a cache copy is made on a computer located in Canada and then retransmitted, there is a distinct violation in Canada of copyright protection. This, as stated, is the issue that divided the Federal Court of Appeal.

* * *

II. Relevant Statutory Provisions

Copyright Act, R.S.C. 1985, c. C–42

2. ... "telecommunication" means any transmission of signs, signals, writing, images or sounds or intelligence of any nature by wire, radio, visual, optical or other electro-magnetic system;

2.4 (1) For the purposes of communication to the public by telecommunication,

. . . . .

(b) a person whose only act in respect of the communication of a work or other subject-matter to the public consists of providing the means of telecommunication necessary for another person to so communicate the work or other subject-matter does not communicate that work or other subject-matter to the public; and

. . . . .

3. (1) For the purposes of this Act, "copyright", in relation to a work, means the sole right to produce or reproduce the work or any substantial part thereof in any material form whatever, to perform the work or any substantial part thereof in public or, if the work is unpublished, to publish the work or any substantial part thereof, and includes the sole right

. . . . .

(f) in the case of any literary, dramatic, musical or artistic work, to communicate the work to the public by telecommunication,

and to authorize any such acts.

* * *

III. Judicial History

A. Decision of the Copyright Board

Tariff 22 proposed the amount and allocation of a royalty payable to copyright owners for the communication of music on the Internet. At the end of the first phase of its proceeding, geared to determining who might be liable to pay royalties, the Copyright Board held that a royalty can be imposed on content providers who post music on a server located in Canada that can be accessed by other Internet users. However, the Board also held that the normal activities of Internet intermediaries not acting as content providers do not constitute "a communication" for the purpose of the Copyright Act and thus do not infringe the exclusive communication rights of copyright owners. The parties did not frame an issue in relation to infringement of the right of reproduction, and its role, if any, did not play a significant part in the Board's decision.

* * *

In order to determine the level of intermediate participation in Internet transmission of musical works that could trigger liability for infringement under s. 3(1)(f) of the Copyright Act, the Board was required to interpret the scope of the limitation in s. 2.4(1)(b), which says that an Internet Service Provider does not "communicate" a copyrighted work if its "*only*" act" is to provide "the *means* of telecommunication *necessary* for another person to so communicate the work".

The Board rejected SOCAN's argument that s. 2.4(1)(b) should be narrowly construed as an exemption to copyright liability. The Board held that where an intermediary merely acts as a "*conduit* for communications by other persons" (emphasis added), it can claim the benefit of s. 2.4(1)(b). If an intermediary does more than merely act as a conduit, (for example if it creates a cache for reasons other than improving system performance or modifies the content of cached material), it may lose the protection. Insofar as the Internet Service Provider furnishes "ancillary" services to a content provider or end user, it could still rely on s. 2.4(1)(b) as a defence to copyright infringement, provided any such "ancillary services" do not amount in themselves to communication or authorization to communicate the work. Creation of an automatic "hyperlink" by a Canadian Internet Service Provider will also attract copyright liability.

As to "authorization", the Board found that knowledge by an Internet Service Provider that its facilities might be used for infringing purposes was not enough to incur liability. The Internet Service Provider needed to grant "the person committing the infringement a license or permission to infringe".

* * *

IV.   Analysis

* * *

A.   Communication under the Copyright Act

It is an infringement for anyone to do, without the consent of the copyright owner, "anything that, by this Act, only the owner of the copyright has the right to do" (s. 27(1)), including, since the 1988 amendments, the right "to *communicate* the work to the public by telecommunication ... and to *authorize* any such acts" (emphasis added) (s. 3(1)(f)). In the same series of amendments, "telecommunication" was defined as "any transmission of signs, signals, writings, images or sounds or intelligence of any nature by wire, radio, visual, optical or other electromagnetic system" (s. 2). The Board ruled that a telecommunication occurs when the music is transmitted from the host server to the end user. I agree with this. The respondent says that the appellants as intermediaries participate in any such transmission of their copyrighted works, and authorize others to do so, and should therefore be required to pay compensation fixed under Tariff 22.

In the United States, unlike Canada, detailed legislation has now been enacted to deal specifically with the liability of Internet intermediaries; see the Digital Millennium Copyright Act, 17 U.S.C. § 512 (1998). Australia has enacted its Copyright Amendment (Digital Agenda) Act 2000, No. 110 of 2000. The European Commission has issued a number of directives, as will be discussed. Parliament's response to the World Intellectual Property Organization's (WIPO) Copyright Treaty, 1996, ("WCT") and the Performances and Phonograms Treaty, 1996, remains to be seen. In the meantime, the courts must struggle to transpose a Copyright Act designed to implement the Berne Convention for the Protection of Literary and Artistic Works of 1886, as revised in Berlin in 1908, and subsequent piecemeal amendments, to the information age, and to technologies undreamt of by those early legislators.

* * *

2.   The Interpretation of the Copyright Act

I therefore turn to the question of the extent to which Canada has exercised its copyright jurisdiction in relation to the Internet Service Providers at issue in this appeal.

SOCAN asserts Canadian copyright in the material transmitted from outside Canada to an end user in Canada. It is true that end users in Canada wind up with copyrighted material in their possession, and a communication to the Canadian user has therefore occurred. The question is whether Tariff 22 imposes a licensing requirement on the appellants and others performing an intermediary function in telecommunications.

At this point the prospect of seeking to collect royalties from foreign infringers is not an attractive prospect for SOCAN. The question therefore is whether any or all of the appellants, in the ordinary course of their business, impart or transmit copyrighted music, and thereby do themselves infringe the copyrights represented by the respondent, within the meaning of the Act.

In Canada, copyright is a creature of statute, and the rights and remedies provided by the Copyright Act are exhaustive.

The respondent must show that the appellants infringed its "sole right", in relation to the musical works at issue, to "communicate to the public by telecommunication".

This will require consideration of two related legal issues:

> i) Can the appellants claim the protection of the limitation in s. 2.4.(1)(b)?

> ii) What is the meaning of "authorization" of copyright infringement, in the context of Internet communications?

> a.   The Section 2.4(1)(b) Protection

A telecommunication starts, as the Board found, with the content provider.

> The fact that [the communication] is achieved at the request of the recipient or through an agent neither adds to, nor detracts from the fact that the content provider effects the communication.

The 1988 amendments to the Copyright Act specify that participants in a telecommunication who only provide "the means of telecommunication necessary" are deemed not to be communicators. The section as presently worded provides as follows:

> 2.4   (1) For the purposes of communication to the public by telecommunication,

> . . . . .

> (b) a person whose only act in respect of the communication of a work or other subject-matter to the public consists of providing the means of telecommunication necessary for another person to so communicate the work or other subject-matter does not communicate that work or other subject-matter to the public[.]

> * * *

Section 2.4(1)(b) is not a loophole but an important element of the balance struck by the statutory copyright scheme. It finds its roots, perhaps, in the defence of innocent dissemination sometimes available to bookstores, libraries, news vendors, and the like who, generally speaking, have no actual knowledge of an alleged libel, are aware of no circumstances to put them on notice to suspect a libel, and committed no negligence in failing to find out about the libel.

The 1988 amendments, including the predecessor to s. 2.4(1)(b), followed on the recommendation of an all party Sub–Committee on the Revision of Copyright of the House of Commons

Standing Committee on Communications and Culture. Its report, entitled A Charter of Rights for Creators (1985), identified the need for a broader definition of telecommunication, one that was not dependent on the form of technology, which would provide copyright protection for retransmissions. This led to the adoption of the broad definition of communication in s. 3(1)(f). In conjunction with this, the Committee recommended that those who participate in the retransmission "solely to serve as an intermediary between the signal source and a retransmitter whose services are offered to the general public" should not be unfairly caught by the expanded definition. The ostensible objective, according to the Committee, was to avoid the unnecessary layering of copyright liability that would result from targeting the "wholesale" stage.

The words of s. 2.4(1)(b) must be read in their ordinary and grammatical sense in the proper context. "Necessary" is a word whose meaning varies somewhat with the context. * * * In context, the word "necessary" in s. 2.4(1)(b) is satisfied if the means are reasonably useful and proper to achieve the benefits of enhanced economy and efficiency.

Section 2.4(1)(b) shields from liability the activities associated with providing the means for another to communicate by telecommunication. "The means", as the Board found, ". . . are not limited to routers and other hardware. They include all software connection equipment, connectivity services, hosting and other facilities and services without which such communications would not occur". I agree. So long as an Internet intermediary does not itself engage in acts that relate to the content of the communication, *i.e.*, whose participation is content neutral, but confines itself to providing "a conduit" for information communicated by others, then it will fall within s. 2.4(1)(b). The appellants support this result on a general theory of "Don't shoot the messenger!".

In rejecting SOCAN's argument on this point, the Board concluded:

> In the end, each transmission must be looked at individually to determine whether in that case, an intermediary merely *acts as a conduit* for communications by other persons, or whether it is acting as something more. Generally speaking, however, it is safe to conclude that with respect to most transmissions, *only the person who posts a musical work communicates it.* [Emphasis added.]

The Board also found, after its analysis of the activities of the various participants in an Internet transmission, that the person who "make[s] the work available for communication" is not the host server provider but the content provider:

> Any communication of a work occurs because a person has taken all the required steps *to make the work available* for communication. The fact that this is achieved at the request of the recipient or through an agent neither adds to, nor detracts from the fact that *the content provider* effects the communication. [Emphasis added.]

This conclusion, as I understand it, is based on the findings of fact by the Board of what an Internet intermediary, including a host server provider, actually does. To the extent they act as innocent disseminators, they are protected by s. 2.4(1)(b) of the Act. As the Board put it:

> As long as its role in respect of any given transmission is limited to providing the means necessary to allow data initiated by other persons to be transmitted over the Internet, and as long as the ancillary services it provides fall short of involving the act of communicating the work or authorizing its communication, it should be allowed to claim the exemption.

I agree with this approach. Having properly instructed itself on the law, the Board found as a fact that the "conduit" begins with the host server. No reason has been shown in this application for judicial review to set aside that conclusion.

* * *

Interpretation of s. 2.4(1)(b) in this way is consistent with art. 8 of the WIPO Copyright Treaty, 1996. In the accompanying Agreed Statements, the treaty authority states:

> It is understood that the mere provision of physical facilities for enabling or making a communication does not in itself amount to communication within the meaning of this Treaty or the Berne Convention.

Similarly, the European E–Commerce Directive provides, in clause 42 of its Preamble that Internet intermediaries are not liable where their actions are confined to

> the technical process of operating and giving access to a communication network over which information made available by third parties is transmitted or temporarily stored, for the sole purpose of making the transmission more efficient; this activity is of a mere technical, automatic and passive nature, which implies that the [Internet intermediary] has neither knowledge of nor control over the information which is transmitted or stored.

While lack of knowledge of the infringing nature of a work is not a defence to copyright actions generally, nevertheless the presence of such knowledge would be a factor in the evaluation of the "conduit" status of an Internet Service Provider, as discussed below.

The Internet Service Provider, acting as an intermediary, does not charge a particular fee to its clients for music downloading (although clearly the availability of "free music" is a significant business incentive).

I conclude that the Copyright Act, as a matter of legislative policy established by Parliament, does not impose liability for infringement on intermediaries who supply software and hardware to facilitate use of the Internet. The attributes of such a "conduit", as found by the Board, include a lack of actual knowledge of the infringing contents, and the impracticality (both technical and economic) of monitoring the vast amount of material moving through the Internet, which is prodigious. We are told that a large on-line service provider like America Online delivers in the order of 11 million transmissions a day.

Of course an Internet Service Provider in Canada can play a number of roles. In addition to its function as an intermediary, it may as well act as a content provider, or create embedded links which automatically precipitate a telecommunication of copyrighted music from another source. In such cases, copyright liability may attach to the added functions. The protection provided by s. 2.4(1)(b) relates to a protected function, not to all of the activities of a particular Internet Service Provider.

On the other hand, as Evans J.A. pointed out, Internet Service Providers who operate a host server would not lose the protection of paragraph 2.4(1)(b) by providing their normal facilities and services, such as housing and maintaining the servers, and monitoring "hits" on particular Web pages, because these added services are merely ancillary to the provision of disk space and do not involve any act of communication.

b.   The Liability of the Host Server

* * *

My [dissenting] colleague LeBel J. * * * relies on art. 8 of the WCT, which gives the copyright owner the exclusive right of "making available to the public ... their works", but as previously noted, the Board found that in copyright terms it is the content provider, not the host server provider, that makes the work available. Accordingly, as I see it, the issue of the relevance of art. 8 to the interpretation of the Copyright Act does not arise.

The Board found that a host server provider like AT&T Canada "merely gives the customer [*i.e.,* the content provider] the right to place information on the servers". Typically the host server provider will not monitor what is posted to determine if it complies with copyright laws and other legal restrictions. Given the vast amount of information posted, it is impractical in the present state of the technology to require the host server provider to do so. In any event, it is unrealistic to attribute to a provider an expertise in copyright law sufficient to "lawyer" all of the changing contents of its servers on an ongoing basis in the absence of alleged infringements being brought to their attention.

However, to the extent the host server provider has notice of copyrighted material posted on its server, it may, as the Board found, "respond to the complaint in accordance with the [Canadian Association of Internet Providers] Code of Conduct [which] may include requiring the customer to remove the offending material through a 'take down notice' ". If the host server provider does not comply with the notice, it may be held to have authorized communication of the copyright material, as hereinafter discussed.

[The Copyright] Board was correct in its general conclusion on this point, which for ease of reference I set out again:

> In the end, each transmission must be looked at individually to determine whether in that case, an intermediary merely acts as a conduit for communications by other persons, or whether it is acting as something more. Generally speaking, however, it is safe to conclude that with respect to most transmissions, *only the person who posts a musical work communicates it.* [Emphasis added.]

In my view, the Federal Court of Appeal was right to uphold this aspect of the Board's ruling.

c.   The Use of Caches

The majority in the Federal Court of Appeal concluded that the use of caching amounts to a function falling outside s. 2.4(1)(b). Evans J.A. took the view that protection is only available "when, without that person's activity, communication in that medium of telecommunication would not be practicable or, in all probability, would not have occurred". This is a high eligibility test which could inhibit development of more efficient means of telecommunication. SOCAN and others representing copyright owners would always be able to argue that whatever the advances in the future, a telecommunication could still have been practicable using the old technology, and that one way or the other the telecommunication would "in all probability" have occurred. In my view, with respect, Evans J.A. has placed the bar too high.

Parliament has decided that there is a public interest in encouraging intermediaries who make telecommunications possible to expand and improve their operations without the threat of copyright infringement. To impose copyright liability on intermediaries would obviously chill that expansion and development, as the history of caching demonstrates. In the early years of the Internet, as the Board found, its usefulness for the transmission of musical works was limited by "the relatively high bandwidth required to transmit audio files". This technical limitation was addressed in part by using "caches". As the Board noted: "Caching reduces the cost for the delivery of data by allowing the use of lower bandwidth than would otherwise be necessary." The velocity of new technical developments in the computer industry, and the rapidly declining cost to the consumer, is legendary. * * * Section 2.4(1)(b) reflects Parliament's priority that this entrepreneurial push is to continue despite any incidental effects on copyright owners.

In the Board's view, the means "necessary" under s. 2.4(1)(b) were means that were content neutral and were necessary to maximize the economy and cost-effectiveness of the Internet "conduit". That interpretation, it seems to me, best promotes "the public interest in the encouragement and dissemination of works of the arts and intellect" without depriving copyright owners of their legitimate entitlement. The creation of a "cache" copy, after all, is a serendipitous consequence of improvements in Internet technology, is content neutral, and in light of s. 2.4(1)(b) of the Act ought not to have any legal bearing on the communication between the content provider and the end user.

As noted earlier, SOCAN successfully relied on the "exigencies of the Internet" to defeat the appellants' argument that they did not communicate a "musical work" but simply packets of data that may or may not arrive in the correct sequence. It is somewhat inconsistent, it seems to me, for SOCAN then to deny the appellants the benefit of a similar "exigencies" argument. "Caching" is dictated by the need to deliver faster and more economic service, and should not, when undertaken only for such technical reasons, attract copyright liability.

A comparable result has been reached under the U.S. Digital Millennium Copyright Act, which in part codified the result in Religious Technology Center v. Netcom On–Line Communication Services, 907 F.Supp. 1361 (U.S. N.D. Cal., 1995), where it was observed, at pp. 1369–70:

> These parties, who are liable under plaintiffs' theory, do no more than operate or implement a system that is essential if Usenet messages are to be widely distributed. There is no need to construe the Act to make all of these parties infringers. Although copyright is a strict liability statute, there should still be some element of volition or causation

which is lacking where a defendant's system is merely used to create a copy by a third party.

The European E–Commerce Directive mandates member States to exempt Internet Service Providers from copyright liability for caching (art. 13(1)).

In my opinion the Copyright Board's view that caching comes within the shelter of s. 2.4(1) is correct, and I would restore the Board's conclusion in that regard.

d. "Authorizing" Infringement

Authorizing a communication by telecommunication is a discrete infringement of s. 3(1).

The respondent argues that even if the appellants did not themselves infringe the copyright, they were guilty of "authorizing" content providers to do so because Internet intermediaries know that material (including copyright material) placed on their facilities by content providers will be accessed by end users. Indeed as Evans J.A. pointed out: "Knowledge of the content available on the Internet, including 'free' music, and of end users' interest in accessing it, are powerful inducements for end users to sign up with access providers, and content providers with operators of host servers."

Of course there is a good deal of material on the Internet that is not subject to copyright, just as there was a good deal of law-related material in the Great Library at Osgoode Hall that was not copyrighted in the recent *CCH* appeal. In that case, as here, the copyright owners asserted that making available a photocopier and photocopying service by the Law Society of Upper Canada implicitly "authorized" copyright infringement. This Court, however, held that authorizing infringement under the Copyright Act is not so easily demonstrated, per McLachlin C.J.:

> . . . a person does not authorize infringement by authorizing the mere use of equipment that *could* be used to infringe copyright. Courts should presume that a person who authorizes an activity does so only so far as it is in accordance with the law. This presumption may be rebutted if it is shown that a certain *relationship or degree of control* existed between the alleged authorizer and the persons who committed the copyright infringement. [Emphasis added.]

SOCAN contends that the host server in essence acts as a commercial partner with the content provider when material is made available on the Internet, but there was no such finding of fact by the Board, and I do not think the rights and obligations of partnership can be so casually imposed.

The operation of the Internet is obviously a good deal more complicated than the operation of a photocopier, but it is true here, as it was in the *CCH* case, that when massive amounts of non-copyrighted material are accessible to the end user, it is not possible to impute to the Internet Service Provider, based solely on the provision of Internet facilities, an authority to download copyrighted material as opposed to non-copyrighted material.

On this point the Board concluded as follows:

> Even knowledge by an ISP that its facilities may be employed for infringing purposes does not make the ISP liable for authorizing the infringement if it does not purport to grant to the person committing the infringement a license or permission to infringe. An intermediary would have to sanction, approve or countenance more than the mere use of equipment that may be used for infringement. Moreover, an ISP is entitled to presume that its facilities will be used in accordance with law.

This conclusion is generally consistent with the decision of this Court in the *CCH* case, although I would point out that copyright liability may well attach if the activities of the Internet Service Provider cease to be content neutral, *e.g.,* if it has notice that a content provider has posted infringing material on its system and fails to take remedial action.

Under the European E–Commerce Directive, access to cached information must be expeditiously curtailed when the Internet Service Provider becomes aware of infringing content. At that time, the information must be removed or access disabled at the original site (art. 13(1)(e)). Under the U.S. Digital Millennium Copyright Act, those who cache information are not liable where they act expeditiously to remove or disable access to material once notice is received that it infringes copyright (s. 512(b)(2)(E)). If the content provider disputes that the work is covered by copyright, the U.S. Act lays out a procedure for the resolution of that issue.

In the present appeal, the Federal Court of Appeal stated that, in the case of host servers, "an implicit authorization to communicate infringing material might be inferred from their failure to remove it after they have been advised of its presence on the server and had a reasonable opportunity to take it down". Reference was made to Apple Computer Inc. v. Mackintosh Computers Ltd. (1986), [1987] 1 F.C. 173 (Fed. T.D.), *aff'd* [1990] 2 S.C.R. 209 (S.C.C.), *i.e.,* an Internet Service Provider may attract liability for authorization because ". . . indifference, exhibited by acts of commission or omission, may reach a degree from which authorisation or permission may be inferred. It is a question of fact in each case."

The knowledge that someone might be using neutral technology to violate copyright (as with the photocopier in the *CCH* case) is not necessarily sufficient to constitute authorization, which requires a demonstration that the defendant did "[g]ive approval to; sanction, permit; favour, encourage" (*CCH*, para. 38) the infringing conduct. I agree that notice of infringing content, and a failure to respond by "taking it down" may in some circumstances lead to a finding of "authorization". However, that is not the issue before us. Much would depend on the specific circumstances. An overly quick inference of "authorization" would put the Internet Service Provider in the difficult position of judging whether the copyright objection is well founded, and to choose between contesting a copyright action or potentially breaching its contract with the content provider. A more effective remedy to address this potential issue would be the enactment by Parliament of a statutory "notice and take down" procedure as has been done in the European Community and the United States.

In sum, I agree with the Court of Appeal that "authorization" could be inferred in a proper case but all would depend on the facts.

D.   Achieving a Balance Fair to Copyright Owners

There is no doubt that the exponential growth of the Internet has created serious obstacles to the collection of copyright royalties. * * *

* * *

Nevertheless, by enacting s. 2.4(1)(b) of the Copyright Act, Parliament made a policy distinction between those who abuse the Internet to obtain "cheap music" and those who are part of the infrastructure of the Internet itself. It is clear that Parliament did not want copyright disputes between creators and users to be visited on the heads of the Internet intermediaries, whose continued expansion and development is considered vital to national economic growth.

This appeal is only tangentially related to holding "the balance" between creators and users. Section 2.4(1)(b) indicates that in Parliament's view, Internet intermediaries are not "users" at all, at least for purposes of the Copyright Act.

V.   Disposition

For the foregoing reasons, I would allow the appeal with costs with respect to copyright liability for caches of data created in a manner that is content neutral for the purpose of economy and efficiency and dismiss the cross-appeal with costs * * *

[Dissenting opinion omitted.]

Notes

1. Proposals for DMCA-type safe harbors in Canada have not yet yielded any legislation. As a result, the U.S. has placed Canada on the Special 301 Watch List.

2. In March of 2009, the New Zealand government withdrew sec. 92A of its Copyright Act, preventing it from going into effect. Sec. 92A, enacted in 2008, would have provided that:

> An Internet service provider must adopt and reasonably implement a policy that provides for termination, in appropriate circumstances, of the account with that Internet service provider of a repeat infringer.

Its enactment was so controversial that it sparked protests. Users and content providers argued that there was too much uncertainty as to how this provision would be implemented—in particular, whether a mere accusation of infringement would be sufficient to trigger termination.

Similar proposals (referred to as "three-strikes" laws) have been rejected by the United Kingdom, Germany, and the European Parliament, although they have been adopted in France, Taiwan, and Australia. In France, however, a recent decision by the highest court, the Cour de Cassation, arguably weakens the French "three-strikes law," requiring a court order before a repeat infringer's Internet access can be terminated. The court cited free speech and due process concerns.

3. The ISP liability provisions of the European Union's Electronic Commerce Directive, mentioned in the *Society of Composers, Authors, and Music Publishers* case, are excerpted below.

DIRECTIVE 2000/31/EC OF THE EUROPEAN PARLIAMENT AND OF THE COUNCIL OF 8 JUNE 2000 ON CERTAIN LEGAL ASPECTS OF INFORMATION SOCIETY SERVICES, IN PARTICULAR ELECTRONIC COMMERCE, IN THE INTERNAL MARKET

* * *

Section 4: Liability of intermediary service providers
Article 12: "Mere conduit"

1. Where an information society service is provided that consists of the transmission in a communication network of information provided by a recipient of the service, or the provision of access to a communication network, Member States shall ensure that the service provider is not liable for the information transmitted, on condition that the provider:

(a) does not initiate the transmission;

(b) does not select the receiver of the transmission; and

(c) does not select or modify the information contained in the transmission.

2.   The acts of transmission and of provision of access referred to in paragraph 1 include the automatic, intermediate and transient storage of the information transmitted in so far as this takes place for the sole purpose of carrying out the transmission in the communication network, and provided that the information is not stored for any period longer than is reasonably necessary for the transmission.

3.   This Article shall not affect the possibility for a court or administrative authority, in accordance with Member States' legal systems, of requiring the service provider to terminate or prevent an infringement.

Article 13: "Caching"

1.   Where an information society service is provided that consists of the transmission in a communication network of information provided by a recipient of the service, Member States shall ensure that the service provider is not liable for the automatic, intermediate and temporary storage of that information, performed for the sole purpose of making more efficient the information's onward transmission to other recipients of the service upon their request, on condition that:

(a) the provider does not modify the information;

(b) the provider complies with conditions on access to the information;

(c) the provider complies with rules regarding the updating of the information, specified in a manner widely recognised and used by industry;

(d) the provider does not interfere with the lawful use of technology, widely recognised and used by industry, to obtain data on the use of the information; and

(e) the provider acts expeditiously to remove or to disable access to the information it has stored upon obtaining actual knowledge of the fact that the information at the initial source of the transmission has been removed from the network, or access to it has been disabled, or that a court or an administrative authority has ordered such removal or disablement.

2.   This Article shall not affect the possibility for a court or administrative authority, in accordance with Member States'

legal systems, of requiring the service provider to terminate or prevent an infringement.

Article 14: Hosting

1.   Where an information society service is provided that consists of the storage of information provided by a recipient of the service, Member States shall ensure that the service provider is not liable for the information stored at the request of a recipient of the service, on condition that:

(a) the provider does not have actual knowledge of illegal activity or information and, as regards claims for damages, is not aware of facts or circumstances from which the illegal activity or information is apparent; or

(b) the provider, upon obtaining such knowledge or awareness, acts expeditiously to remove or to disable access to the information.

2.   Paragraph 1 shall not apply when the recipient of the service is acting under the authority or the control of the provider.

3.   This Article shall not affect the possibility for a court or administrative authority, in accordance with Member States' legal systems, of requiring the service provider to terminate or prevent an infringement, nor does it affect the possibility for Member States of establishing procedures governing the removal or disabling of access to information.

Article 15: No general obligation to monitor

1.   Member States shall not impose a general obligation on providers, when providing the services covered by Articles 12, 13 and 14, to monitor the information which they transmit or store, nor a general obligation actively to seek facts or circumstances indicating illegal activity.

2.   Member States may establish obligations for information society service providers promptly to inform the competent public authorities of alleged illegal activities undertaken or information provided by recipients of their service or obligations to communicate to the competent authorities, at their request, information enabling the identification of recipients of their service with whom they have storage agreements.

* * *

Note

In the 2009 *Pirate Bay* case, the Stockholm District Court held that the operators of a file-sharing service were criminally liable for the infringing activities of their users. Key passages from the lengthy opinion, which has since been affirmed on appeal, are reproduced below.

VERDICT*

Stockholm District Court
Division 5, Unit 52
17 April 2009
Case No. B13301–06

* * *

Acts of complicity

– Complicity—objectively

In accordance with * * * Chapter 23, § 4 of the Criminal Code, not only the person who has committed the act (principal offence), but also other persons who have aided and abetted this person in word and deed (act of complicity), will be held liable for a specific act. This rule is applicable to all individual criminal offences for which a sentence of imprisonment may be imposed. Criminal liability rests also with anyone who has aided and abetted the act in a physical or psychological sense. The accomplice must have facilitated the execution of the principal offence. There is no requirement for the accomplice's actions having been a precondition for the accomplishment of the principal offence. Liability for complicity can apply even to someone who has contributed only insignificantly to the principal offence.

The District Court has already concluded that punishable offences have been committed in accordance with the District Prosecutor's indictment. The issue which the District Court now must decide on is whether Fredrik Neij, Gottfrid Svartholm Warg, Peter Sunde Kolmisoppi and Carl Lundström have aided and abetted the principal offence by enabling users to upload and store torrent files for the filesharing service The Pirate Bay, by providing a database linked to a catalogue of torrent files, by enabling users to search for and download torrent files and by providing the functionality with which users who wished to share files could contact each other through the filesharing service's tracker [*i.e.*, search and indexing] function.

The defendants have, inter alia, argued that liability for complicity is out of the question since the principal offences, and how the defendants have influenced these offences, are not sufficiently precise, bearing in mind that the perpetrators are not known. The District Court has concluded that the District Prosecutor has succeeded in proving that the alleged principal offence has taken place in the way claimed. There is no requirement for the perpetrators to be known for liability for complicity to be considered. The District Court has already stated that it is sufficient for the District Prosecutor to prove that the

---

* Translated by IFPI (International Federation of the Phonographic Indus- try). This is not an official court version of the decision.

objective requisites for the principal offences have been fulfilled. If a certain action is regarded as having aided and abetted the principal offence, liability for complicity comes into play.

The investigation into the case has shown that, during the time period specified in the indictment, The Pirate Bay was a popular website with a large number of users around the world. The purpose of The Pirate Bay was to create a meeting place for filesharers. The website was, according to details which have emerged during the examination of Fredrik Neij and Gottfrid Svartholm Warg, under constant development. New hardware was purchased continuously, and improvements made to the search functions and tracker, all with the aim of providing efficient access to, and transfer of, uploaded material. Some users of the website used it and the functions mentioned in such a way that the users committed a breach of the Copyright Act in the manner alleged in the indictment (the principal offences). In accordance with what will be further demonstrated below, all the defendants were aware that a large number of the website's users were engaged in the unlawful disposal of copyright protected material. By providing a website with advanced search functions and easy uploading and downloading facilities, and by putting individual filesharers in touch with one other through the tracker linked to the site, the operation run via The Pirate Bay has, in the opinion of the District Court, facilitated and, consequently, aided and abetted these offences.

Liability for complicity does not require The Pirate Bay's operation to be essential to the making available to the public of rights or works. The fact that the copyright-protected works may possibly have been made available to the general public on other websites before they were made available on The Pirate Bay, or that they may possibly have been made available on other websites at the same time as they were made available on The Pirate Bay, is, in the opinion of the District Court, irrelevant to any liability for complicity which may fall on the defendants as a result of their actions.

The defendants have argued that any complicity on their part has not taken place before the completion of the principal offence. Some offences, continuous offences, are regarded as taking place throughout the duration of a certain circumstance. One example of a continuous offence is unlawful deprivation of liberty. The offence comes to an end only when the circumstance which occasioned the commission of the offence ceases. The making available which constitutes the principal offence in the indictment is, as far as the original seeder [*i.e.*, the person providing the file] is concerned, completed once he/she uploads the torrent file to The Pirate Bay's website and then starts making the work available to others. Other seeders have completed their individual offences when, after downloading segments of the protected work, they have made it available to others. Nor does anyone have to make available a whole work to be in breach of the Copyright Act. The making available of a segment of a work is sufficient for the offence to be completed. The offence continues for the full duration of the making available. The criminal action—aiding and abetting a crime—for which the defendants have been indicted refers, in each case, to the time before the principal offences were completed.

In summary, the operation carried on by The Pirate Bay does, objectively, constitute complicity in breach of the Copyright Act. The question is then whether the defendants can be held responsible for this complicity. This would, firstly, require them to be in a position where they can be held responsible for what took place within the framework of The Pirate Bay's operations. Secondly, their intent must cover all the objective circumstances on which the offences are based.

* * *

The fact that the defendants intentionally brought about the actual circumstances which constituted aiding and abetting must be regarded as established. The defendants have, however, argued that they should not be held liable since they have had no knowledge of the existence of the rights or works specified in the indictment and, therefore, have not intentionally committed the principal offences. It has not been demonstrated that the defendants knew that the specific works listed in the indictment had been made available via The Pirate Bay. The defendants' intent does not, however, have to cover the specific works which it is alleged have been made available. It is, rather, sufficient for them to have had the intent to bring about the existence of copyright-protected material on the website. The examination of the defendants, the letters from rightsholders published on the website, The Pirate Bay, and the e-mail correspondence indicating that the operation involved pirate copying make it clear that the defendants have been aware that copyright protected works were available via the website, and were shared via the tracker embedded within the framework of The Pirate Bay's operation. Despite this knowledge, they have elected to take no action to prevent the infringement of copyright. Based on their positions in relation to the filesharing service, The Pirate Bay, they have, in the opinion of the District Court, together and in collusion knowingly aided and abetted infringements of the Copyright Act by the individual users.

* * *

According to what has emerged during the investigation into the case, there were a very large number of torrent files uploaded to The Pirate Bay's website during the time period of interest to this case. Confirmation of the allegation that the majority of these torrent files related to copyright-protected rights and works requires a reliable investigation of all, or at least a large number, of these. The District Prosecutor has not, however, referred to any such investigation, so the allegation cannot, consequently, be regarded as confirmed. The examination of Anders Nilsson has, however, shown that the most popular torrent files, at least with reference to films, in principle related exclusively to copyright-protected works. Carl Lundström has confirmed that The Pirate Bay's website attracts visitors because it offers the opportunity to utilize copyright-protected works free of charge. In an e-mail sent by him to his legal representative, he wrote that the purpose of the website was pirate copying, and he stated, during the main hearing, that the purpose of the website was, *inter alia*, pirate copying. The 33 works which are the subject of the indictment, and the extent to which these have been downloaded, indicate that the torrent files which relate to copyright-protected works were extremely popular and generated numerous visits and a great deal of activity on The Pirate Bay's website. Although the District Prosecutor has not been able to prove his general allegation that "most of the files which are made available for filesharing via The Pirate Bay contain copyright-protected works and performances", it has, for the reasons specified above, been established that the torrent files on the website related to a significant extent to copyright-protected material.

* * *

Freedom from liability under the Electronic Commerce Act?

The District Court's assessment of the indictment for complicity in breach of the Copyright Act means that the defendants are liable for the offence. The question is then whether the freedom from liability provisions relating to punishment—but also to the liability to pay damages—of a "service provider" contained in the Electronic Commerce Act are applicable. The Electronic Commerce and Other Information Society Services Act contains, for example, provisions relating to freedom from liability for a service provider, with reference to issues of both a legal and compensatory nature. The Act was adopted in response to the implementation of the European Parliament and Council's directive 2000/31/EC on certain legal aspects of information society services, specifically electronic commerce, on the internal market (the e-commerce directive).

The initial issue on this point is whether The Pirate Bay is a service provider which provides any of the services of an information society? A service provider, under the terms of the Electronic Commerce Act, is a physical or legal entity which provides any of the services found in an information society. The defendants' involvement in the operation of the filesharing service must be regarded as such that they can be considered service providers. In § 2 of the Services Act, information society services are specified as services which are normally provided against payment, and which are supplied at a distance, electronically and at the individual request of a service receiver (the user of the services). The service offered by the filesharing service The Pirate Bay includes enabling users to upload or download torrent files on The Pirate Bay's website and, via The Pirate Bay's tracker, establish contacts with other users who have/would like the file the torrent file relates to. In the opinion of the District Court, it is, therefore, clear that the services from The Pirate Bay website have been supplied at a distance, electronically and at the individual requests of the users. Even if the users have not paid for the services, the requirement for compensation has still been met since the operation of The Pirate Bay has, at least to some extent, been financed by advertising revenue. The Electronic Commerce Act is, consequently, applicable to the filesharing services supplied from The Pirate Bay website. The grounds for freedom from liability for service providers are found in §§ 16–19 of the Electronic Commerce Act. The provisions correspond to articles 12–14 of the e-commerce directive.

While articles 12–14 of the e-commerce directive refer to all types of liability in all legal areas, §§ 16–18 of the Electronic Commerce Act focuses specifically on, inter alia, liability for compensation and § 19 on legal liability. The content of §§ 16–19 of the Act does, however, correspond to articles 12–14 of the e-commerce directive.

The grounds for freedom from liability in § 16 of the Electronic Commerce Act covers solely service providers who only transfer information provided by a service receiver in a communications network, or provide[] access to such a net, and where the storage of information is carried out purely for the purpose of the transfer and does not continue longer than required by the transfer. The provisions of § 17 cover the type of transfer where information is stored for the specific purpose of making the transfer of information more efficient. The provisions of § 18 cover a service provider who stores information provided by a service receiver. § 19 cover both types—transfer and storage—by the service provider.

The purpose of the Pirate Bay's services was, inter alia, to provide server space so that users could upload and store torrent files on the website. This storage means that § 16—which covers only services where some form of automatic and temporary intermediate storage takes place as a result of a particular transfer—and § 17—which covers only storage carried out for the explicit purpose of improving the efficiency of the transfer of certain information (caching)—do not apply. The fact that The Pirate Bay offered a service where the user could upload and store torrent files on the website means, instead, that it is a matter of the type of storage service covered by the provisions of § 18 of the Electronic Commerce Act.

According to § 18, a service provider who stores information provided by a service receiver is not, as a result of the content of the information, liable to pay compensation for injury, provided that the supplier was not aware of the existence of the illegal information or operation, and was not aware of facts or circumstances which made it obvious that the illegal information or operation existed or who, as soon as he received knowledge about or became aware of this, prevented the spread of the information without delay.

The case has demonstrated that the filesharing service The Pirate Bay was, *inter alia*, used to provide the opportunity to make available copyright-protected works. It must have been obvious to the defendants that the website contained torrent files which related to protected works. None of them did, however, take any action to remove the torrent files in question, despite being urged to do so. The prerequisites for freedom from liability under § 18 have, consequently, not been fulfilled.

§ 19 of the Electronic Commerce Act is also applicable to service providers who store information. Under § 19, a service provider who stores information on behalf of others can only be held liable for an offence relating to the content of the information if the offence was a deliberate act. The District Court has previously concluded that all the defendants were aware that copyright-protected works were being made available through torrent files uploaded to The Pirate Bay, and that they deliberately chose to ignore this fact. Even if the defendants were not aware of precisely those works covered by the indictment, they have, according to the previous findings of the District Court, at least been indifferent to the fact that it was copyright-protected works which were the subject of filesharing activities via The Pirate Bay. Considering that it is a matter of deliberate offences, the actions of the defendants do not enjoy immunity from prosecution under § 19 of the Electronic Commerce Act.

* * *

C. LIABILITY OF VENUES AND SUPPLIERS

In a pair of cases involving karaoke bars, the Supreme Court of Japan was asked to determine whether and under what circumstances parties other than the individual customer-performers should be held liable for infringing public performances.

INFRINGEMENT OF COPYRIGHT BY SINGING AT A KARAOKE OUTLET*

Supreme Court of Japan, 1988
Case No. 1984(*o*) No. 1204
Minshu Vol. 42, No. 3, at 199

[Majority Opinion:]

On the ground of judgment by the representative for the appeal:

According to the fact findings of the lower court, the appellants installed in their jointly owned snack bars karaoke equipment and karaoke tapes incorporating copyrighted musical pieces whose copyrights and performing rights are licensed through the appellees. There, hostesses and other employees of the snack bar operated the

* Translation provided courtesy of the
Institute of Intellectual Property, Tokyo.

equipment, gave customers an indexed list of the musical pieces, handed them a microphone and encouraged them to sing, and had the customers sing in the presence of other customers accompanied by the music recorded in the karaoke tape. They often made the hostesses sing alone or together with the customer, and thus enhanced the lively atmosphere of the snack bar with the intention of attracting customers and increasing profit. Under such circumstances, not only in cases where the hostesses sang, but also when the customers sang, the parties who used the copyrighted music by performance (singing) were the appellants, and the performance was in public and for profit making purposes. This is because it is evident that the singing by the customers and hostesses was intended for the public to listen to directly, and even when only the customers were singing, they were not singing without the involvement of the appellants; through the appellants' soliciting of the customers to sing, the appellants' choice of music from the karaoke tape provided by the appellants, and the operating of the karaoke equipment by the employees, the customers are understood to have been singing under the management of the appellants. The appellants treated singing by customers as part of the snack bar's business strategy, and by using this, enhanced the atmosphere as a karaoke snack bar, and also intended to attract customers who prefer such an atmosphere and thus increase profit. Thus, the singing by customers as indicated above can be seen as equivalent to the appellants themselves singing from the viewpoint of the regulation of the Copyright Law.

Therefore, the appellants have infringed the performing rights which are derived from the copyright on the musical work by allowing the hostesses and other employees and customers to sing, accompanied by the karaoke music[,] the pieces which are copyrighted works managed by the appellee, without obtaining the consent of the appellee, and cannot be exempted from tort liability for the infringement of performing rights, because they are the parties responsible for the performance Although when producing the karaoke tape, fees were paid to the holder of the copyright, the fees are for allowing the reproduction (recording) of the copyrighted music and as such, the karaoke tape can be freely replayed as the reproduction of the lawfully recorded copyrighted music, it cannot be construed that singing by customers accompanied by karaoke, which is a completely different manner of use of copyrighted music from the replay of a karaoke tape, should be allowed to be done freely without the consent of the holder of the copyright, solely because the singing is accompanied by karaoke which merely has a supplementary role.

The ruling of the original instance court, which is in line with the above, is justifiable, and there is no breach of law in the judgment as was argued by the appellant. * * *

* * *

Therefore, * * * except for the opinion of Justice Masami Itoh, the justices unanimously rule as the main text of the judgment.

[Concurrence:]

The opinion of Justice Itoh is as follows:

I concur with the conclusion of the majority opinion which confirmed the lower court's ruling that the appellants are liable for the tort of infringing the performance right and acknowledged the appellee's claim for compensation based upon tort liability, but cannot concur with the reasoning which leads to the conclusion on the following grounds. The majority opinion, based upon the lower court's finding that the appellants installed karaoke equipment and tapes in the snack bars which they own, that the hostesses and other employees operated the equipment, gave customers an indexed list of musical pieces, handed them a microphone and encouraged them to sing, that the appellants let the customers sing in the presence of other customers accompanied by the replay of the music recorded in the karaoke tape, and that they often made the hostesses sing alone or together with the customer, and thus enhanced the lively atmosphere of the snack bar with the intention of attracting customers and increasing profit, ruled that not only in cases where the hostesses and the others sing, but also in cases where only the customers sing, the parties responsible for the use of the copyrighted music by performance (singing) are the appellants, who are the entrepreneurs, and because the performance was for profit making purposes and made in public, the appellants who failed to obtain the consent of the appellee cannot be exempted from tort liability for the infringement of the right to perform.

I have no objection, in cases where the hostesses and other employees sing with karaoke accompaniment, to regarding the appellants, as entrepreneurs as the parties responsible for using the copyrighted music by performance (singing), and in cases where the hostesses and other employees sing together with customers, the appellants may also be regarded as the parties responsible for using the copyrighted music by considering the singing of the hostesses and customers as a whole. However, it is rather unnatural to regard the appellants, as are entrepreneurs, as the parties responsible using the copyrighted music when only the customers sing; as an interpretation, this has gone too far. The majority opinion, as mentioned above, even in cases where it was only the customers who sang, took into consideration the solicitation to sing by employees, the choice of the music from the karaoke tape supplied by the appellants, along with the operation of the karaoke equipment by the employees, and concluded that the customers were singing under the control of the appellants, and on the other hand, found that the appellants adopted the singing by customers as part of their business strategy to pursue profit, and thus found the singing by customers to be the equivalent to the singing by the appellants from the viewpoint of the regulation of the Copyright Law. Even by taking into account the circumstances such as the solicitation of singing as referred to in the majority opinion, the customers are not singing on the basis of employment or work contract with the appellants, nor do they have any obligation to the appellant to sing; whether to sing or not is entirely left to the choice of the customers, and the copyrighted music is used by their free will. Therefore, it cannot be said that the appellants were actively involved in the use of the copyrighted music, and the singing by customers should be distinguished from the singing by hostesses and other employees in relation to the use of the copyrighted music. Treating the singing of customers as an equivalent of the singing by the appellant is too fictional and unacceptable.

I believe that regarding karaoke performance, the matter should be approached not from the aspect of singing with karaoke accompaniment as above, but by focussing on the karaoke equipment and considering the replay of the karaoke tape by the karaoke equipment itself as an infringement of the rights to performance. [Ed. note: As Justice Itoh discusses below, under the Japanese Copyright Law that was in effect at the time of these events, it was generally not an infringement of copyright to publicly perform lawfully recorded music. However, this public performance privilege did *not* extend, *inter alia*, to performances in certain establishments which used music for a profit-making purpose, such as "music tearooms, dance halls, discos," etc.] Article 14 of the Rules Attached to the Copyright Law provides that, concerning the replay of the performance of copyrighted music which has been lawfully recorded, for the time being, Article 30, para. 1. subpara. 8 of the previous Copyright Law, which provided that "providing for entertainment and broadcasting of works lawfully copied on equipment which mechanically reproduces the sound shall not be deemed as forgery," is applicable except for broadcasting, or cable transmission, and profit-making businesses using copyrighted music which are designated by cabinet order, and on this basis, Art. 3, para. 1 of the Implementation Order of the Copyright Law lists "cafes and other businesses providing food and drinks to customers which advertise as part of the business that the customers are able to enjoy music, or which have special equipment installed for the customers to enjoy music," as among the designated businesses mentioned above. The majority opinion seems to understand that the installed karaoke equipment was not "special equipment installed for the customers to enjoy music". However, karaoke equipment is special equipment with which, by replaying the karaoke tape, customers sing directly to the public accompanied by the recorded music, and although the installation of karaoke equipment with such a purpose may not be [in] a place "which has special equipment enabling the customers to enjoy music" *per se*, nevertheless it should be regarded as something similar, and therefore, because the replaying of the karaoke tape by karaoke equipment is for business purposes, it is reasonable to understand that Article 30, para. 1. subpara. 8 of the previous Copyright Law is rendered inapplicable by Article 14 of the Rules Attached to the Copyright Law. Since, at the time of the enactment of the Copyright Law, the popularity of karaoke equipment of today was not foreseen, Art. 3, para. 1 of the Implementation Order of the Copyright Law was not written with karaoke equipment in mind, but in light of the intention of the law to [exempt only] * * * those businesses in which the provision of music was not directly linked to the profit, the above interpretation is thought to be in line with such an intention of the law.

DUTY OF CARE OF THE LESSOR OF KARAOKE EQUIPMENT FOR BUSINESS USE*

Supreme Court of Japan, 2001
Case No. 2000 (Ju) No. 222
Minshu Vol. 55, No. 2, at 185

On the ground of certiorari by the representatives for the appeal:

I.   The facts lawfully ascertained by the original instance court are as follows:

1.   The appellant is the authorized licensing agent for the copyrighted musical works at issue. The appellant is the sole organisation for the intermediation of copyright on musical works in Japan, and handles the licensing for the majority of musical works (hereinafter, "the Work entrusted for management"). The appellee is a limited liability company engaged in the leasing and selling of karaoke equipment for business use in the area south of the Ibaragi prefecture. A is one of the joint owners of the "B" and "C" (hereinafter, "the Outlets").

2.   The appellee concluded a lease agreement for karaoke equipment with A on September 30, 1991 for B, and, on December 27 of the same year, for C (hereinafter, "the Lease Agreements"),

* Translation provided courtesy of the
Institute of Intellectual Property, Tokyo.

and transferred sets of karaoke equipment for laser discs to him. In the Lease Agreements, it was stipulated in writing that "if the present equipment is to be used for business purposes, the lessee is required [by the appellant] to conclude a license agreement for the copyright. In concluding the present agreement, the lessee is asked to be responsible for taking these measures." The appellee, when concluding the contract, also orally explained this to A, but did not verify if A had concluded a licensing agreement or offered to conclude one. A and others played laser discs using the above karaoke equipment in the Outlets from the date of the conclusion of the lease agreement to June 8, 1995 without the consent of the appellant, played the music and displayed the lyrics which are the Work entrusted for management, allowed the customers and employees to sing, and thus enhanced the atmosphere with the intention of increasing profit.

3.   The appellee became aware that A had been served an interim order to prohibit the use of the karaoke equipment which is the object of the appeal by the appellant, and came to realise for the first time that A had failed to conclude a licensing agreement for the use of the copyright. However, because A promised the appellee that it would solve the dispute in a responsible manner and would not trouble the appellee, the appellee concluded new lease agreements for the karaoke equipment for the Outlets and transferred sets of karaoke equipment to A. A and others utilised the karaoke equipment transferred by the appellee in the Outlets without the consent of the appellant in B, until December 20, 1996, and in C, until October 20, 1995, played the music which was the Work entrusted for management, allowed the customers and employees to sing them, and thus created a lively atmosphere with the intention of increasing the profit.

4.   The royalty which the appellant is entitled to receive from the Outlets is 73,452 yen per month per outlet.

II.   The present case involves a claim by the appellant for compensation equivalent to the amount of the royalty on the ground that the act of the appellee constitutes a joint tort with A as an infringement of the copyright.

III.   The original instance court held that the appellee was liable, and ordered the appellee to pay compensation, from September 1995, but denied liability on the part of the appellee up to June 8, 1995 and ruled as follows.

1.   Entrepreneurs who are lessors of karaoke equipment have a general duty of care to ensure that the karaoke equipment will not be used as an instrument of infringement of copyright. This duty of care should be regarded as having been fulfilled, if the lessor advises the lessee in writing or orally at the time of conclud-

ing the agreement that the lessee is under a legal obligation to obtain a copyright license. The lessor of karaoke equipment is under an obligation to take measures to prevent the infringement of copyright by not transferring the equipment to the lessee if there is a foreseeable possibility that the lessee will not obtain a copyright license or if, after the execution of the lease agreement, there are special circumstances giving reasons to suspect that the licensing agreement has not been entered into. The lessor is also under an obligation, where the equipment has already been transferred, to retrieve the equipment from the lessee. However, the lessee is not under any general obligation to verify, before entering into the lease agreement, whether or not the lessee has offered to obtain a copyright license from the appellant, or to verify the existence of such a license at any time after the execution of the lease agreement.

2. In the lease agreement in the present case, there is a statement that a copyright license should be obtained from the appellant, and that the appellee has orally explained this to A. The lower court found no special circumstances that would give reasons to suspect that A had no intention to obtain a copyright license from the appellant at the time of the lease agreement, or had not obtained such a license after entering the lease agreement. Therefore, the court held, there was is no breach of the duty of care until June 8, 1995.

IV. However, the above ruling of the original instance court cannot be upheld from the following reasons.

1. In cases where the owners of restaurants and other similar outlets install karaoke equipment for laser discs * * *, encouraging the customers to sing, reproducing the piece of music chosen by customers, showing the lyrics and playing the songs which are copyrighted, letting the customers and employees sing accompanied by this music, and, by creating a lively atmosphere, intend to solicit more customers and to increase profit, the owner of the venue is not exempted from tort liability for the infringement of the right to perform and the right to show on the screen in relation to the singing of the customers and employees and the showing or reproduction of the lyrics and the song by the use of the karaoke equipment, unless he has obtained the consent of the holder of the copyright of the music.

2. It is reasonable to consider that the lessor of karaoke equipment, when entering into a lease agreement for the equipment, bears a duty of care not only to advise the lessee to obtain a license for the use of the copyrighted work, but also to transfer the equipment to the lessee only after verifying that the lessee has obtained such a license or has offered to obtain such a license from

the holder of the copyright, if the equipment is solely for showing on the screen and playing the copyrighted music and letting the public directly watch or listen to it. This is because: (1) in light of the fact that most of the works shown or played by karaoke equipment are copyrighted, such equipment generally has a high probability of being used in infringement of copyright (as mentioned above in 1) by the owners of the outlets with such equipment, unless there is a license from the copyright holder, (2) an infringement of copyright is a criminal offence (Article 119 and the following), (3) karaoke lessors profit from leasing the karaoke equipment which has a high probability of being used in breach of copyright, (4) it is publicly known that, in general, the rate of licensing by the owners of karaoke outlets is not especially high, and the lessor should have foreseen the probability of the infringement of copyright unless it could verify that the lessee has obtained, or offered to obtain, a copyright license, (5) it is easy for the lessor of the karaoke equipment to verify whether the lessee has obtained, or offered to obtain, a copyright license, and thus, it is possible to take measures to prevent the infringement of copyright. Therefore the existence of the above duty of care should be acknowledged.

3. In the present case, it is evident that A intends to use the karaoke equipment to show and play the Work entrusted for management to the public for direct viewing and listening. The appellee was under a duty of care to prevent the infringement of copyright by A by verifying whether A has obtained, or offered to obtain, a copyright license at the time of the transfer of the karaoke equipment to A pursuant to the Lease Agreements. Nevertheless, the appellee merely advised A to obtain a copyright license, but failed to verify whether he had obtained, or offered to obtain, a copyright license, and transferred the equipment to A. This is contrary to the above-mentioned duty of care based upon Reason. The infringement of copyright by A and others resulted from this omission, and therefore, there is a causal link between the failure of the appellee to fulfill the duty of care and the damage incurred by the appellant caused by the infringement of copyright by A.

Thus, the above ruling of the original instance court which found that there was no breach of the duty of care on the part of the appellee until June 8, 1995 erred in the interpretation and application of law, and it is evident that this error affects the conclusion of the judgment of the original instance court, and the grounds of appeal are well-founded.

[Accordingly, the court ordered the appellee to pay the appellant the full amount of the royalties incurred by both of the lessee's karaoke establishments throughout the lease periods, plus interest.]

* * *

Notes

1.   Consider the singing of "Happy Birthday" in a restaurant: How would this be analyzed under Japanese law when the singing includes restaurant employees? What if it involves customers only? How does U.S. law address these situations?

2.   How does the Japanese Supreme Court's theory of lessor liability compare with that of the lower court? How would the lessor's liability be assessed under U.S. law? Which approach makes the most sense in terms of policy?

3.   It is speculated that the reason why the Japanese music industry sought recourse against the lessors of karaoke equipment is the difficulty of collecting royalties from karaoke bars in Japan, which are often operated by criminal syndicates known as "Yakuza."

4.   The Japanese Supreme Court may soon be asked to reconsider its karaoke rulings. A recent decision by the Intellectual Property High Court held that a company providing a system that enables users to record television programs and play them back (a permissible private use) was not liable for infringement, because the user and not the company controlled which programs would be recorded, even though the recording and transmitting equipment was controlled by the company. The case is likely to be appealed.

   In the meantime, the karaoke rulings have been used to enjoin a Napster-like file-sharing service, on the theory that the service provider controled the activities of its users.

*

Index

References are to pages.
Page numbers in bold indicate significant treatments of the topic.

Adaptations 18, 98–113
Anticircumvention laws 4
Assignments 90–92, **96–97**, 98
Attribution, right of
  See Moral rights
Authorizing, liability for
  See Secondary liability
Authorship
  In general 67–92
  Cinematographic works 88–92
  Joint works 67, **82–89**, 92
  Works made for hire 1, 17, **67–82,**
    89, 99
Authors' rights 1, 24, 43–44, 47–48, 59
Berne Convention 3–5, 25, 67, 69,
  75–77, 95–99, 102, 104, 116–17,
  122, 167–68, 173–76, 178, 182,
  185–87, 197–98, 239
Broadcasters 1, 3, 6
Caching 235–48, 250–51
Choice of law 67–81, 102–07
Cinematographic works 5, 17, 67, 76,
  81, **88–92**, 95, **99–113**, 123–24,
  128, 129–45, 153–62, 166
Collective works 25, **67–80**, 81
Colorization 99–108
Compilations
  See Collective works
  See Data compilations
Computer programs 5–6, 17, 81, 123,
  131–32, 166
Conflicts of law
  See Choice of law
Contributory liability
  See Secondary liability
Copyright term
  See Term of protection
Creativity
  See Originality
Crown copyright 92–94
Data compilations 4–6, **24–61**
Database Directive (EU) 26, **38–61**
Databases
  See Data compilations
**Digital Millenium Copyright Act
  (DMCA)** 239, 245, 247, 249
Digital Rights Management (DRM)
  4
Distribution, right of 98, **124–72**, 233

Divulgation, right of
  See Moral rights
Droit d'auteur
  See Authors' rights
Droit de suite
  See Resale right
Economic rights
  See Patrimonial rights
European Union
  Directives 26, 38–61, 89, 95–96, 98,
    109, 123–44, 153–62, 167–72,
    192–93, 199–201, 228, 242,
    246–47, 249–52, 255–56
  Treaty 3-4, 124–29, 156, 167
Exhaustion of rights 2, 124, 126–27,
  146–72
Fair dealing
  See Fair use
Fair practice
  See Fair use
Fair quotation
  See Fair use
Fair use 2, 24, **197–228**, 232
Fashion design 6, **17–24**, 228
File sharing 195–96, **236–59**, 265
Films
  See Cinematographic works
First sale
  See Exhaustion of rights
Fixation 15, 17
Folklore 92–94
Fragrance
  See Perfume
Geneva Phonograms Convention 4,
  95, 98, 199
Government copyright
  See Crown copyright
Harmonization 2, 5–6, 43, 50, 59, 127,
  135–38, 158–61, 168–69
Hyperlinks 52
Importation right
  See Parallel imports
Industrious collection
  See Sweat of the brow
Integrity, right of
  See Moral rights
**Internet, infringement via 188–96,
  234–57**
ISP liability 234–57

Page numbers in bold indicate significant treatments of the topic.

Joint authorship
  See Authorship
Joint works
  See Joint authorship
Karaoke 257–65
Labels 146–53
Lending right 1, 122–29, **130–32**, **138–45**, 155
Licenses 2, 96, 98
Maastricht Treaty
  See European Union
Making available 4, 154, 157, 192, 195
Moral rights
  In general 1, 4, 81, 89, 92, 96–99, 211
  Attribution (Paternity) right 98, 108, 116, 122, 211
  Berne Convention 98–99, 102, 104, 116–17, 122
  Destruction as violation 113–22
  Divulgation right 98, 116, 122, 211
  Integrity right **98–122**, 211
  Performers 188
  Waivers 113
  Withdrawal (Retraction) right 96, 98, 116, 122
Motion pictures
  See Cinematographic works
Neighboring rights 2, 6, 95, 98, 187–88
Newspapers
  See Collective works
Nondiscrimination 2–3, 167–68, 187
North American Free Trade Agreement (NAFTA) 37
Notice-and-take-down 244, 248
Originality **24–38**, 43–50, 59–61
Ownership **67–97**
Parallel imports
  See Exhaustion of rights
Parody 201, 211, **226–28**
Patrimonial rights 1, 4, 6, 81, 89–90, 95–97, 98, 104, 106
Performance right 2–3, 6, 98, 127, **172–87**, 235, 257–65
Performers' rights 2–3, 6, **187–88**
Perfumes **6–18**
Phonograms 2–3, 5–6, 82, 88, 95, 98, 123–45, 163–66, 187–88
Preemption 62

Public domain 2
Reciprocity 106, 167–69, 171, 187, 192
Rental right 2, 4, 6, **122–38**, 143, 155, 166, 188
Resale right 1, **167–72**
Rome Convention 3, 95, 98, 187–88, 198–99
Secondary liability 229–65
Software
  See Computer programs
Sound recordings
  See Phonograms
Stage direction 24
Sweat of the brow **24–38**, 43, 47, 59–60
Term of protection 6, **95–96**, 171–72, 188
Termination rights 1
Territoriality 67, 146, 191–93
Three-strikes laws 249
Trademarks 146–53
Transmissions, infringing **188–96**, 234–57
TRIPS Agreement 3, 6, 67, 95–97, 98–99, 123, 128, 146, 172–86, 188, 197
Unfair competition 62–66
Universal Copyright Convention 4, 101
Videograms 132–39
Visual Artists Rights Act (VARA) 122
WIPO
  Copyright Treaty 4–5, 38, 67, 95, 98, 123, 146, 158–59, 192, 197, 239, 242–43
  Performances and Phonograms Treaty 4, 6, 67, 95–98, 123, 146, 158, 188, 197, 239
Withdrawal, right of
  See Moral rights
Works made for hire
  See Authorship
World Intellectual Property Organization (WIPO)
  See WIPO
World Trade Organization (WTO) Agreement
  See TRIPS Agreement

†